THE WAL-MART EFFECT

THE WAL-MART EFFECT

How the World's Most Powerful Company Really
Works—and How It's Transforming the American Economy

CHARLES FISHMAN

The Penguin Press
New York
2006

THE PENGUIN PRESS
Published by the Penguin Group
Penguin Group (USA) Inc., 375 Hudson Street, New York, New York 10014, U.S.A. • Penguin Group
(Canada), 90 Eglinton Avenue East, Suite 700, Toronto, Ontario, Canada M4P 2Y3 (a division of
Pearson Penguin Canada Inc.) • Penguin Books Ltd, 80 Strand, London WC2R 0RL, England • Penguin
Ireland, 25 St Stephen's Green, Dublin 2, Ireland (a division of Penguin Books Ltd) • Penguin Books
Australia Ltd, 250 Camberwell Road, Camberwell, Victoria 3124, Australia (a division of Pearson
Australia Group Pty Ltd) • Penguin Books India Pvt Ltd, 11 Community Centre, Panchsheel Park,
New Delhi – 110 017, India • Penguin Group (NZ), Cnr Airborne and Rosedale Roads, Albany,
Auckland 1310, New Zealand (a division of Pearson New Zealand Ltd) • Penguin Books
(South Africa) (Pty) Ltd, 24 Sturdee Avenue, Rosebank, Johannesburg 2196, South Africa

Penguin Books Ltd, Registered Offices:
80 Strand, London WC2R 0RL, England

First published in 2006 by The Penguin Press,
a member of Penguin Group (USA) Inc.

Copyright © Charles Fishman, 2006
All rights reserved

ISBN 1-59420-076-9

Printed in the United States of America
1   3   5   7   9   10   8   6   4   2

Designed by Stephanie Huntwork

For my mom and dad, Suzanne and Lawrence Fishman,
who taught me the importance of asking questions,
and listening closely to the answers

CONTENTS

ONE
WHO KNEW SHOPPING WAS SO IMPORTANT?

I'm probably not the best negotiator in the world; I lack the ability to squeeze that last dollar.

—*Sam Walton, founder of Wal-Mart*

STARTING IN THE early 1990s, a change swept through a line of products that most adult Americans use every day. Until then, nearly every brand and style of deodorant—roll-on and solid, powder-fresh and unscented—came in a paperboard box. You opened the box, pulled out the container of deodorant, and pitched the box in the garbage. In the early 1990s, Wal-Mart, among other retailers, decided the paperboard box was a waste. It added nothing to the customer's deodorant experience. The product already came in a can or a plastic container that was at least as tough as the box, if not tougher. The box took up shelf space. It wasted cardboard. Shipping the weight of the cardboard wasted fuel. The box itself cost money to design, to produce—it even cost money to put the deodorant inside the box, just so the customer could take it out. With the kind of quiet but irresistible force that Wal-Mart can apply, the retailer asked deodorant makers to eliminate the box. Unbox the antiperspirant.

The box turned out to cost about a nickel for every container of deodorant. Wal-Mart typically split the savings—letting deodorant makers keep a couple pennies and passing a couple pennies in savings along to its antiperspirant customers.

Walk into a Wal-Mart today, and pause in the deodorant aisle: eight shelves of deodorant, sixty containers across. In a well-tended Wal-Mart store, nearly five hundred containers of deodorant face you. Not one box. Walk into any store now, Walgreens, Target, Eckerd, CVS, and go to the deodorant aisle. Not one box.

Whole forests have not fallen in part because of the decision made in the Wal-Mart home office at the intersection of Walton Boulevard and SW 8th Street in Bentonville, Arkansas, to eliminate the box. The nickel savings may seem trivial, until you do the math. With two hundred million adults in the United States, if you only account for the nickel on the container of deodorant in the medicine cabinet right now, that's a savings of $10 million, of which customers got to keep half, $5 million, just for one small change, unnoticed by consumers, more than a decade ago. But the change, and the savings, is recurrent, and permanent. We're saving $5 million in nickels five or six times a year—as often as we need a new container of deodorant. The nation has saved hundreds of millions of dollars since the deodorant box disappeared. It's a perfect Wal-Mart moment—the company used its insight, and its muscle, to help change the world. Millions of trees were not cut down, acres of cardboard were not manufactured only to be discarded, one billion deodorant boxes didn't end up in landfills each year. It's all unseen, all unnoticed, and all good.

Unless, of course, you were in the paperboard-box-making business. That couple years where you took a call from every single deodorant maker in America, with each one canceling their standing order for boxes, those were rough times.

THE WAL-MART EFFECT

Wal-Mart changes the world like that every day, and has been for forty years. A wasteful routine, often long entrenched, is detected and eliminated, establishing a new standard of efficiency, lowering costs for everyone, especially ordinary customers. And in the wake of the change comes a ripple of unintended consequences, or if not quite unintended, at least unacknowledged. That is the Wal-Mart effect— the ways both small and profound that Wal-Mart has changed business, work, the shape and well-being of communities, and everyday life in the United States and around the world.

At about the same time deodorant was coming out of the box, Wal-Mart was experimenting with the idea of doubling the size of some of its new stores in order to start selling groceries alongside general merchandise in a format it called supercenters. When Wal-Mart first started nudging into the grocery business, everyone in the United States already had well-established grocery-buying habits. No one was waiting for a Wal-Mart to open to buy a gallon of milk or a jar of spaghetti sauce or a package of boneless chicken breasts. The supermarket business was dominated by well-established, deeply experienced, well-run national chains. Albertsons was founded in 1939. Safeway was founded in 1915. Kroger was founded by Barney Kroger in 1883. Into that familiar group fifteen years ago stepped Wal-Mart. At the end of 1990, Wal-Mart had just nine supercenters.

Ten years later, at the end of 2000, Wal-Mart had 888 supercenters— it had opened an average of 7 new supercenters a month, 120 months in a row—and Wal-Mart was the number-one food retailer in the nation. In little more than a decade, from a standing start, Wal-Mart mastered the U.S. grocery business and remade what turned out to be a complacent industry in its wake. It is an astonishing achievement. Today Wal-Mart sells more groceries than any company not just in the United States but in the world; it has 1,906 supercenters, 1,000 more than it had five years ago. That is, in the last five years, having already conquered the supermarket business, Wal-Mart has dramatically increased the pace of its grocery invasion; it has opened an average of 16 new supercenters a month for five years.

In groceries, as in other areas of retail, Wal-Mart isn't just the first among equals; it is unchallenged. The company that essentially didn't exist as a grocer fifteen years ago now sells more food than Kroger and Safeway combined. Nationwide, Wal-Mart has about 16 percent of the grocery market. In many individual cities, though, it has 25 or 30 percent of the grocery market—one out of four, or one of three families do their food shopping at Wal-Mart.

Wal-Mart's grocery departments—in supercenters, about 40 percent of the floor space is devoted to groceries—are not particularly appealing places to shop. The aisles are long, the staffing is thin, the stocking often spotty and chaotic, the produce ample but undistinguished. But when Wal-Mart starts selling groceries in a new city—Dallas, Memphis, Oklahoma City—it quickly wins business in a simple, potent way: Its prices are about 15 percent lower on exactly the same foods sold elsewhere. You can buy fresh salmon from the Wal-Mart seafood display case for $4.84 a pound, a price so low it almost seems too good to be true. For a family of four who might spend $500.00 a month on groceries, Wal-Mart's 15 percent lower prices translate into savings of hundreds of dollars a year, just for driving to a different store.

Wal-Mart didn't just change the lives and spending habits of grocery shoppers, though. It changed the very ecosystem and rhythm of the supermarket business, often with devastating consequences for those who couldn't adjust. In the same decade that Wal-Mart has come to dominate the grocery business in the United States, thirty-one supermarket chains have sought bankruptcy protection; twenty-seven of them cite competition from Wal-Mart as a factor. That, too, is the Wal-Mart effect.

Wal-Mart isn't just a store, or a huge company, or a phenomenon anymore. Wal-Mart shapes where we shop, the products we buy, and the prices we pay—even for those of us who never shop there. It reaches deep inside the operations of the companies that supply it and changes not only what they sell, but also changes how those products are packaged and presented, what the lives of the factory workers who make the products are like—it even sometimes changes the countries where those factories are located. Wal-Mart reaches around the globe, shaping the work and the lives of people who make toys in China, or raise salmon in Chile, or sew shirts in Bangladesh, even though they may never visit a Wal-Mart store in their lives.

Wal-Mart has even changed the way we think about ourselves—as shoppers, as consumers. Wal-Mart has changed our sense of quality, it has changed our sense of what a good deal is. Wal-Mart's low prices routinely reset our expectations about what all kinds of things should cost—from clothing to furniture to fresh fish. Wal-Mart has changed the lens through which we see the world.

The Wal-Mart effect touches the lives of literally every American every day. Wal-Mart reshapes the economic life of the towns and cities where it opens stores; it also reshapes the economic life of the United States—a single company that steadily, silently, purposefully moves the largest economy in history. Wal-Mart has become the most powerful, most influential company in the world.

Who knew shopping would turn out to be so important?

MORE THAN HALF of all Americans live within five miles of a Wal-Mart store, less than a ten-minute drive away. Ninety percent of Americans live within fifteen miles of a Wal-Mart. On the nation's interstates, it is rare to go a quarter hour without seeing a Wal-Mart truck.

Wal-Mart now has 3,811 stores in the United States (including 10 in Alaska and 9 in Hawaii); that is more than one Wal-Mart store for every single county in the country. The stores are so large that they do not fade into the landscape the way that Starbucks and McDonald's do. The stores sit on vast aprons of asphalt parking, usually at a slightly different grade from the nearby roads, so they look dug into the ground or popped out of it. Wal-Mart stores aren't just big inside; they present big, flat planes of concrete—sides and roofs—which catch the eye because they are out of scale. You do not pass a Wal-Mart without noticing it. The stores have a gravitational force, bending the land, the circulation, the rhythms of the communities where they are planted.

In most of America, Wal-Mart is not just unavoidable, it has become a kind of national commons. Every seven days more than one hundred million Americans shop at Wal-Mart—one third of the country. Each year 93 percent of American households shop at least once at Wal-Mart. Wal-Mart's sales in the United States are equal to $2,060.36 spent there by every U.S. household in the last year. (Wal-Mart's profit on that $2,060.36 was just $75.00.) If your family didn't spend $2,000.00 at Wal-Mart last year, well, someone else's spent $3,000.00.

And it's not just the United States. Wal-Mart is the largest retailer in both Mexico and Canada, and the second largest grocer in Britain. Worldwide, so many people shop at Wal-Mart that this year 7.2 billion people will go to a Wal-Mart store. Earth's population is only 6.5 billion, so this year the equivalent of every person on the planet will visit a Wal-Mart, with more than half a billion visits left over.

Wal-Mart's scale can be hard to absorb. The company isn't just the largest retailer in the nation and in the world. For most of this decade, Wal-Mart has been both the largest company in the world, and the largest company in the history of the world. In 2006, Wal-Mart will be bumped from the number-one spot on the Fortune 500 list of the largest companies by ExxonMobil, whose sales will surge past Wal-Mart's, but only because the world price of oil has risen 50 percent in the last year. Wal-Mart's dominance really remains unrivaled, as is revealed by a single statistic. ExxonMobil employs about 90,000 people worldwide; Wal-Mart employs 1.6 million. ExxonMobil is growing by raising prices; Wal-Mart is growing despite lowering prices. As a store, Wal-Mart isn't just the largest; it no longer has any near rivals. Wal-Mart is as big as Home Depot, Kroger, Target, Costco, Sears, and Kmart combined. Target, which is considered Wal-Mart's nearest direct rival and its most astute competitor, is small by comparison. Each year Wal-Mart sells more by Saint Patrick's Day, March 17, than Target sells all year.

On top of that, Wal-Mart is the nation's, and the world's, largest private employer, with 1.6 million "associates," as the company refers to its employees. In the United States, another 3 million people have jobs directly dependent on purchases from Wal-Mart, according to Wal-Mart's figures. Most of us shop at Wal-Mart, but many of us are also dependent on the company for our income, or know someone who is, even if that person doesn't actually work at Wal-Mart.

It's not just Wal-Mart's presence as a merchant and employer that is so pervasive. In a single typical day of media coverage, Wal-Mart is mentioned significantly in more than one hundred stories around the country. Each month Wal-Mart's announcement of its sales is good for a full twenty-four-hour cycle of news coverage, more if Wal-Mart surges or stumbles, because Wal-Mart's performance is considered a vital indicator of trends in the U.S. economy overall—are we spending confidently or not? It is a rare day that the *Wall Street Journal* does not have a story that mentions Wal-Mart; most days the company is cited multiple times.

In the last five years, a national debate about Wal-Mart's impact—about the wide spectrum of the Wal-Mart effect—has escalated into a series of skirmishes being fought not only in print and at zoning hearings but also in the courtroom. Wal-Mart's practices, the way it treats its employees, the way it treats its suppliers, the way it treats communities, and its motivation—its very soul—are all subjects of such bitter contention that it is hard to imagine that partisans are actually describing the same institution. Wal-Mart is either one of the boldest, most democratic creations in human history, a validation of free markets, harnessing its enormous power on behalf of the needs of ordinary people, or it is an insatiable, insidious beast, exploiting the people it pretends to defend.

WAL-MART'S BIRTH in a remote corner of Arkansas is now, quite rightly, the stuff of American business legend. The first Wal-Mart opened in 1962; that same year also saw the opening of the first Target and the first Kmart. Wal-Mart was the creation of a single man, Sam Walton, who latched on to a single idea that he somehow knew in his gut was singularly powerful: Sell stuff that people need every day just a little cheaper than everyone else, sell it at that low price all the time, and customers will flock to you. That single idea drove Walton to keep the costs of his own company as modest as possible, and soon caused Wal-Mart to ask whether its suppliers couldn't be more frugal too and lower the price of their products. As Wal-Mart gained scale, growing in rural areas where it brought a range of selection and price not previously available, the questions to suppliers became a way of doing business, a culture of looking for every penny of cost savings that could be wrung out of designs, packaging, labor, materials, transportation, even the stocking of stores. It is that cascade of frugality, questions, and pressure that creates the Wal-Mart effect.

The phrase itself—"the Wal-Mart effect"—has made its way into the culture, shorthand for a whole range of impacts resulting from Wal-Mart's way of doing business. As a phrase, "The Wal-Mart effect" itself reveals our own conflicted feelings about Wal-Mart. The Wal-Mart effect is never used as simply a description; it is never neutral. But neither is the Wal-Mart effect presumptively negative, or presumptively positive. It takes its coloration from its context.

The Wal-Mart effect—when Wal-Mart starts selling groceries in a new area, bringing lower prices to its own shoppers and, through competition, driving down the prices of established grocery stores as well.

The Wal-Mart effect—when Wal-Mart, or any big-box retailer, comes into town, reshapes shopping habits, and drains the viability of traditional local shopping areas.

The Wal-Mart effect—the relentless downward pressure on the prices of everyday necessities that a single vast retailer can exert on behalf of consumers.

The Wal-Mart effect—the suburbanization of shopping; the downward pressure on wages at all kinds of stores trying to compete with Wal-Mart; the consolidation of consumer product companies trying to match Wal-Mart's scale; the relentless scrutiny of unnecessary costs that allows companies to survive on thinner profits; the success of a large business at the expense of its rivals, and the way in which that success builds on itself.

A second phrase, also increasingly common, captures the ill-defined fears that the Wal-Mart effect has come to stand for: "the Wal-Mart economy." The Wal-Mart economy describes the nagging sense that there might be some unseen but terrible cost to be paid for "always low prices." The Wal-Mart economy is a place where the jobs are traps: low wages, miserly benefits, stultifying work, no respect, no future. In the Wal-Mart economy, we as consumers often buy too much just because it's cheap. We are slaves to our impulse for a bargain. The lights are always on in the Wal-Mart economy—it's open twenty-four hours a day, seven days a week, and it's never a bad time to wheel into a Wal-Mart and buy some stuff. The Wal-Mart economy extends far beyond the borders of the United States to the countries whose names are on the labels of everything we buy, where an endless peasantry is always waiting to work for $10 a day, or $5 a day.

Still, we find the pull of Wal-Mart irresistible, and Wal-Mart has not hesitated in the face of our appetite. In 2004, in the United States, the company opened 244 new supercenters—the combined general merchandise and grocery stores—in thirty-seven states. That's 4 new supercenters a week. Although 90 percent of us already live within fifteen miles of a Wal-Mart, the company picked up the pace in 2005. Through the first ten months of the year, Wal-Mart opened 232 new supercenters—5 per week.

In the last two years, Wal-Mart has added more dollars in sales than Target's total sales. It is precisely that scale, built out of our own purchases, $5 and $10 and $20 at a time, that powers the Wal-Mart effect. In many ways, we all now live in the Wal-Mart economy—the literal version, if not the metaphoric one. The reach would be bemusing if it weren't so encompassing.

In its June 2004 issue, *Music Trades* magazine, a monthly devoted to the business of making and selling musical instruments, featured this blunt editorial: "Is Wal-Mart a Real Threat?" The editorial said that Wal-Mart's decision to start selling inexpensive guitars and horns was sending shudders through independent musical instrument dealers, a corner of retail still mostly the province of local shops run by people who know something about musical instruments. A long analytical story on the same topic a few issues later quotes an instrument retailer saying, "After seeing an $89 guitar in Wal-Mart, if they walk into your store and see a guitar for $500, their immediate reaction is, 'This guy's ripping me off.'"

In January 2005, Bloomberg News reported a story about nickel's prospects on the London commodity markets. "Nickel, the best performer on the London Metal Exchange since 2003, may record its first annual drop in four years as buyers such as Wal-Mart Stores Inc. and Ikea International use cheaper alternatives in products ranging from coffee tables to desks and mirrors." Soaring nickel prices were causing Wal-Mart to look at home furnishings that use cheaper grades of stainless steel with little or no nickel content. Potential result: softening worldwide demand for nickel, softening nickel prices worldwide—and on the London Metal Exchange too. (Wal-Mart's instincts were good; the price of nickel rose 25 percent during the first five months of 2005. But in the last half of 2005, nickel prices turned, falling more than 30 percent through October.)

No business comes close to Wal-Mart's dominance across not just the consumer economy, but the economy as a whole, or ever has. The Wal-Mart effect is evident every day. Sears and Kmart were crippled by effective competition from Wal-Mart—their merger is just a desperate grasp at survival in the face of Wal-Mart's relentless competence. It won't be clear for several years whether their marriage will reveal some previously hidden strategy for success. Still, Sears and Kmart combined are now the size Wal-Mart was in 1993, one fifth Wal-Mart's current size.

Toys "R" Us, the company that invented the "category killer" store back in the 1950s and transformed the way toys were sold in the United States, wilted in its race against Wal-Mart. Since 1998, Wal-Mart has sold more toys in the United States than Toys "R" Us. In early 2005, Toys "R" Us sold itself to a trio of private equity investors who were as interested in the chain's real estate as its toy business.

Toys "R" Us is expected to shrink further rather than win back toy customers from Wal-Mart.

Winn-Dixie, the venerable if increasingly shabby $11 billion grocery chain, was forced into bankruptcy in 2005 because of its inability to compete with Wal-Mart. It closed one third of its 920 stores, and laid off twenty-two thousand employees.

Procter & Gamble and Gillette, two of the world's most stable and innovative consumer products companies, agreed to a merger that will cost P&G $57 billion and create a single company that sells everything from Duracell batteries to Tampax tampons, Pringles potato chips to Oral-B toothbrushes. Together, the companies have twenty-one brands that each has $1 billion in sales or more. The merger was motivated in part by the companies' need to maintain scale in the face of Wal-Mart. The combined company will have sales of $68 billion a year, of which at least $10 billion will be at Wal-Mart, 15 percent of the business. Deep inside its financial filings with the U.S. government, P&G reports that before the merger, Wal-Mart was 16 percent of its business. It also reports that its top ten retail customers are 32 percent of its business. What that means is that Wal-Mart is not just P&G's number-one customer—it's as big as the next nine customers *combined*. So the really interesting question is whether the purchase of Gillette by P&G gives the company more leverage with Wal-Mart— or whether it gives Wal-Mart yet more muscle with a bigger P&G.

AMERICANS MAY THINK of Wal-Mart as a kind of faceless, tireless corporate monolith that operates with almost total control, total information, and total competence. That impression is only reinforced by some of the company's contemporary, and obsessive, data-gathering habits. Wal-Mart, for instance, keeps track of the number of items per hour each of its checkout clerks scans at every cash register, at every store, in every state, for every shift as a means of measuring their productivity. (A typical checker scans four hundred to five hundred items an hour—six to eight a minute.)

But many of Wal-Mart's vaunted areas of innovation, including warehousing, logistics, data management, and merchandising, were areas the company ignored for years, and perfected only slowly and with deliberation. When Wal-Mart stores first opened, Sam Walton didn't even bother to divide the merchandise into departments. He just had his managers pile the deals up on the shelves or on tables in the aisles. The company now measures sales per running foot of shelf space for every item and category to make sure stores and individual products are productive, and to compare their profitability.

Although Wal-Mart has stayed true to its original core value— always low prices—the company has now grown so large, and evolved in so many ways, that it no longer truly understands its own culture clearly or effectively—or understands how it is perceived by the rest of us. The mascot of the company is the bouncing yellow smiley-face price chopper. But while the prices at Wal-Mart may make us smile, Wal-Mart itself almost never does. This, too, is part of the Wal-Mart effect—turned back on Wal-Mart itself. One of the great ironies of Wal-Mart's success is that the very things that allowed it to thrive so inexorably are now the source of so much criticism.

Sam Walton's ability to find, recruit, and inspire ordinary people was the source of Wal-Mart's discipline, its growth, its innovation. Thousands of people found their life's work at Wal-Mart, and became millionaires while doing it. And yet the same company now finds itself under attack, both politically and legally, for its treatment of workers—including a lawsuit on behalf of 1.6 million women who have worked for Wal-Mart that alleges systematic sex discrimination in promotion and pay. Wal-Mart's wages, the adequacy of the health insurance it offers, the fact that some managers have required employees to work off the clock, or locked employees in stores overnight all make it seem as if our low prices may come at the expense of the people ringing up our purchases.

Being headquartered in Bentonville has always been a source of Wal-Mart's strength—planted in a small town, cultivating an ethic of frugality, focus, and hard work, undistracted by the temptations of the big cities. But Wal-Mart's isolation in Bentonville is also the source of the company's lack of perspective—about itself, about its public perception, about the difference between running a store in Rogers, Arkansas, and running one in Philadelphia, Pennsylvania.

Wal-Mart's brilliant, obsessive focus on a single core value—delivering low prices—created what became the largest and most powerful company in history. And yet the drive for low prices is also the cause of the troubling elements of the Wal-Mart effect: low wages, unrelenting pressure on suppliers, products cheap in quality as well as price, offshoring of jobs.

Wal-Mart's inability to see itself clearly begins at the home office. The company earnestly portrays itself as family friendly both inside and outside the company. But in Bentonville, there is a well-known role: the Wal-Mart wife. It's just like being a military wife: She has to run her family as if her spouse were never coming home. In January 2005, Wal-Mart CEO Lee Scott kicked off an aggressive nationwide campaign to correct what he says are the misimpressions Americans have of Wal-Mart. Tackling wages, for instance, Scott has said again and again, and with evident pride, that the average wage of hourly store employees is "almost twice the federal minimum wage." But it isn't clear that Scott has any idea what that means. In Wal-Mart's home state of Arkansas, the company says it pays store employees an average of $9.18 an hour. For a single mom with two kids who opts to buy health insurance from Wal-Mart, that translates to take-home pay of $290 a week. If our single-mom Wal-Mart associate is living in an apartment that costs only $500 a month, she's got just $660 a *month* left for everything else: the electric bill, car insurance, feeding and clothing her kids, saving for retirement. Even if she shops at Wal-Mart, that's lean living.

Wal-Mart has recently taken to explaining that retail jobs like those it offers, although paying double the minimum wage, are nonetheless intended as supplemental income, not as support for a family. The problem with that is that for two thirds of Americans, Wal-Mart is the single largest employer in the state where they live.

The misperceptions cut both ways. Critics often glibly describe Wal-Mart as just another big, greedy corporation. If you took the company's total profit from 2004 ($10.3 billion) and gave every dollar to Wal-Mart's employees (1.6 million), you would distribute about $6,400 per employee.

Microsoft had an even larger 2005 profit of $12.3 billion. But Microsoft has just one twenty-sixth the number of employees as Wal-Mart—its profits come to $200,000 per employee, or thirty times those at Wal-Mart.

More to the point, perhaps, for its hourly employees, Wal-Mart's total profit comes to $3 an hour over a typical year. So although there may be some dispute about whether the average Wal-Mart store associate earns $8 an hour or $9 an hour, Wal-Mart could not afford to pay those people $12 an hour. There isn't enough money—at least not without raising prices.

A TYPICAL WAL-MART has 60,000 different items for sale. You could fill a shopping cart with 50 items every day for three years without buying the same thing twice. A Wal-Mart Supercenter offers 120,000 items. Step inside a Wal-Mart, pause briefly at the threshold—with two, or three, or four acres of brand-new goods before you piled to the ceiling—and at that moment you command a cornucopia from every corner of the globe that wasn't available, not even to the richest and most powerful, one hundred years ago.

The Wal-Mart effect begins on the shelves, it begins with the allure of the low prices, it begins with us, the shoppers, putting stuff we need in our shopping carts, with a little reinforcing thrill if we know how much we're saving on laundry detergent and disposable diapers and boxes of breakfast cereal.

I am myself a Wal-Mart shopper. In the last year, I went to Wal-Mart fifty-eight times, sometimes to answer a question for this book, but mostly to shop for my family. More typically, I'd go to Wal-Mart a couple times a month, perhaps every two weeks.

I don't actually shop at Wal-Mart. I go to buy things. I know what I need as I walk in the door, and I always work the same path through a particular kind of store—there are only a few different store layouts. My goal every time is to get through the place and emerge with the basic necessities we need without surrendering too much money, or too much of my time. The only things I impulse-buy at Wal-Mart are things I'd forgotten we were out of, items that suddenly remind me as I churn through the aisles: Oh yeah, we need 75-watt lightbulbs. As doleful as it sounds, each expedition has a certain hunter-gatherer quality for me. In most Wal-Marts, getting from one end of the place to the other (baby products and health and beauty products, for example, are often in opposite corners of the stores) requires determination, energy, a refusal to be discouraged, a certain wiliness, and a big-box sense of humor. A successful Wal-Mart shop instills in me a small sense of triumph. I know enough about prices after twenty-five years of shopping that I'm aware of when I'm saving money. Often I know exactly how much money I'm saving (the Johnson's baby shampoo is 79 cents cheaper than at other places, the cans of Snow's minced clams are 17 cents cheaper).

Every Wal-Mart has its own personality, its own character. Some have soaring ceilings, and skylights, and toys piled cheerfully up the walls to the roof. Some have ceilings so low that you can't see the walls of the store in the distance.

Some stores are well organized and well tended. In others, you wander into the diaper aisle, or the toy department, and it looks as if someone went through and swept the merchandise onto the floor.

At some stores, the parking lots are sprinkled with trees and small islands of grass, the shopping carts are collected diligently, and the Wal-Mart sign is brightly lit. At other stores, the parking lots are barren of anything but asphalt, so many shopping carts are scattered around outside that there are no carts to use inside, and the sign says W L MA T because the lights in the A and the R are burned out, with the ★ dark for good measure. (In general, when a Wal-Mart can't keep the letters in its sign lit, the store is a mess.)

I am both amazed by Wal-Mart, and appalled. I am never bored. The GE lightbulbs we use were $2.19 for four 60-watt or 75-watt bulbs five years ago. Now, at the Wal-Mart where we shop most often, those same four bulbs sell for 88 cents. From 55 cents a bulb to 22 cents a bulb, almost literally while I've been watching. I have bought hundreds of GE lightbulbs from Wal-Mart during the last ten years. I have never pulled one from the corrugated paperboard box and found it broken; I've never screwed one into a socket and had it not work. How is it that the price has fallen 60 percent, and yet the bulbs keep coming, good as ever? The Wal-Mart effect.

At one Wal-Mart where we shopped regularly, I noticed they were getting ready to renovate. Supplies like pallets of floor tile and new, shrink-wrapped checkout stands were piling up outside on the sidewalk and in the parking lot. I asked someone when the store would be closing. "Oh no," the associate told me, "we're going to stay open right through the renovation. We're going to replace all the store fixtures, and all the flooring, and all the checkout lines. But we won't have to close for a day." The associate was proud. "Just watch," she said.

It was incredible to behold. They did, indeed, renovate that store from south to north, one strip of flooring, one aisle, one checkout line at a time. When they started, the place was a kind of unashamed dump. Grungy floor, battered shelving, chaotic stocking. Each week they ripped out a section of the store interior from front to back and replaced it with all new fixtures and flooring. During the weeks of renovation, the store was flooded with Wal-Mart staff. If you turned once in a circle with a baffled expression on your face, wondering where your dishwasher detergent had gone, someone would say, "Sir, can I help you find something? We've moved a few things around here temporarily."

When the renovation was over, though, the store drifted back to its original character. New floor, but with a coating of grit; new shelves, but you still had to push around all the megapacks of Pampers to find the right size and quantity because they were never where they should have been on the shelf. If you needed help, you could walk briskly down a long side-to-side aisle, peering down the crossing aisles, and never find anyone in a blue vest. The checkout stations were new; the listless checkout clerks remained. That, too, is the Wal-Mart effect: The refurb team came eleven hundred miles from Bentonville, and they did a beautiful job on the fixtures; they did nothing about the deeply entrenched store culture that had drifted as far from Sam Walton's ideal as the store itself was from headquarters.

So I went shopping at Wal-Mart dozens of times in the last year, with a certain grim satisfaction. My wife went shopping once at Wal-

Mart in the last year, and vowed not to return anytime soon. My wife doesn't go to stores to buy things, she goes to shop. Even a weekly trip to the grocery store is occasion for pitching something new in the shopping cart, just to see. She's optimistic; she's always bringing home some "discovery" we've been walking by for a decade. My wife wants to explore, to be surprised and persuaded. She doesn't want to work while she's shopping. She finds Wal-Mart harsh, disorienting, exhausting, frustrating. For her, the prices aren't worth the cost.

The difference between my perception of Wal-Mart and my wife's is not that large. Our descriptions of Wal-Mart are the same, it is our response that is different, and our goals. That, in fact, is how we all pick where we shop. We go where the products and the price and the experience match our sensibility and our sense of value. We shop where it's convenient and comfortable. We don't tend to think about it analytically. We might think about whether it's okay to eat at Mc-Donald's, but that is fundamentally a personal question. Should I really be eating this food? What does it do to me? How does it make me feel? People pondering the drive-through typically aren't thinking about America's industrial-food complex.

But as Wal-Mart's presence and power have grown, as the Wal-Mart effect has become more obvious and more widespread, a new kind of question has arisen: Should I shop at Wal-Mart? You can type that full question into Google—"Should I shop at Wal-Mart?" or "Should we shop at Wal-Mart?" or "Should you shop at Wal-Mart?"— and find several dozen thoughtful discussions.

It's an amazing question. It's hard to know even what kind of question it is: A political question? An economic question? A moral question? A values question? The question is really shorthand for the whole set of larger questions, the mystery at the heart of Wal-Mart: What is the Wal-Mart effect? Is Wal-Mart good for America or bad? Is Wal-Mart itself good or bad? When we spend our money at

Wal-Mart, are we helping companies and the economy and factory workers along with ourselves? Or are we just adding drops of acid to the corrosion of the very system we value?

Wal-Mart's very familiarity in the landscape, in the economy, in the media, in our own psychology is itself seriously misleading. It leaves us with the sense that we know Wal-Mart, that we know its impact, that we understand the Wal-Mart effect. In fact, Wal-Mart is hiding in plain sight. For all its power, for all its ubiquity, for all the ink and airtime devoted to talking about Wal-Mart, we know very little for certain about the company. Wal-Mart is arguably the world's most important privately controlled economic institution. It not only has no rivals, it often seems impervious to challenge, let alone accountability. Many of the most basic, and most urgent, questions about Wal-Mart, those at the core of the public debate, are unanswered. Wal-Mart's own forty-year history of absolute secrecy, including forbidding its suppliers to talk about their relationship with Wal-Mart, has only deepened the mystery of Wal-Mart's impact.

How much does Wal-Mart really lower prices?

Does Wal-Mart raise our standard of living while it lowers prices?

Does Wal-Mart bring businesses to the communities where it opens, or does it kill businesses already in them?

Does Wal-Mart create new jobs as it opens stores? Or does it just create new Wal-Mart jobs at the expense of other businesses?

Does Wal-Mart really make its suppliers more efficient?

Is doing business with Wal-Mart good for a company's financial health?

Does Wal-Mart drive creativity and innovation at its suppliers, or is so little profit left that there is no money left for innovation?

Does Wal-Mart send factory jobs overseas?

And where exactly does all that merchandise made overseas come from, who makes it, and are they happy new members of the global economy or indentured factory serfs? Are we shopping ourselves out of not only good factory jobs in the United States but also out of a safe environment, since overseas factories make toys and bikes and power tools for us without the need to adhere to safety and pollution regulations?

In the end, how much does Wal-Mart really save us? And do those savings dramatically offset all the costs of the Wal-Mart effect? Or is it the other way around: Do the costs of the Wal-Mart effect, scattered in factories and towns across the country and around the world, add up to far more than the dimes and dollars Wal-Mart allows each of us to keep in our pockets?

And if, as the debate about Wal-Mart indicates, we are so concerned about the company's impact, why do we continue to shop there with such loyalty, such devotion? If Wal-Mart is so infuriating, why is it also so irresistible?

The very range of questions, their complexity, and their significance show the importance of the Wal-Mart effect. Answering the questions is vital—not just to understanding the impact of Wal-Mart but to understanding the behavior and impact of all kinds of companies in the global economy. Wal-Mart is so large, its reach so great, that it has created an ecosystem in which its suppliers and competitors, and their suppliers and competitors, and their customers, all operate. Wal-Mart sets the metabolism, it sets the rules, of that ecosystem. Wal-Mart has inexorably changed our expectations as shoppers—and the Wal-Mart effect also extends to consumers who never shop at Wal-Mart. Likewise, Wal-Mart has reshaped the companies that supply it—and it has also reset the pace and the competitive landscape even for companies that try to do business without Wal-Mart.

It is time to look at Wal-Mart anew, to see in a fresh way what has become utterly familiar, even prosaic. From Bentonville, Arkansas, to Dhaka, Bangladesh, from McDonough, Georgia, to Puerto Montt,

Chile, the Wal-Mart effect doesn't just shape the lives of companies and communities, it shapes the lives of real people every day. In offices, on factory floors, and in our own shopping carts and checking accounts, it is possible to get beyond the noise about Wal-Mart, to penetrate the wall of secrecy that Wal-Mart itself has imposed, and get at the truth of the Wal-Mart effect.

TWO
SAM WALTON'S TEN-POUND BASS

People say Wal-Mart is making $10 billion a year. But that's not how the people inside the company think of it. If you spent a dollar, the question was, How many dollars of merchandise do you have to sell to make that $1? For us, it was $35.

—*Ron Loveless, one of Sam Walton's early managers,*
who rose from stock boy to senior vice president

LARRY ENGLISH, now fifty-seven years old, grew up in Harrison, Arkansas, which even today is a small town, and a couple hours' twisty two-lane ride from bigger towns like Fayetteville. At fourteen, Larry English got a job at Wal-Mart #2, which was in a strip mall and had more the air of today's dollar stores than a modern Wal-Mart. The ceilings of the original #2 were so low English could stretch up and touch them, the fixtures were improvised.

"The frills of things like a tile floor, particularly in Harrison, Arkansas, wasn't there," says English. "It was just a cement floor, it was bare bones." English started at #2 just a few months after it opened, and at fourteen, he imbibed a culture, a philosophy, and a work ethic that would shape the rest of his life.

His first boss was Don Whitaker, a legendary, one-eyed Wal-Mart

manager so gruff he was called the Bear. "He was like a drill ser-
geant," says English. The very first assignment Whitaker gave his
young stock boy was to go out in back of #2 and load boxes and trash
into a cattle truck, because the store had no trash pickup. "I worked
for thirty or forty-five minutes on that trash. I thought, Am I going to
do this? Or am I going to quit? Then I thought, If that old man wants
to run me off, I'm just going to show him what I'm made of."

The point of Wal-Mart was firmly established by store #2, and it
made a vivid impression on a fourteen-year-old boy. "If we could do a
10 percent discount versus the downtown drugstore on the square,"
says English, "we were king. A 45-rpm record was a dollar at the drugstore. We sold them for 77 cents."

Before English was twenty years old, he would be an assistant
manager at Wal-Marts #5, #1, #10, and #3 (Conway and Rogers,
Arkansas; Tahlequah, Oklahoma; Springdale, Arkansas). He got to be
the manager of his own store at age twenty, in 1970: #18, Newport,
Arkansas.

"It was 29,500 square feet and the manager literally did everything," says English. "We had thirty-five different departments. We
hired our own staff. We ordered anything we felt we were big enough
to order." Bear Whitaker and Sam Walton taught Larry English to be
a merchant during his teenage years. And at twenty, he was accountable for the business of #18.

"We had numbers to hit. Mr. Walton was a numbers man. If he
called you at eight A.M. on Saturday, you better know your sales for
the week, by day. And you by damn better know what your payroll
[cost] was, by percentage of sales."

With just a few dozen stores, the key elements of the Wal-Mart
culture were already firmly anchored. Buy stuff cheap, sell it cheap.
And if you're going to sell the same stuff as every other store, but
cheaper than they sell it, controlling your own costs has to be more

than a goal. It has to be a fundamental element of your business every day. One of the costs store managers could control then, and still control today, are payroll costs—the cost of staffing and stocking the store.

When English was manager of #18, the Bear, Don Whitaker, would turn out to be his boss yet again, his district manager. "Well, I had a payroll budget of 8 percent at this store I was managing," says English. "I had just gotten a new assistant manager—a second assistant manager. I was so grateful.

"One day, Whitaker calls up and he says, 'What's your payroll?' I said, 'It's 8.1 percent.' And Whitaker says, 'What did I tell you your budget was? Eight percent.'"

In that era, in a store doing about $1 million in sales a year, Larry English's "missed" payroll number, his excess cost, amounted to $1,000 over a year—$20 in extra labor cost for a week, $3 a day. The Bear acted immediately. "He said, 'Since you can't control your payroll, I'll control it for you. Send that new assistant on to Poplar Bluff, Missouri.'"

Larry English would go on to become in his own right almost as legendary a field manager for Wal-Mart as Bear Whitaker. English would open the first 80,000-square-foot store (#278, Shreveport), the first 110,000-square-foot store (#512, El Paso), and the first store to do $1 million in business—not in a year but in a week (also #512). But that day thirty years ago, he was just a green store manager who worked for the Bear and had busted his payroll by $20 a week, and lost a desperately needed assistant as a result. English remembers his reaction. "You had a little disappointment. And by the same token, you were disappointed in yourself, because you hadn't managed the people with the dollars you had. The goal was to manage the business like it was your own money."

For competitors and businesspeople, and even for shoppers, one of the most fundamental questions about Wal-Mart is also the simplest: How do they do it? How do they sell the very same stuff—the same toothbrush, the same twenty-pound bag of dog food, the same bin of LEGO—for less than the grocery store down the street or the nearby Target? The answer begins in the education of Larry English, and the education of a whole generation of Wal-Mart managers who formed the foundation not just of the company's early stores, but of its headquarters staff and its powerful corporate culture as well.

While most people have a strong sense of what working in Wal-Mart's stores is like—if only from shopping in them—they have no sense of what working for Wal-Mart in headquarters is like, of what being a manager is like. What is the culture inside the building where what became the largest company in human history is run? We all have some impression of what it was like to work for General Motors in the fifties, or to be an "IBM man" for Big Blue in the sixties and seventies, or what working for Amazon or Apple was like in the dot-com era. Wal-Mart is the iconic company of the American economy right now. Its managerial culture is crucial to the company's success, and its influence. Yet the Wal-Mart white-collar culture is a blank because Wal-Mart managers and executives so rarely talk about their experiences.

The financial discipline that Larry English—a man who never went to college—learned in #18 in Newport, Arkansas, is just one element of that culture. But thirty-five years after English first became a manager, that discipline can be seen clearly on Wal-Mart's financial statements today. To sell $100.00 worth of merchandise, Wal-Mart spends $3.10 less than Target does to sell the same $100.00 worth of merchandise. In retail, that's a huge advantage. It means that Wal-Mart can price an item Target would sell for $100.00 at $96.97. Or Wal-Mart can shave 31 cents off the price of something that Target typically sells for $10.00 and sell it for $9.69. That margin is at the core of the Wal-Mart effect—it's where the power to pull in customers begins.

The durability and the primacy of that financial discipline is clear today in another way. It is the root cause of the most serious accusations and problems facing Wal-Mart: a series of lawsuits and investigations and revelations about Wal-Mart's labor practices. From one side of the country to the other, there are dozens of lawsuits alleging that store managers routinely forced hourly employees to punch out at the time clock, then return to work, putting in hours of unpaid labor. Wal-Mart recently settled a federal investigation of its use of hundreds of illegal aliens to clean its stores, making a record-setting payment to the federal government. The company faces the largest class action workplace lawsuit in history: the sex discrimination suit on behalf of 1.6 million current and former female employees that alleges that Wal-Mart managers systematically underpaid women and denied them promotions. A front-page story in the *New York Times* in 2004 revealed Wal-Mart's routine practice of locking employees inside about 10 percent of its stores overnight, a practice the company altered even before the *Times* could publish its story.

The wave of accusations and revelations about Wal-Mart's workplace practices seemed to catch the public, and ostensibly the company, by surprise. What Wal-Mart's senior management seems not to fully appreciate is that, in fact, those practices spring from the same source as Wal-Mart's cost advantage over Target: an unrelenting focus not on profits but on controlling costs. Financial discipline, cost control, had become for some an excuse for exploitation and mistreatment. The virtue had morphed.

The bedrock values instilled by Sam Walton and his early lieutenants were all-American values: hard work, frugality, discipline, loyalty, a restless effort at constant self-improvement. Those values trained and inspired a set of pioneering storekeepers who revolutionized retailing in the United States. When you talk to those men and women today, they are clearly not just competitive businesspeople, intuitive retailers, and loyal employees, but fundamentally decent, thoughtful managers and people. When they talk, you can hear the voice of Sam Walton himself.

L OWELL KINDER STARTED at Wal-Mart in 1975, when the company had about a hundred stores. He had moved his family to the Bentonville area from Overland Park, Kansas, to try his hand at selling real estate, and found he didn't care for it. He had managed a large store back in Kansas, so he applied to work at Wal-Mart.

"Sam was very particular about the people he hired," says Kinder. "I was interviewed seven times. The entire philosophy of the company then was the people." During one of Kinder's interviews, he remembers saying to a personnel manager, "I've been down here four times already. My references check out. What's the holdup? He said, 'We have to be sure you're right for us.' He asked me a question: 'Are you willing to put everything you've ever done behind you and learn what we're doing?' "

Kinder quickly discovered that Sam Walton took the education of his staff in hand himself.

"We would sit around a big table, and Sam would talk to us like a Dutch uncle. He would say, 'You see this pen? We're selling it for 88 cents. It's a good pen. We're paying 60 cents for it. We could write an order for this at 60 cents and sell it at 97 cents. But we don't. We want to sell a good product at the best price. And make sure we've always got it.' "

And Sam's philosophy was working. "In those early days," says Kinder, "the stores were very poorly merchandised. Old fixtures, old tables, old racks. And they were still doing business like crazy. . . . The company was the most interesting thing you ever saw. The entire thing was optimism."

It can be hard to look around today and remember that Wal-Mart has not always dominated the landscape, or American retailing. As recently as 1985, ten years after Lowell Kinder signed on, Wal-Mart was still a regional outfit, with $8.5 billion in sales and 882 stores. Kmart then had 2,180 stores—and $22.4 billion in sales. Sears had $36.4 billion in revenue.

A *New York Times* story in February 1986 was headlined KMART CLOSING THE SEARS GAP. The story asked, "Will the Kmart Corporation edge out Sears, Roebuck & Company before the 1980s end and become the nation's largest general merchandise retailer?" The story did not mention Wal-Mart.

By the end of 1990, Wal-Mart was bigger than Kmart. Two years later Wal-Mart passed Sears. By the end of 1994, Wal-Mart was bigger than Sears and Kmart combined.

Wal-Mart's surge was driven by many things, but the real engine was deep inside the company, in the workplace habits instilled by Sam Walton. The key ideas of Walton's work philosophy are so simple that it is easy to overlook their driving power. The values are so elemental—they are really Ben Franklin-esque—that it seems hard to believe they are the foundation of the largest corporation in history.

Wal-Mart's headquarters staff works relentlessly hard, and always has. At headquarters, buyers and midlevel staffers get to work at 6:30 in the morning. Senior executives often arrive even earlier—at 6:00. Routine quitting time ranges from 5:00 to 7:00 P.M., depending on the job, the season, and the workload. And all white-collar employees work from 7:00 A.M. to 1:00 P.M. on Saturday, including attending the legendary Saturday-morning meeting. So a headquarters staffer who manages to scoot out the door every day at 5:00 P.M.—who would be rare—is putting in a typical week in the office in excess of fifty-eight hours. Even if you assume that Wal-Mart and its competitors are hiring equally talented staff—which is not a safe assumption—the standard Wal-Mart headquarters staffer is working at least 15 percent more hours in a routine week, even if his or her competitors are logging fifty hours.

Wal-Mart's corporate culture is instinctively, reflexively frugal, as was Sam Walton himself. Indeed, frugal is too pale, too dilute a word for how Wal-Mart and its managers have come to think about spending the company's money. To this day, Wal-Mart's vendors are required either to provide a toll-free phone number for their company or accept collect calls from Wal-Mart buyers. For decades, Wal-Mart has not wanted to pay for the telephone calls necessary to talk to its own suppliers. In the offices at headquarters, even the offices of senior merchandising and store executives, the furniture is often a mismatched hodgepodge of colors and styles, including samples of chairs from suppliers that Wal-Mart, having assessed for purposes of selling them in its stores, has put into everyday service. Most Wal-Mart staffers who travel are only reimbursed for tipping up to 10 percent of the cost of a meal. Staffers routinely bring basic office supplies like pens from home rather than go to the trouble of requisitioning them.

"Sam valued every penny," says Ron Loveless, another of Sam's early, legendary store managers, who started as a stock boy in #21 (St. Robert, Missouri) and rose to be senior vice president in charge of Sam's Club stores. "People say Wal-Mart is making $10 billion a year, or whatever. But that's not how the people inside the company think of it.

"If you spent a dollar, the question was, How many dollars of merchandise do you have to sell to make that $1?

"For us, it was $35. So, if you're going to do something that's going to cost Wal-Mart $1 million, you have to sell $35 million in merchandise to make that million."

It's a sobering way of thinking about spending money, even for a big company. For Wal-Mart, every $1 million in spending amounts to a whole year's worth of purchases for 485 families.

In addition to diligence and frugality, Sam Walton insisted on accountability. His oldest son said Walton was reviewing store-level sales data, in his hospital bed, days before he died. The company's Saturday-morning meeting for headquarters staff served many purposes—information sharing, brainstorming, bonding, benchmarking—but a key element of the meeting was, and still is, a discussion of the dollar performance of Wal-Mart's sales, category by category. There was no hiding.

And Sam Walton was competitive, competitive the way some people are smart: He never let up, whether he was trying to beat a Kmart store that was going head to head against a Wal-Mart, or playing tennis.

"Sam was no genius," says Loveless, whose mom once worked as a housekeeper for the Waltons. "Sam was a workaholic. He wanted to be the best at whatever he did. He was not driven by money, but by competition. Sam was one of the most competitive tennis players I've ever met. He could be playing a one-legged man in a wheelchair, and he would show no mercy."

But along with accountability and competitiveness, Walton had a core respect for his colleagues in retailing, and saw them as the source of a constant stream of good ideas for Wal-Mart. Even as he was urging his managers to beat their competitors, he insisted that managers of all ranks visit competing stores on a regular basis to learn everything they could. Walton believed in continuous improvement before the phrase existed in American business—and what better way to sustain respect for your rivals, while denying them any edge, than to constantly shop their stores for things they were doing well?

The Wal-Mart culture was from the beginning, and remains, incredibly demanding. Wal-Mart managers convey a sense not just of challenge and achievement, but also of being on a mission: Delivering low prices is worthwhile, it changes the lives of customers. Walton gave his managers serious responsibilities early on, and for many the mission was completely absorbing. Between his first job as a stock boy at his hometown Wal-Mart in Harrison and his first shot at running his own store, Larry English did a stint as an assistant manager at Wal-Mart #1, in Rogers, Arkansas, just a few miles from headquarters in Bentonville.

It was 1967, and English, then nineteen, was married with a young daughter. One Sunday he was working and had brought his daughter, Windy, along. In those days, the Rogers store had a basement, and Windy English, not quite a toddler, was hanging out in a walker.

"She went down the stairs in that crawler," says English. "She went down the stairs. By the time I got to the hospital, I had decided, I'm not having any more children. No more children. I thought, What if I had two kids down here at the store in a stroller, and they went down the stairs?"

Windy wasn't seriously injured, but Larry English stuck to the decision he made on the way to the hospital that Sunday. "She's the only child I have, and that's part of the reason. Did Wal-Mart run my family? Not really, but yes. You ate, breathed, and lived Wal-Mart. Out of a desire to be the best. It is a sacrifice."

Wal-Mart likes to portray itself as a family-oriented company—in 2004, it was running TV ads featuring employees talking about Wal-Mart's family-friendly policies. But no less an authority than Sam Walton's wife, Helen, is quoted saying in her husband's memoirs that the demanding work culture started with him. "During one period . . . he would work until ten on Saturday night, and then he'd get up and go right back in Sunday morning. We were supposed to be taking turns about getting the kids to Sunday school, and to get four little kids dressed for church with nobody to help me was a little unreal. It's true we had less time with Sam after Wal-Mart [started in 1962], but don't get the idea that he wasn't working most of the time before that."

Wal-Mart has often been a family experience in another way. Larry English, now fifty-seven years old, is the oldest of eight children. "All of us, including my mother, have worked at Wal-Mart," says English. The three brothers—Larry, Terry, and Marty—have a combined sixty-eight years of Wal-Mart service. Windy's stepfather has another thirty years of service. Windy lived in six states growing up, and went to fifteen schools. Larry English has been married four times.

The level of commitment required of managers starts in the stores. Terry English, one of Larry's younger brothers, spent nineteen years as a district manager supervising ten stores, based in Oklahoma. "A good manager will come to the store about six-thirty in the morning, and get his sales for the store by department. Typically, managers work until five P.M.," says English. "They'd work late a couple nights a week, until nine-thirty or ten. Managers are typically off on Wednesday and Sunday, then they would take one full weekend off once a month." That typical workweek English just described amounts to more than sixty hours. "In my experience, even my weak managers didn't look at the clock."

If anything, Terry English's own hours as a more senior manager were even more daunting. "Technically, Wal-Mart wants you to be family oriented. But you have to work from six-thirty in the morning until six-thirty at night, and at least half a day on Saturday. You spend

Saturday afternoon and Sunday doing family chores—and then suddenly it's Monday morning again. You do get three or four weeks of vacation eventually, but you can't take more than a week at a time." Terry English retired in early 2004—he was only forty-eight years old, and working at Wal-Mart had made him a millionaire. "I love Wal-Mart," he says. "I love the company. It's made up of common people, and I love the people. Why did I retire? After thirty-two years, I'm tired."

Sam Walton died in 1992, working right up to the end, but all the elements he imprinted indelibly on Wal-Mart's corporate culture remain: the accountability, a devotion to numbers-based performance measures for people, products, shelves, and stores; the competitiveness, reinforced with a constant nagging sense that you weren't doing things quite as well as you could; and a vigilance about your competitors. All together, the early elements of the Wal-Mart way are a kind of reinforcing loop of discipline, reality, humility, and direction. Get to work early, check your own numbers constantly, don't spend money you don't have to spend, notice specifically what your competitors are doing well, then get to work the next morning before they do.

But all that overlooks the fabric that knit it all together for Sam Walton—he loved the stores themselves, his own stores and other peoples' stores. "Sam Walton," says Ron Loveless, "was a merchant. He loved to go buy stuff cheap." And sell it cheap too.

AFTER LOWELL KINDER survived the rigors of seven interviews, and before he was called back to Bentonville to run Wal-Mart's auto service business, he spent a half dozen years managing Wal-Mart stores and being a field-based district manager supervising ten stores in Texas. He remembers a meeting one year before Christmas where the topic of extension cords came up.

"We'd order cases of those 88-cent extension cords, the brown ones," says Kinder. "We'd display them next to the Christmas trees and the Christmas lights, and on an end cap." And they'd sell cases of them too.

David Glass, who went on to be CEO of Wal-Mart, was at the meeting. He said, "I'd like you to try something different. We've got the big orange extension cords, and those are $12 or $13 each. I'm not saying do away with the 88-cent ones. I'm just saying, cut a couple of cases of the orange ones open and leave them next to the Christmas trees too. If we sell three of those, we make more than on a whole pile of brown 88-cent ones."

"David was big on this," says Kinder. "If you've got a customer in to sell him something, how do you get him to buy something else?"

Retail is not rocket science. It's not like designing a new generation of microchip, or deciphering the human genome. Yet because retail is so familiar—we all shop, but few of us understand the relationship between enzymes and gene expression—the idea of innovation in stores can get lost. How much has the typical Sears, or the typical Kmart, changed in the last thirty years? The allure and success of Apple Computer's high-fashion retail stores, of Whole Foods' mouthwatering grocery stores, is a reminder of the enchanting power of retail innovation—and of how unusual it is.

Today's warehouselike Wal-Marts hardly seem like a lab of retail creativity. But Sam Walton's restlessness—he spent part of most weeks flying from town to town, visiting Wal-Marts—was aimed as often at finding new ideas for his stores as it was at simply inspecting them. The point of innovation, of experimentation, was simply to get more merchandise to the customers. Walton insisted on learning from the people who were selling to ordinary people every day.

"When I was managing the store in Fayetteville, Arkansas, #6, Henrietta Davis was the fabric department manager," says Lowell

Kinder. "She was one of my best people, one of the most loyal. Sam came in one day, and he said, 'Is Henrietta here?' " Someone went and found Henrietta.

"Sam said to her, 'Henrietta, what are you doing that's new and different?' And he listened. And then he said, 'Boy, Henrietta, that is just *great*.' And then he would whip out his tape recorder or his legal pad and start writing."

Wal-Mart's dominance of whole retail sectors—toys, eyeglasses, DVDs—makes it easy to overlook the experiments. Wal-Mart has never been afraid to step gingerly into a business, or a way of doing business, stumble around, figure it out, and then take it chainwide. In the old days, the company was so small that its experiments went unnoticed along with the company itself; now, the chain is so large that people often overlook the innovations until they are rolled out across the country.

Auto service popped up on Wal-Mart's radar screen in 1981 for two reasons: Sears and JCPenney were doing it. And very soon after Wal-Mart opened two or three auto service areas, Kinder says, "I noticed that the store with the auto center is doing twice as much [auto department] business—motor oil, batteries, and so on." Those were—those are—the kinds of connections Wal-Mart managers are always searching for in the sales data that pours from the stores. It doesn't always need to make sense—if the store is offering oil-change and battery service, why would it sell more of those supplies to do-it-yourselfers?—but finding the connections between how a store is managed and what motivates people to buy is essential. Cut open some cases of orange extension cords and put them out too.

Kinder's auto service division, known as TBA—tires, batteries, and accessories—was a typical experiment. "We didn't even sell tires, and everybody convinced Sam you had to have service bays and so forth, and do service work. Sam opened two or three of these, but he didn't have anyone to take care of them. I moved back to Bentonville to run that division. I had no direction. Nobody in the company knew anything about it. So why not me? When I took that division over, they just handed it to me. There were no instructions. I did have a guy to report to. He had no idea what I did."

Except that, like every other person who managed an in-store department for Wal-Mart, Kinder had to report how TBA was doing every Saturday morning. "Everybody simply lived off results," he says.

The division grew rapidly, and like many home office executives, Kinder spent much of his week traveling. "I spent two days a week in the office—Monday and Friday, and of course Saturday. The rest of the time I spent in the stores."

Even Sam Walton was the occasional car-care customer. One year, with the company's year-end meeting coming up, someone at headquarters told Kinder to collect Walton's car, take it to the Bentonville store (#100), and let his auto service team put the car back in shape. It was 1985, the first year as it happens, that Forbes ranked Walton as the richest person in America (net worth then $4.5 billion).

"Sam had a 1975 Chevy," says Kinder. "The car was quite something. He'd been hauling his bird dogs around in it. The hubcaps were gone. It was dirty and muddy. And the dogs had been chewing on the steering wheel.

"We did everything," says Kinder. "We reupholstered the seats, we gave him new brakes, new tires, new hubcaps, a new battery. We detailed it and cleaned it." Kinder had the car delivered back across Walton Boulevard, along with a bill, to Sam's secretary, Loretta Boss Parker. "Then here comes Sam, back from some meeting, and he says, 'Hey, Lowell, let's go look at my old car.' So we go out to the parking lot, and he says, 'That old car is like brand new! If your boys are doing that kind of work, Lowell, you'll have all kinds of customers!' And he winked."

By the time Kinder had four hundred or five hundred service centers, he says, "It became obvious that the thing was becoming unmanageable. Mechanics are temperamental. It was hard to keep the mechanics, and it was hard to keep them honest. They all worked on commission—they didn't understand anything different than that, and we never really came up with a solution to that. And cars were really becoming too technical for us anyway."

Wal-Mart learned a lot about the economics and the challenges of the auto repair business. They learned that it wasn't really a Wal-Mart business. Wal-Mart now has in excess of two thousand auto service departments (along with auto parts departments), but they keep it simple. They do nothing but tires, batteries, and oil changes.

SAM WALTON WAS always looking for experienced managers to bring aboard from other retailers, especially to help with areas where Wal-Mart's own experience was a little thin. If you can crib their ideas, why not their talent? Clarence Archer came to Wal-Mart in 1981, when he was forty-eight years old and had already had a full career, first as a pharmacist, then running pharmacies for Kroger, which operated a drugstore chain called SuperX (with the "Rx" standing for pharmacy). The chain was much like today's Eckerd or CVS. Archer had also worked for the jewelry store company Zales, which owned a chain of drugstores for a while.

One of Archer's jobs in his early days at Wal-Mart was another of Sam Walton's experiments. He ran a group of "deep-discount" drugstores called Dot Discount Drugs, designed to compete with Phar-Mor. "Sam simply saw what Phar-Mor did to Wal-Mart when they came into a town. It was a big subject at Saturday-morning meeting. We would talk about their pricing, we would talk about how many cars they had in their parking lots, how many checkout lanes they had running. The prices at Phar-Mor were excellent."

Archer eventually had fourteen Dot stores. "I visited every Phar-Mor I could get into," says Archer. "Sam would say to me, 'I visited another Phar-Mor, it was very busy.'"

Wal-Mart tried to match Phar-Mor's operating philosophy and store culture, which was even more austere than Wal-Mart's own. "We used fixtures that were old Wal-Mart fixtures," says Archer. "Wal-Mart didn't throw them away, so I said, Give 'em to me." Phar-Mor was running with costs something like 25 percent lower than Wal-Mart's, a fascinating achievement for someone as cost obsessed as Sam Walton.

"We learned what you had to do to operate the store with those costs," says Archer. "You have to beat the salesmen for the best deal. You have to keep wages completely down. . . . You have to keep staff down. The moment the checkers didn't have any customers in line, they were to be out in the store, stocking shelves."

It was too much even for Sam Walton. "We learned what we wanted to learn," says Archer. "You learn what your competitor knows." Phar-Mor eventually went through bankruptcy twice, and is permanently out of business.

Clarence Archer's main job, however, was creating the pharmacy business in which Wal-Mart has become a major force. When Archer—known to everyone simply as Arch—came on board in the summer of 1981, Wal-Mart had three hundred stores. It had sixteen pharmacies of its own, and another one hundred stores had pharmacy space that had been leased out (the way some Wal-Marts now have nail salons).

The very day Arch was hired, Paul Carter, the executive vice president to whom Arch would report, told him, "Clarence, I just want you to make sure you understand that this may last only six months. We'll see if it works." The pharmacy division, too, was an experiment, but no one in five interviews had mentioned that to Archer. "We didn't sell our house in Dallas for a year, till we knew they were going to stick with it, and till we knew that I was happy."

At forty-eight, Arch saw in Wal-Mart an opportunity few other companies could offer. "The thing I liked about it was that I could start something. I could start my own drugstore chain and run it, backed by real resources. It might only last a short time, but at least I would get a whack at it. At Wal-Mart, I was the CEO."

On day one, Paul Carter told Arch that something had come up, and Arch would have a new boss, Dave Washburn. "He took me over and introduced me to Washburn, and Carter left," says Arch. "Washburn says, 'I don't know a goddamn thing about pharmacies. So don't bring me your problems.' I don't think I saw him again for five or six months."

Wal-Mart, it was quickly clear, was a very different kind of company from the retailers where Arch had worked. "The mood at headquarters was very friendly," he says, "but not as friendly as Kroger. At Kroger there was a lot of drinking coffee and bullshitting. We did have break rooms at Wal-Mart, but you didn't go in there and sit."

The pharmacy business was going to be a challenge for Wal-Mart, and Arch knew it. "People I worked with at Kroger and SuperX told me when I took the job, 'You will never get pharmacies to work in Wal-Mart. People just don't go to Wal-Mart for prescriptions.'"

It wasn't just that the feeling of a Wal-Mart Discount City, the original nickname of the stores, wasn't quite pharmacylike. "It was also a question of convenience," says Arch. "The parking lots of Wal-Mart, even then, were enormous. People who go to drugstores to get their prescriptions don't like that."

Arch moved slowly the first year. He opened the pharmacies that had been scheduled to open, he traveled to understand the business, and he developed a two-pronged key to success: price and people.

"In those days, pharmacies weren't like today," says Arch. "Most of the prescription business was a cash business"—people paid directly for their medicine. "You had cash, and you had Medicaid/Medicare. So people knew the price of their medicine, and price made a difference."

But the biggest thing, says Arch, "was hire the number-one pharmacist in the market. People will follow their pharmacist because of the way a good pharmacist communicates with you. When we would open a store, we would hire the best pharmacist in town, no matter the price." He started with one pharmacist per store, with sometimes a relief pharmacist for the weekends; pharmacists were expected to fill one hundred scrips a day—now the number is two hundred to three hundred per day.

Arch came to Wal-Mart with a philosophy that matched Sam Walton's almost precisely. "From day one," he says, "Arch was known for one thing: sales, sales, sales. Sales cure all illnesses. Sales cure all sicknesses. I taught my staff one thing: sales, sales sales. And what drives sales? A $5-off coupon." That is, price.

Arch adapted pharmacy to Wal-Mart, and he adapted Wal-Mart to pharmacy. "For years, I was the pharmacy division. I set up the stores, I hired the pharmacists, I trained the pharmacists, I laid out the pharmacies—everything." Arch eventually insisted on taking command of a few of the aisles of medicine and first-aid supplies that Wal-Mart traditionally positions right near the pharmacy. "In the early years, there were always a lot of out-of-stocks in that area. You know, on Saturday and Sunday, they would be out of Tylenol, Bayer, Maalox. They didn't have high-caliber people on the weekend assigned to stock, to keep them 'faced up.' We preached: Never have an out-of-stock. Who wants to come in to buy Tylenol because they have a headache, and you're out of it? They have a headache, and now they have an even bigger headache because they have to go somewhere else."

Arch came to Wal-Mart with another element of the Wal-Mart culture already in his character: He was tirelessly competitive. He opened a pharmacy at the Wal-Mart in Mena, Arkansas, #67, in 1982 or 1983. "There was already a pharmacy in the shopping center there. I opened with a coupon in the newspaper for $5 or $10 off, with the grand opening of our pharmacy, and the 9-cent rubbing alcohol special or something."

The next day, the pharmacist in the shopping center announced that he would match Arch's coupon. "So the day after that, I ran a coupon for $20 off your next prescription. And I never heard another word from the guy after that."

At that week's Saturday-morning meeting, a regional manager stood up and told of Arch's brief battle, holding up the newspaper ads, which took up most of a page in the local paper.

"Mr. Sam looks at those ads and he smiles and he says, 'You can get pretty rough out there, Clarence, can't you?'" At Wal-Mart, only Walton used Archer's given name. "I said, This guy wanted to play hardball. . . ."

"Well," said Walton, "congratulations."

Arch got a significant break that demonstrated both Wal-Mart's patience and its determination to make the pharmacy business a success. He got five years to turn a profit. But Sam Walton seemed to lose sight of that pretty regularly—once a month, on Saturday morning.

"You don't start pharmacies up and make a profit," says Arch, who opened an average of 150 per year—3 per week—during his sixteen years at Wal-Mart. "The pharmacist costs a bundle, in those days, we were paying $40,000 in salary. To recoup that, you have to write quite a few scrips.

"Every month, at Saturday-morning meeting, when the P&Ls came out for each division, Sam would stand up on the stage, and we would go over the profitability of each division of the stores—the general merchandise, the snack bars, the shoe department, jewelry.

"I'd be sitting with the guy from automotive and the guy from jewelry. Every single division made a profit. Except pharmacy. For five years. Mr. Sam would say, 'Clarence, when are we going to start making a profit there?' And every time, Jack Shewmaker"—one of Sam's senior-most lieutenants—"he'd jump up and say, 'Remember what I told you, Sam: Pharmacy is going to take time.'"

Even losing money, Arch had numbers to make, and rules to follow. "I could lose $500,000 a year. But once I lost $500,000, I wasn't allowed to open any more new pharmacies that year," says Arch. "It was hard. Some pharmacies were making money, some were losing big. What I figured out was, Hey, Arch! Just open all your stores for the year in the first four months of the year, before you've lost $500,000."

Arch's competitive nature, and Wal-Mart's work practices, did not make them friends in the pharmaceutical business. "Wal-Mart is not well liked in the pharmacy business because of our pricing," says Arch. "And everyone knows that everyone goes to Wal-Mart once a week anyway." The sprawling nature of Wal-Mart's business has become an advantage to both Wal-Mart's pharmacies and its pharmacy customers, especially regular customers who are on the whole range of maintenance drugs, like cholesterol-lowering medicines: You really can walk in the store, drop off your prescription, do your shopping, and pick up the prescription on the way out. "Once, Mr. Sam said to me, 'Clarence, tell those pharmacists to slow down a bit, so we get the carts filled up some more.'"

By the time Clarence Archer retired in January 1997, Wal-Mart had 2,200 pharmacies, 5 separate warehouses dedicated to distributing pharmaceuticals, and 200 people working on pharmacy at headquarters. Today, Wal-Mart does about $11 billion in pharmacy business a year and has 3,535 pharmacies. Interestingly, Wal-Mart is just number four in the business—behind Walgreens, CVS, and Rite Aid. In part, that's because it's hard for Wal-Mart to beat competitors on the price of medicine because what consumers pay is generally set by insurers, and consumers continue to focus on convenience and ease of pickup.

Arch persuaded Walton to join the National Association of Chain Drug Stores (NACDS)—Walton and Wal-Mart had a deep-seated aversion to joining trade groups, and almost never did—because, says Arch, "we needed to know what was going on in the business, and with other retailers."

The first annual meeting Arch and his colleagues attended was chilly. "I knew people didn't like us," says Arch, "but this was something. That first year we went down, and you get a great, big name tag, and if it's your first year as a member, you get a pink sticker. People would see the sticker—they were coming up to us, to meet us and introduce themselves—and they'd see we were from Wal-Mart, and they'd just drop their hand and turn away."

WAL-MART'S RELATIVE isolation in Bentonville, and its imperviousness to, indeed its disregard for, outside opinion go a long way toward explaining the gap between how the public sees the company and how the company insists on seeing itself. Wal-Mart's culture, and its sense of its culture, hasn't changed in the last twenty years. But the reality of Wal-Mart—its size, the company connection and mission its employees feel, the way those employees are compensated—all those things have changed dramatically. Wal-Mart has outgrown its culture, it has outgrown its personality, but it has not yet come to terms with that new reality.

From all accounts, Sam Walton truly wanted his workers to be happy. Lowell Kinder remembers flying down from Bentonville to Texas with Walton to visit what was then the company's first ninety-thousand-square-foot store (#330), in Victoria. Actually, Walton was going down for the opening of the store in Cuero, Texas (#385). He had told Kinder, among others, that he thought the Victoria store's location was a mistake. So when they were done in Cuero, Walton did what he often did. "He said, 'Let's borrow a car and go to Victoria and see that store.'" As managers often did, Kinder called ahead to tip off the Victoria manager that they were coming by for a visit.

The store looked good, says Kinder, it was busy, and as was his practice, Walton shooed the manager away, gathered the associates around, and had some frank talk about how things were going.

"When he would go out to the stores," says Kinder, "people would be this high up off the floor to see him. And Sam was beside himself; he was happy. When it was time to leave Victoria, all the people were coming up and hugging him, and me, and saying good-bye."

It was 1981. "We're on the plane flying home," says Kinder, "and Sam says to me, 'Lowell, tell me something. What do you do in your spare time?'

"I said, 'Sam, who do you know at Wal-Mart that has got any spare time?' Then I said, 'I do fish a little.'

"And Sam said, 'What's your goal with that, Lowell?'

"I thought a minute, and then I said, 'Well, I'd like to catch a ten-pound bass someday.'

"And Sam said, 'You know, Lowell, you were right about that store. That's a good store in Victoria. And when we were fixing to leave, and all those people were waving and hugging me—I caught my ten-pound bass right there.'"

Few Wal-Mart managers in the first decades made great salaries, and many took pay cuts to come to Wal-Mart. But in addition to a kind of missionary zeal that Walton was able to infuse into the work, another element fired Wal-Mart along: growth. Growth of the stores, growth of the business, and growth of the stock. Part of the unspoken bargain was this: You might not be earning a grand salary as the years ticked by (especially compared to the hours you spent at work), but in the end there would be an incomparable reward, because of the vitality you were investing in Wal-Mart.

If you were a smart enough, or loyal enough, employee to buy just 100 shares of Wal-Mart stock the first year they were available, in 1970, and simply sat on the shares—adding nothing, but also taking nothing—by 2000 you would have had 204,800 shares, worth roughly $11.25 million. Terry English, who retired in early 2004 after thirty-two years, has an Arkansan's natural reserve about money. But he will say, "Most of my stock went through nine splits." Even just 100 shares of Wal-Mart stock that go through nine splits end up as 51,200 shares, worth more than $2 million.

In the era when Sam Walton was alive, it was not hard to create a substantial nest egg as a Wal-Mart employee—it required a certain amount of faith and patience, but it didn't require much money. Just 100 shares purchased anytime between 1970 and 1981, held fifteen years, would have yielded in excess of $150,000. Those same 100 shares held twenty years—you didn't have to keep working at Wal-Mart, just buy the stock and hold fast to it—would have yielded anywhere between $300,000 and $1.7 million, depending on when you bought it between 1970 and 1981.

But the bargain has broken down as Wal-Mart has grown and absorbed hundreds of thousands of new employees. Here's how dramatic the change has been: If you came to work at Wal-Mart anytime after June 1990—that is, anytime in the last fifteen years—and bought your 100 shares, the *most* your stock could be worth would be $20,000. If you started work July 1, 1980, bought your 100 shares, stayed fifteen years, left the company and sold your stock on June 30, 1995, you'd have $340,000. But if you started work July 1, 1990, bought your 100 shares and stayed fifteen years, you'd walk away with only that $20,000. It didn't matter how hard you—as a more recent associate—were working; your stock was working only one seventeenth as hard.

That's what happens as companies grow phenomenally, and as they grow up. But it's a problem that goes much deeper than Wal-Mart's stock price (which from 2000 to 2005 did not appreciate at all). The surest indicator of Wal-Mart's failure to evolve is the wave of workplace problems the company is facing, the manner in which it handles them, and the way the problems can be traced back to the virtuous elements of Sam Walton's original culture. Those values—hard work, cost control, discipline—remain admirable, and they are key to Wal-Mart's success. We want companies that value hard work and thrift. But their application inside Wal-Mart today often looks much different than it did in 1965, or 1975, or even 1985. What looks like missionary zeal when you're a quirky regional retailer comes across much differently when you're the most powerful company, and the largest employer, in the world.

By the fall of 2005, Wal-Mart faced forty separate lawsuits, filed by employees from one end of the country to the other, alleging that they were forced to work off the clock, either working through scheduled breaks or punching out and continuing to work for no pay. In 2002, Wal-Mart lost the first such case to come to trial, in Oregon, although both the number of plaintiffs and the award were small. But in 2000, it settled a class action suit on similar charges brought by sixty-nine thousand current and former Wal-Mart employees in Colorado, for $50 million. What better way for a store manager to control payroll costs than to have employees work free?

In October 2003, federal agents raided sixty Wal-Mart stores in twenty-one states in a single day before dawn, arresting 245 illegal aliens who were cleaning the stores overnight as employees of sub-contractors. Wal-Mart consistently denied knowing its cleaning companies were using illegal immigrants, but to resolve the investigation, it paid the federal government $11 million in 2005. The payment, not technically a fine, was four times the size of any previous settlement involving accusations of employing illegal aliens. The $11 million was also more than twice the amount that Wal-Mart's cleaning contractors themselves paid as a result of the investigation.

The single-mindedness with which Wal-Mart still regards controlling its costs is so great that it would sooner give up business than cede a measure of control. In August 2004, a union was certified at a Wal-Mart store in Québec, and it was authorized to negotiate a labor contract with Wal-Mart on behalf of the store's 190 employees. Ten months later Wal-Mart closed the 130,000-square-foot store in Jonquière, laying off all the associates. In eleven years of doing business in Canada, where Wal-Mart is the largest retailer, the company had never permanently closed a store. A Wal-Mart spokesperson said simply that the union's contract demands would have required the store to add thirty new jobs—a 15 percent increase in payroll for a company that operates on a 3 percent profit margin.

It's unclear how well Sam Walton himself realized that the culture of the company he created would have to change as the scale of the enterprise changed. In any case, when Sam Walton died in 1992, Wal-Mart was a $44 billion-a-year company with 370,000 employees. Plenty big. But in the thirteen years since his death, the number of Wal-Mart employees has grown by 1.2 million; sales have grown by $240 billion. Wal-Mart is not only not the company Sam Walton founded, it is no longer even the company he left behind.

That Sam Walton's core values seem to have become inverted, that they now sometimes drive behavior that is not only exploitive but perhaps illegal, is a sign that even worthwhile cultures need to question themselves constantly and examine the consequences of their values. If the denials and protestations of Wal-Mart's executives are to be believed—that they knew nothing about any of the current questionable workplace practices and certainly never condoned or encouraged them—then the inversion of those values is a sign of something more profound: Even Wal-Mart's senior executives have lost track of the consequences of the Wal-Mart effect, even closest to home, right inside the company's own stores. But the Wal-Mart effect only starts with Wal-Mart's employees and its own stores. For the companies that supply Wal-Mart and for their employees, the impact of the Wal-Mart effect—both beneficial and corrosive—is, if anything, even more dramatic.

THREE

MAKIN BACON, A WAL-MART FAIRY TALE

You'd have to trick me into saying anything bad about Wal-Mart.
—*Gary Ramey, who worked on Sara Lee's Wal-Mart team*

THE THINGS THAT Jonathan Fleck didn't know during his first trip to Bentonville were many, but he wasn't confused about one thing: the opportunity.

Cheryl Knight, a woman responsible for buying kitchen gadgets for Wal-Mart, wanted to talk to Fleck about stocking his kitchen gadget. In 1992, Fleck's eight-year-old daughter, Abbey, had come up with the idea for a nifty way to cook bacon: a dish with small crossbars in which bacon cooks as it hangs suspended in a microwave oven. The dish catches the grease as it drips down, and the bacon cooks up crispy and relatively grease free. They called their invention Makin Bacon. Together, father and daughter spent two years refining a design that worked, figuring out how to get the dish manufactured, then finding someone to sell it. They share the patents.

By the time Fleck went to Bentonville in the spring of 1995, he was already selling the plastic Makin Bacon dish faster than he could make it, using a mold that turned out just one dish at a time. Fleck had taken a run at the major retailers, including Wal-Mart, without any luck. When retailers showed no interest in Makin Bacon, Fleck literally talked his way into the offices of bacon seller Armour, which decided in the fall of 1994 to put a coupon offering the dish on the back of 15 million packages of bacon. Send in two Armour bacon proofs of purchase and $6.99, and get the newfangled bacon-cooking dish.

Then, in November 1994, *Good Housekeeping* ran an item on Makin Bacon on its page devoted to microwave cooking—"Abbey's Bright Idea"—and the orders flooded in.

By the time Wal-Mart reached out to Fleck a few months after the Armour promotion started, he was selling thousands of dishes a week—and not filling the orders fast enough to meet the coupon's "4 to 6 week" delivery promise. Sharon Franke, still with *Good Housekeeping,* remembers the magazine being "inundated with letters and calls from people who sent a check and didn't get their product. . . . He made good on that. Every person who wrote to us got one direct from him"—and another one once his fulfillment house caught up with the backlog. The Armour promotion was great. An order from Wal-Mart, though, could turn a quixotic effort into a real business.

Wal-Mart, says Fleck, "that's every inventor's wet dream."

Fleck met Cheryl Knight, the gadgets buyer, in the stark cubicles where Wal-Mart conducts almost all its vendor meetings. "Cheryl had seen the dish, and she wanted it," says Fleck. "It was going out at $6.99, and the first thing Cheryl said is, 'The only way we can offer this is at something less than that price.' They wanted me to sell it for something less than it was being sold for on the back of Armour bacon."

Cheryl Knight, of course, could order with a single form as many Makin Bacon dishes as Armour's customers would order in nine months. Fleck looked Cheryl Knight in the eye and said, "Sorry, I can't do that.

"Cheryl was pretty dumbfounded. She said, 'You are crazy. You are nuts to turn me down.'" But Fleck really couldn't have said yes. He couldn't make enough Makin Bacon dishes to keep up with the Armour demand as it was. What's more, he says, "Armour gave me a huge opportunity. If Mabel and Fred see what they just bought for 2 cents less on the shelf at Wal-Mart, they will be pissed at me. And I didn't want to do that to Armour either."

So Fleck told Cheryl Knight, "After the program closes out with Armour, I'll be back." A guy whose entire company was running out of a mail-order fulfillment house in Grand Rapids, whose R&D adviser was a fifth grader—that guy told the largest retailer in the United States to wait.

Many things go unappreciated about Wal-Mart. One is this: The company often knows exactly what it wants and is willing to wait—not always patiently—to get what it wants. Six months later, in October 1995, the Armour promotion ended, and Wal-Mart was still game. "Cheryl said, 'Let's do it, or I'm gonna move on.'" The deal was done by phone. Cheryl Knight wanted to launch Makin Bacon in Wal-Mart with an end-cap display, that is, set up on shelves at the end of an aisle, where the novel bacon-cooking dish could make a splash.

It was a great order—two hundred thousand Makin Bacon dishes—and it was a great day. Except for one problem. "As soon as you get the order, you start to do the math," says Fleck. "Financially, going into Wal-Mart puts you on the brink of bankruptcy." It put Fleck and his family there anyway.

The nice thing about the Armour bacon promotion had been that people mailed their money to Jon Fleck before he had to make them a dish. The whole thing was self-financing. Orders poured in, along with the cash to buy plastic and packaging, and pay the manufacturing plant, which was then in Utah.

The Wal-Mart deal was completely different: Fleck needed more than a hundred thousand dollars, in advance. He had to buy sixty thousand pounds of high-grade plastic, he had to have a package designed (a friend did the design he still uses, for free), then he had to buy cardboard and get the packaging manufactured. And, of course, he had to get the dishes manufactured too.

From Bentonville, Fleck received a currency, of sorts. "Cheryl presented me with mountains of 'blue stripers,' that's what they called them. Paper purchase orders, from the preelectronic days." They were distinguished by alternating pale blue and white stripes running across the purchase orders. With the blue stripers in hand, Fleck turned to an unlikely source for a hundred thousand dollars in working capital: a seventy-eight-year-old retired Whirlpool refrigeration engineer who was living in Arnegard, North Dakota, raising durum wheat, Fleck's father, George.

Jon Fleck—energetic, restless, entrepreneurial—is the youngest of eleven children. He started a custom wheat-harvesting business with a brother when he was sixteen—and retired from it when he was twenty-four, and had finished college. His parents, Helen and George, who lived most of their lives in St. Paul, Minnesota, and raised their kids there, had never borrowed money, had never taken out a loan, until Jon got the Wal-Mart blue stripers. George Fleck, who grew up in North Dakota, walked into a bank in western North Dakota, and with the blue stripers and the farm as security, he got a credit line for several hundred thousand dollars for his youngest son. "My dad was skeptical," says Jon. "But it was a done deal, we had the purchase orders." You can still feel the excitement, the urgent persuasion, in Fleck's voice, a decade later. *It's a done deal.* All Jon Fleck had to do was make the dishes, start delivering them, and the money would come right back from Wal-Mart.

And Fleck did deliver. Oh, there was a problem—Fleck is mortified by it to this day. He sent Wal-Mart prepacked displays with twelve dishes. Those prepacks were eighteen inches deep. The problem? The end-cap shelves were twelve inches deep. "I screwed up," says Fleck. "It was disastrous. A mistake like that today with Wal-Mart would not be good—it would be the end of your business with them."

It wasn't too disastrous, though. Fleck and Wal-Mart worked out a slightly different display for those first dishes. George Fleck's first loan was paid off in sixty days. And Jon Fleck's business has never had to take another. He has sold about 1.25 million Makin Bacon dishes through Wal-Mart, and more than 4 million nationwide. You can find Makin Bacon in virtually every Wal-Mart, in the aisle with the microwave ovens, still with a picture of Abbey on the package—frozen in time as an adorable ten-year-old. Today's she's finishing UCLA as a comparative religion major.

The story of Jonathan Fleck is a fairy tale. It's an improved version of *The Wizard of Oz*—about a character, an innocent, who treks to the source of all power, pulls back the curtain, and is welcomed inside.

WHEN YOU ENTER the world headquarters of Makin Bacon today, you are also entering the basement of the house near White Bear Lake, Minnesota, that Jon Fleck shares with his wife and kids. In fact, Makin Bacon's headquarters makes do with about a third of the basement—the rest is set up as a game room and sitting area.

Jon Fleck's relationship to Wal-Mart would be surprising and noteworthy on its own—that the largest company in history, with 1.6 million worldwide employees, would do business with the smallest company in history: one guy, with a home office, who doesn't actually have to tend Makin Bacon full-time these days. What's really remarkable is that Jon Fleck's business, and his relationship with Wal-Mart, works in some important ways just like Procter & Gamble's or

LEGO's—it's a perfect miniature of the Wal-Mart effect. It's an example of how, when things go well with Wal-Mart, it's good for everyone: vendors, factory workers, customers, even the customers of Wal-Mart's competitors, people who refuse to shop at Wal-Mart. Of course, like any business doing business with Wal-Mart, Fleck lives with his share of Wal-Mart oddities.

On opposite ends of his long, angled desk sit two computers: a modern, stylish Macintosh, which is Fleck's preferred machine, and a utilitarian PC. "The PC is just for Wal-Mart," he says. "I'm a Mac guy. I'd love to get rid of it, but Wal-Mart insists on the PC." That's how Wal-Mart's orders come in; that's how Fleck can drill into Wal-Mart's vast database, Retail Link, and sift for insights into how people are buying Makin Bacon, and how he might sell more.

The electronic ordering process—even on a PC—is a huge improvement over the hard-copy blue stripers, of course. After Fleck's initial order, the blue stripers came on a regular basis, in their own peculiarly Wal-Mart fashion. "The blue stripers would arrive on Tuesdays," says Fleck, "Airborne Express. Then you'd get the bill for the Airborne Express delivery of your purchase orders the next week—by regular mail. About $8."

The profile of the Makin Bacon business is also very similar to the profile of much larger consumer product companies supplying Wal-Mart. Fleck does about 25 percent of his volume each year—give or take—with Wal-Mart. Wal-Mart is his largest single customer, but he still does 75 percent of his business with other outlets. Occasionally, Target sells more dishes than Wal-Mart. But Target has been a more fickle Makin Bacon customer—enthusiastic some years, uninterested others. "We've been with Wal-Mart continuously, uninterrupted," says Fleck. "That's key. They are reliable. You can be out of Target on a week's notice. Wal-Mart doesn't play that game. If you're in there, if you're not in there, you know." Indeed, Target can go large just as quickly as it goes small—a couple Christmases ago, for example, "Target ordered a boatload of product for the fourth quarter. I had no clue the order was coming."

In fact, the ability to be nimble, to respond just like a major corporation with factories warmed up and ready, is why Fleck has his dishes made in the United States, just thirty-five miles north of his home, at a plastic-injection-molding facility in St. Croix Falls, Wisconsin. When the unexpected Target order tumbled in, the St. Croix Falls factory ran Makin Bacon twenty-four hours a day to fill it, and it went to Target by truck. Coming by container ship from China, it never would have happened. "I can fill on a time frame that over the water you can't."

Makin Bacon is also available, depending on the season, depending on the year, at Kmart and Walgreens, Linens-n-Things and Le Gourmet Chef stores, and a range of smaller, high-end cookware stores. Another steady outlet for Makin Bacon is an old-fashioned one: catalogs from companies like Carol Wright, mailed directly to homes. "We do a boatload of business with mail-order outfits you've never heard of," says Fleck, "the catalog grandma gets that sits next to the chair in front of the TV." And Fleck gets a dozen or so orders a week sent directly to Makin Bacon headquarters, with a check.

Wal-Mart sells the dish for $6.97, just like they did in 1995, cheaper than anyone else. Target sells it for $6.99. "It costs 2 cents more at Target," says Fleck, "and Target keeps the 2 cents." Everywhere else, the dish is higher priced. During a 2005 test in Walgreens, preparatory to what Fleck hopes will be a huge order, it sold for $7.99. At Le Gourmet Chef, it's $11.99. At Carol Wright Gifts' Web site recently, it was "reduced" from $12.95 to $7.99, with $3.95 in postage bringing the cost to $11.94. If you buy it directly from Makin Bacon, using ordering instructions on the Web site, you send a check for $10.00, including postage, for each dish you want.

Retailers, of course, decide individually what price to charge for the dish, based in part on Fleck's price to them. As in any business, Fleck's wholesale prices are based on volume and the level of service the account requires. But, in fact, everyone gets a deal because of Wal-Mart. Wal-Mart literally pays to turn the factory on. Indeed, without Wal-Mart, or a customer of equivalent scale and steadiness, Makin Bacon would be a much tougher business proposition all the way around.

"The economies of scale that Wal-Mart gives me to purchase my raw material, and to run at the level I do at the factory—that's a huge thing," says Fleck.

"There's no way I would be able to sell this at the price point I'm selling it for at the small specialty retailers, or at mail order, if it weren't for that. The price would be at least 50 percent higher." The Makin Bacon dish is a charming, useful item—but a good deal more appealing at $6.97 or $11.99 than at $15.00 or $18.00. It's not clear, in fact, how well it would sell at all at that price.

There's an important distinction, too, between the economics of efficiency and the economics of competition. They often reinforce each other, of course. Wal-Mart and Target keep their Makin Bacon prices within pennies of each other for competitive reasons. But the price break for all Makin Bacon buyers that comes from Fleck's having Wal-Mart as a foundation customer—that's different. That's a powerful, invisible Wal-Mart effect that has to do simply with scale, focus, efficiency, predictability. And the story of the Makin Bacon dish makes it crystal clear that the benefit goes beyond allowing Fleck to sell the dish more cheaply to everyone—the pricing and economics of the whole business might not make sense at all without Wal-Mart.

"And these dynamics don't change with large companies," says Fleck. "There have been studies of Wal-Mart's impact on the rate of inflation. This is what they're talking about. And I don't think Wal-Mart gets credit for that."

So even if you're buying Makin Bacon at Le Gourmet Chef for $11.99—and, says Fleck, "a lot of the people who go to Le Gourmet Chef would not even walk into a Wal-Mart"—even those customers are getting their dish at a Wal-Mart price.

WALTON CLARK REMEMBERS clearly the call from his client in Bentonville. The members of the senior team he dealt with there were climbing on a company jet and flying out to Englewood Cliffs, New Jersey, for a visit. They wanted a look into the future. They wanted to know Clark's plans for the next three years: What was he going to do to take market share from his competitors? What was he going to do to create some excitement for Wal-Mart's customers, the consumers? What were the creative sparks that were going to grow the business, for him and for Wal-Mart?

"In one sense," says Clark, "we were very flattered. That's a very positive mode. But in the other sense, you're a little nervous. If your funnel is weak, if they are weak ideas, they are not going to be polite. They'll tell you, That's weak. That's bad. You don't have enough."

What caused the group from Wal-Mart to fly to Clark was their concern about innovations in a category most of us think of as pretty well settled, for about the last century: spaghetti sauce. Walton Clark was the director of marketing for Ragu (part of the conglomerate Unilever), with years of experience dealing with Wal-Mart. It was Clark's three-year plan for innovations in pasta sauce that the Bentonville team wanted to scrutinize. "I better be doing a good job," says Clark. "Every category has room to grow. Cleaning floors was dead, but look at Swiffer." (Launched by Unilever rival P&G in August 1999, Swiffer now sells more than half a billion dollars a year in disposable floor-cleaning wipes.)

Wal-Mart does not believe in complacency for itself. Sam Walton's strategy of shopping at his competitors ceaselessly, looking for what they did better than Wal-Mart, is still in use—and Wal-Mart transmits that restless dissatisfaction outward to its suppliers. As the company has gotten bigger, its ability to reach deep inside the day-to-day operations of its suppliers has increased, has in fact become all but irresistible. And that is the most potent, least public, least well-understood power of the Wal-Mart effect: the impact Wal-Mart has in shaping the operations, the choices, the product mix of its suppliers. It is harder to discern, and much harder to get people to talk about, at the giant companies that service Wal-Mart, but it is also richer and more far reaching in those settings than in a tiny operation like Makin Bacon.

Walton Clark worked in the food divisions of Unilever for seventeen years, from 1986 to 2003, a period, he says, "when Wal-Mart went from an unknown to the number-one account." Not only was Wal-Mart interested in new ideas from standard categories, Wal-Mart offered the ability to launch those new products dramatically, widely, quickly.

"If you launch a new item, they want to be 25 percent of your new-item share volume," says Clark. "At Ragu, we launched something called Rich & Meaty—we were putting half a pound of meat in a jar of Ragu sauce." It was 2002.

"Normally, when I ship a new item, I would allow ten to twelve weeks from my first ship date for start-up advertising." If you start shipping January 1, you start advertising in mid-March. "You have to get it to the warehouse, you have to get it onto the shelf. When Wal-Mart takes a new item, two weeks later they want an end-aisle display up in every store, and they want it supported on the shelf"—they want plenty of stock available to keep shelves full if the product takes off. "That's amazing. When they want to, they can turn on a dime."

Clark also learned the power of Wal-Mart's focus on price. One of Sam Walton's retailing innovations was to break the decades-long high-low cycle of pricing of consumer products. For example, something like Coke will have a typical shelf price—say, $1.39 for a two-liter bottle—that is discounted every few weeks to, say, $1.09 for the two-liter bottle, or even 99 cents. Anyone who shops is familiar with those promotional bursts that last a few days—alert, savvy consumers never pay $1.39 for the Coke, they just stock up when it's 99 cents. The promotional discounting is scheduled well in advance, but it still drives large waves and troughs of consumption. Consumers become addicted to the lower price and resist the standard price; suppliers get addicted to the bursts of volume the discounting inspires, but need to sell at the standard price too in order to maintain a reasonable profit margin. And stores go crazy stocking for the promotions, resetting displays, and dealing with a pileup of product that doesn't move when the discounting stops.

Wal-Mart has done away with it all, to the quiet relief of some suppliers who still endure the cycle at other retailers. Wal-Mart wants its vendors to add up all the discounts it would normally give during the course of a year, and take them off the price of an entire year's worth of products. Come up with a single, everyday low shelf price. Teach consumers that Wal-Mart always has the product at that price—better than the standard price elsewhere, close to the discount price. Smooth out and rationalize the demand from consumers—they buy it when they need it. That makes the supply more predictable. Everyone saves—customers and companies.

Wal-Mart's insistence on an "every day low price" on the shelf has had another effect: It has become almost self-fulfilling for suppliers, causing many, including Clark and his colleagues, to hesitate to talk to Wal-Mart about price increases, even when they seem completely justified.

"In early 2003, Bertolli Olive Oil [also a Unilever product] took a price increase," says Clark. "Bertolli is 100 percent imported from Italy. The Euro exchange rate to the dollar had gone from 90 cents or 95 cents to $1.15. That's a huge increase. At the same time, olive oil is a bit of a commodity product. It was a bad crop year, and the price of olive oil went up—a 10 to 12 percent increase. At the previous price, they weren't covering their full costs.

"So before Bertolli took the price increase, they went to Bentonville with a six-page presentation to explain it. Wal-Mart rejected it."

That was a critical moment: Bertolli wasn't trying to make more money, or add profit to reinvest in the business. The world had changed, the price of olive oil had changed, the price to Wal-Mart simply wasn't realistic anymore. Wal-Mart didn't care.

In this case, says Clark, Bertolli didn't accept Wal-Mart's refusal to accept the price increase. "For two or three months, Wal-Mart didn't buy olive oil from them. Eventually, they came back, with the increase. Eventually, everybody in the market had to go up, and Wal-Mart accepted the increase as real."

Wal-Mart executives, says Clark, "see themselves as the advocate of the consumer. If they don't stand up, who will?" And, says Clark, Wal-Mart's scale has made it sensitive to price increases of any kind for another reason. "They go into a little town, people say, run all the local merchants out of business, and a year later, their prices are higher. You have predatory pricing—they are worried about being sued." In fact, the company does not raise prices in small markets if the competition goes out of business. But, says Clark, "they didn't want any examples."

The moral of the Bertolli olive oil price story, says Clark, was clear:

"They have a potent effect on keeping prices stable, even without ever talking about it."

Wal-Mart officials talk often about their "partnership" with their supplier companies, sixty-one thousand in the United States alone. In a 2004 speech to a group of antitrust lawyers, Wal-Mart board chairman (and oldest son of Sam) Rob Walton said, "Our supplier relationships are special. We do not consider ourselves customers of our suppliers. Instead, we are partners." The symbol of the partnership is the "Wal-Mart team," which hundreds of companies have established to tend exclusively to their business with Wal-Mart. Each team is staffed with people who do nothing but analyze and strategize a company's products and relationship with Wal-Mart. It's unclear if this idea of a team of vendor staff members dedicated to the needs of a single customer started with Wal-Mart. When Wal-Mart suppliers started doing it, it was typical for companies to service their customers according to product categories or geography or the size of customers. But Wal-Mart adopted the idea aggressively, and the Wal-Mart team has itself become a symbol of Wal-Mart's power—more than seven hundred companies now have offices in Bentonville or nearby towns to make sure their Wal-Mart team members are as available to Wal-Mart as possible.

The most famous Wal-Mart team is Procter & Gamble's, which was first, and now has a 250-person team based in an office building south of Bentonville, where the staff works every day on servicing P&G's products in Wal-Mart stores. Bill Caldwell helped create and lead the second such team, starting in 1989, on behalf of Sara Lee's apparel group, which includes brands like Hanes, L'eggs, Playtex, and Champion. The idea, says Caldwell, who came out of retirement as a vice president to head the initiative, was "to look at our organizations as one continuum of activity, starting with the time Sara Lee buys raw materials, through the manufacturing process, the distribution process, the merchandising process, and the time the consumer buys it and takes it home and uses it satisfactorily. If we can disregard this artificial barrier"—the barrier, that is, between vendor and retailer—"we can take costs out of the system."

This kind of "partnership" was another Wal-Mart innovation. The "barrier" Bill Caldwell is talking about isn't really artificial—it's the division between the employees and the responsibilities and the finances of one company, the manufacturer, and another company, Wal-Mart. The idea of the partnership was to share a good deal more information than had been typical in such a relationship in order to find areas of inefficiency that could be eliminated, and areas of opportunity that could be exploited. The barrier is simply a means of protection for both companies; the partnership requires a large measure of trust.

Gary Ramey, an early member of the Sara Lee Wal-Mart team, remembers the genesis a little more vividly. "Senior officials were always coming down there [to Bentonville] for meetings, and they always had their sheets of paper bent up so the Wal-Mart person couldn't see them. The idea was, Why don't we just put the sheets of paper on the table?"

As soon as the team was formed, Sara Lee reaped rewards. The company was already using a fair amount of offshore manufacturing in Latin America in the late 1980s, and bringing the clothing in through ports in the southeastern United States, from where it then traveled by truck to Sara Lee distribution centers and then from Sara Lee warehouses to Wal-Mart warehouses. The team quickly discovered that Wal-Mart had hundreds of trucks driving north on I-95 from Florida, mostly empty after delivering merchandise to Florida stores. Why not fill those empty trucks with underwear and socks, and stop using Sara Lee trucks altogether?

"We said, let's bring that product into the port at Jacksonville, set up a distribution center, and those Wal-Mart trucks can stop off in

Jacksonville, pick the product up, and deliver it to their distribution center at a lower rate than we can ship it to them." The arrangement, says Caldwell, saved time, money, gasoline, and the labor involved in unnecessarily loading and unloading merchandise.

At the time, Hanes was sending men's and boys' underwear to Wal-Mart stores in cases of six-dozen packages. "It was more than a store could handle," says Caldwell. "The store would order half a case. So Wal-Mart was picking the underwear up at our distribution center, hauling it to their place, breaking open the case to supply underwear on a partial-case basis." Sara Lee's people said, "That's crazy." They quickly came up with a three-dozen package case to allow stores to order the underwear in smaller quantities without having to have someone manually open every shipping carton and break the packages out into smaller groupings. "Imagine how much money that saved in Wal-Mart's distribution centers, at a very modest out-of-pocket cost to Sara Lee," says Caldwell. "And that cost was more than made up for in the increased sales in the stores as a result of a reduction in stock-outs." Stores ordered more precisely, more routinely.

Those two changes in distribution, says Caldwell, "reduced total costs for the two companies between 1.5 percent and 2 percent"—large amounts of money, given the volumes involved. More important, those savings of what would ultimately be millions of dollars caused benefit for everyone: truck drivers, warehouse workers, people wearing underwear. The changes eliminated the corporate equivalent of pure waste, like turning out the light in an empty room. "One of the things we talked about early on," says Caldwell, "was that from any savings, one third would go to Sara Lee as profit, or funds to use; Wal-Mart would keep one third; and one third would be passed on to the consumer in price reductions.

"What really happened over the next four or five years was that Sara Lee got more than one third, and the consumer got most of what was left. Wal-Mart took a little bit." But what Wal-Mart really liked was the increase in sales from Sara Lee's apparel.

Part of what drove that increase was a new way of displaying products—not on shelves, but planted directly on the floor of an aisle in Wal-Mart, still on its wooden shipping pallet, a single product stacked chest high, ready to buy.

Typically, finished merchandise leaves a factory, by truck, on those slatted wooden (now often plastic) pallets, forty-eight inches by forty inches. Stacked on the pallets, the merchandise is then strapped or shrink-wrapped in place, and the load is easily moved and loaded by forklift. At a store, the pallet has typically been relegated to the storeroom—merchandise is unloaded from it and stocked on shelves as needed.

In 1991 or 1992, says Bill Caldwell, Sara Lee president Paul Fulton was traveling in Europe, and at the French discounter Carrefour he saw products displayed, on the shopping floor, piled on prepacked shipping pallets. Fulton was so struck by the idea that Caldwell went to France to look at it himself. "It was such a powerful merchandising concept," says Caldwell. They brought the idea home to Bentonville, and Caldwell thinks the Sara Lee Wal-Mart team was the first to use the pallet in the United States.

The pallet was easy—position it on the floor, remove the shrink-wrap, tape up some price signs, and the "stocking" work was done.

The pallet got large quantities of merchandise into stores quickly, with minimal labor.

The pallet was dramatic. "It's statement merchandising," says Caldwell. "It's stacking it high and selling it cheap." It's a 360-degree display of stuff, the customer's view not even hampered by shelving.

In an era of true technological revolution, what amounts to innovation in retailing is often more basic—and pallet selling was a revolution in thinking about merchandising.

Surprisingly, Wal-Mart was initially reluctant. "It was a difficult sell," Caldwell says. "When we first started doing it, Wal-Mart didn't have nearly as many stores of the size they do today. Putting a pallet in an aisle was relatively difficult to do, and inconvenient for the consumer."

But pallets did two things Wal-Mart loved: They took costs out of the system, and increased sales. And as with Wal-Mart's other innovations—the elimination of high-low pricing, increased information sharing—the pallet's success was all the persuasion Wal-Mart ultimately needed. Today every Wal-Mart has something known in the trade as Action Alley, the wide central path through each store that is considered prime selling space—because of the pallet. Action Alley is lined with one pallet after another of deals, often on seasonal merchandise. Indeed, the pallet, piled high with a single kind of merchandise—underwear, pickles, antifreeze, ammunition—is now a symbol of the value proposition at Wal-Mart: lots of stuff, cheap. Companies design pallet displays with built-in cardboard shelving facing out in all four directions. "I can't say for certain that was the first time any U.S. manufacturer had used that approach with a U.S. retailer," says Caldwell, "but I don't remember one before we did it." These days, it's hard to imagine big-box retailing without pallets.

Fifteen years ago, even as Wal-Mart was commencing the growth that would take it to complete dominance, the familiar culture was in place. "The ambience at the home office—using that term loosely—was utilitarian to the nth degree," says Caldwell. "I don't think I ever sat on a lawn chair at a meeting, but I have sat on a box, because the two chairs in the office were taken by somebody else." His main point of contact at Wal-Mart was often Bill Fields, executive vice president for merchandise and sales. "I used to go to work at six-thirty in the morning. I'd look at that first hour, from six-thirty to seven-thirty in the morning, as very productive time, because the phone didn't ring.

At seven-thirty, I'd often call Bill Fields, and they all answered their own phones, of course—and it was six-thirty in the morning in Bentonville. He'd pick up. He was there. And he wasn't there by himself."

David Glass, Wal-Mart's then CEO, told Caldwell his competitive philosophy was simple: "He said, 'We want everybody to be selling the same stuff, and we want to compete on a price basis, and they will go broke 5 percent before we will.'"

The lack of complacency was also evident. Gary Ramey remembers one year's "extremely successful back-to-school season with fleece. The buyer said to us, 'Great, but what can we do to make it better next year?' He was happy, but that lasted ten seconds. I was ready to take my wife out to dinner. All he wanted to know was, what can we do next year?"

The Sara Lee Wal-Mart team was such a success that Caldwell immediately duplicated the idea. "Within a year, we set up a Kmart team. Shortly thereafter, a Target team, and shortly after that, a warehouse club team. We were applying the learning from Wal-Mart to Kmart and Target and the warehouse clubs." The Wal-Mart effect was not only cascading outward, it was actually benefiting Wal-Mart's competitors.

Removing the barrier between supplier and customer, says Caldwell, "scares a lot of people." But the impact was palpable. "The relationship we had with Wal-Mart made us a substantially better company than we had ever been before," says Caldwell. It was more than palpable, it was measurable. In the five years Caldwell led the Sara Lee Wal-Mart team, sales to Wal-Mart rose from $88 million a year to $1 billion a year. Says Caldwell, "It's a lot of pallets."

Willie Pietersen, now a professor of management at Columbia University's business school, has decades of experience in consumer products as president of Unilever's Lever Foods group, president of Seagram's U.S. liquor business, and president of Tropicana, the dominant orange juice brand in the United States. He learned quickly, he says, that the few things that matter to Wal-Mart are nonnegotiable. "They won't relent. They'd just as soon do business without Tropicana, and keep faith with their customers," says Pietersen. "That hurts if you're a supplier. If you want to protest, and writhe around in agony, fine. But this is the real world, what these people are doing is, they are revolutionizing the supply chain. Instead of being a victim, the trick is, how can we get superefficient?

"And once you are, that efficiency washes over not just your Wal-Mart business, but the total business. If you do it, then you have to doff your hat and say, 'Thank you, Wal-Mart, for putting the pressure on us.' "

But Pietersen says that, teams notwithstanding, the idea that suppliers have a partnership with Wal-Mart is a little silly. "I think it's a misnomer to call it a partnership. They might want to dress it up and call it a partnership. It's not. They're saying, I take care of my customer. They are saying, On behalf of that customer, for whom I am the champion, I'm going to use leverage of scale and power. There is a tension in that situation that needs to exist for that to work. But that doesn't sound like a partnership."

In all the struggle—the drive for efficiency, growth, and innovation—it is possible to lose track of the ultimate point of the creativity and exertion, whether the product is spaghetti sauce, or white cotton briefs, or orange juice. During the early years of Sara Lee's Wal-Mart team, when their basic apparel business with Wal-Mart was growing dramatically, what was actually happening in the business? Where were the hundreds of millions of dollars of "new" sales coming from? Was Hanes taking market share in underwear and athletic socks from competitors? Were people replacing their underwear sooner?

"Both," says Bill Caldwell. "And a third item that is a strange one:

increased wardrobe inventory. I can remember sitting around in the office time and time again, looking at increased industry sales in category after category—increases substantially in excess of population growth—and wondering where the hell that stuff was going."

They concluded, says Caldwell, "people just had more underwear stored in their house than they really needed, or had had in the past." The underwear was so cheap, and so irresistibly displayed on those pallets, that people just bought it and took it home. That kind of consumption doesn't trouble Caldwell at all—his job was to sell underwear. It's always nice to have a fresh pair of athletic socks, of course, but consumption driven strictly by price and impulse—consumption that answers no need at all—well, that's curious. Wal-Mart was saving its customers money, and they were literally tucking the savings away in the underwear drawer.

A T ZOOS AND MUSEUMS and aquariums in the sixties and seventies (and still sometimes today), there was often a miniature, coin-operated factory, under a large plastic bubble, that would make an injection-molded plastic souvenir—an elephant, a sailfish, a *Tyrannosaurus rex*—while you waited. Drop in three quarters, and two halves of a metal mold would slide together, heated plastic would be pumped in, then the mold halves would slide apart, and the waxy blue sailfish would be perched under the dome until a small metal spatula nudged it, and it toppled into a compartment at the front of the vending machine. It emerged warm, smelling faintly of melted plastic.

That, in a much more sophisticated form, is precisely how Jon Fleck's Makin Bacon dish gets made. He has them made in the United States not out of sentiment or stubbornness or inertia. Information travels at the speed of light in a global economy, but real stuff still travels mostly at about twenty knots, the speed of a container ship crossing the Pacific Ocean. Responsiveness is something Wal-Mart and the other megaretailers require, and when it comes to responsiveness, geography matters.

So the machine that makes Makin Bacon, about the size of a mid-sized SUV, is in a small factory in western Wisconsin. Just like the souvenir-making machine, the two enormous steel halves of the mold slide together, and melted plastic is pumped in. Fleck runs a double-cavity mold—when the steel mold separates, the parts for two complete Makin Bacon dishes are ready. Two men staff the press that is known around ITP Molding as "Jon's machine." "It's our machine, of course," says Neil Johnson, president and co-owner of ITP, and Makin Bacon's de facto vice president of manufacturing. Says Fleck, "I've bought and paid for the machine a couple times over."

One of the men pulls the parts free from the molds as they open, then cuts the parts from stringers with snips; the other man assembles the dishes one at a time, slides each dish into its Makin Bacon package, and slots the packaged dish into a box, eight to a box. The dishes are still warm when he tapes the box closed and stacks it on a pallet. The shipping box doubles as the display unit at Wal-Mart—it slices open on an angle along the sides to reveal the product inside.

In an era of sophisticated microchip etching and highly automated high-speed consumer products factories, there is something almost craftlike about ITP. A full molding cycle of the press takes fifty seconds—the two men can make and package 144 dishes in an hour. When a production run starts, ITP runs Makin Bacon—or any of the products it molds, many of which are medical devices—continuously, three shifts a day. "You get poor quality and wasted material on start up and shut down," says Johnson. "Once you heat those machines up and get them running, you keep running."

Over a decade, Fleck has developed a close and easy relationship with ITP. He walks into the warehouselike one-story buildings like a staff member, and although Johnson says Makin Bacon is only about 8 percent of ITP's overall business, Fleck's relationship is unique. "Other customers, we're a little protective, we don't let 'em wander into our shop any old time," says Johnson. "Jon, he wanders in and out whenever he darn pleases."

Fleck takes his orders—by fax, electronically—and transmits them all electronically to ITP. At ITP, a staff person named Kimberly rides herd on the orders, makes sure manufacturing time is scheduled, deals with shippers who arrive to carry the dishes away, and invoices Fleck. Most ITP customers require only a single operator for each machine, but ITP double staffs Makin Bacon because they pack and palletize the products for shipping. "When we're done, it's ready for UPS," says Johnson. "We do provide his logistics. It's the only customer we do that way. The UPS man is simply amazed by how many years he's picked up Makin Bacon dishes from us to send out."

Fleck pays for all those ITP services, per dish. He strides into another ITP building, a warehouse. Here, on ceiling-high shelves are cardboard cartons filled with polymethylpentene—called TPX in the trade—a high-quality plastic, transparent to microwaves, resistant to high heat, and so low density that the entire Makin Bacon dish floats. The TPX is another way Fleck's business is a little different. He buys his own raw material—he literally owns the cartons sitting in the warehouse—often on the reuse market, constantly working to keep that key cost down as petroleum prices soar. ITP buys the raw material for every other product it makes, to ensure quality, says Johnson. "If I let the customers buy it, they could send us junk material and expect Cadillac parts out of it."

ITP, and Fleck's relationship with them, is one of the critical elements to his success. Fleck trusts them completely, and although he often dashes up to the plant on his motorcycle to do a test run with some samples of TPX he's thinking of buying, ITP doesn't need hand-holding.

"We are his business," says Johnson. "We bend over backwards for him, and we don't do it for anybody else." ITP is one of the key reasons that Fleck doesn't consider taking Makin Bacon offshore. He's been to China—he had a manufacturing mold made there, they only last about one million cycles—and while it would be cheaper, the long lead times and the potential for having containers of product trapped on the docks in California could cripple his business. And Fleck would have to find a way of handling logistics that ITP handles effortlessly now.

In fact, in order to be as responsive as possible to customers like Wal-Mart, Johnson and ITP don't always wait for Fleck's orders. "We cheat," says Johnson. "We make some of 'em ahead of time. Just ready to ship."

Makin Bacon isn't just a single-employee company and a single-product company; it's a single-item company—one SKU, as a product's bar code is called—and despite being a single-SKU company, Jon Fleck has had the full global economy experience in the last ten years.

The dish looks exactly like the kind of thing that an offshore factory could produce mountains of so cheaply that although there isn't a lot of room between free and $6.97, a clever knockoff could quickly suck away his business. Wal-Mart's shelves are filled with entry-level generic products of every stripe—can openers, combination locks, baby wipes, transparent tape—that are half the price of the name brands.

"I'm not a wizard," says Fleck. "I'm watching China." He has been there several times. For a single person, managing contractors in China is daunting. The manufacturing mold Fleck bought cost $25,000 instead of $100,000, but the quality was poor; getting it fixed required months of negotiations, and it didn't produce the consistency Fleck requires. In terms of molding in China, "I'm worried about the security of the product." Fleck has heard stories of companies who ended up competing against Chinese-made items that looked eerily identical to their own—under a generic brand name.

Fleck and his daughter Abbey have been smart: the Makin Bacon dish has three patents, and they've trademarked the phrase Makin Bacon. It was a prescient. In 1996, just months after launching in Wal-Mart, Fleck sued Tristar Products, a then $100 million Pennsylvania company, in federal court for patent infringement over a similiar competing Tristar product called the Incredible Bacon Cooker. A year later Tristar settled the suit with a letter acknowledging the Makin Bacon patents and a $150,000 check. Tristar also surrendered its molds, shipping the steel blocks used to make the Incredible Bacon Cooker to Fleck in St. Paul. He's still got them in storage.

On the retail side, Fleck has had a brush with the new reverse-auction technique. Retailers looking to buy merchandise—bed linens, sheets and towels—announce a set of quality specifications and the size of the order they are looking to place, then allow vendors around the world to bid against one another, typically on the Internet, to see who will offer their products most cheaply, in wave after wave of time-limited bidding in which everyone can see huge chunks of business landed while profits are washed away.

A buyer at Target decided to manage shelf space, using a reverse auction, in a category that included Makin Bacon. "She said, 'We're going to offer this [space] up to thirty items. In two days' time, it's going to be down to twenty-three; in two more we're going to whittle it down to eighteen.' She said, 'So, what can you do for me on price?'

"I said, 'I'm not doing anything on price. If you tell me you want me in a reverse auction, you will see me out the door.' "

As remarkable as Fleck's success and survival have been, he says, "I've lost my hairline."

Even his relationship with Wal-Mart has had its bumps. The dish has sold well with other microwave cookware on shelves in the aisle where Wal-Mart sells microwave ovens. "It really found its home there," says Fleck. Then, a couple of years ago, the aisle was re-designed, the microwave ovens were raised to eye level, and the microwave cookware shelf above the ovens was raised too, to six feet high. "It killed the category," says Fleck.

But Wal-Mart is nothing if not data driven, and in 2005, the microwave section was redesigned again—the ovens got lower, the microwave cookware is right back at eye level, and sales perked up. Like all Wal-Mart's other sixty-one thousand U.S. suppliers, Fleck can tap the company's Retail Link sales database to monitor how Makin Bacon is doing. Retail Link is a proprietary system that Wal-Mart first made accessible to vendors in 1991. Back then they had to have a special computer and a phone line; today Retail Link is accessed over the Internet. Retail Link contains a record of every sale of every individual item at every Wal-Mart store, every hour of every day for the last two years. Wal-Mart has pioneered making such data available— vendors typically only get to look at sales data for their own products—as a way of requiring suppliers to do some basic analysis and as a way of encouraging them to understand where, and when, and why their products sell at Wal-Mart. The data that pours out of Retail Link for even modest-sized suppliers is so enormous, so complicated, and so rich that companies now specialize in teaching vendors how to mine the data for insight. Retail Link has become so valuable to Wal-Mart's suppliers in driving sales of their products at Wal-Mart that competing retailers eventually attempted to imitate it, with mixed success. Few retailers gather data with the microscopic diligence, or the speed, of Wal-Mart.

Jon Fleck turns up the occasional nugget about Makin Bacon. He knows that the dish sells better at supercenters. "It's just the volume of traffic," he says, but it can't hurt that you can buy the Makin Bacon dish, and some bacon to test it out, in the same place. (Retail Link could show whether people who purchased bacon were more likely to purchase the dish—or vice versa.) The data about this one product at individual stores is so detailed that Fleck knows that at certain times of year, the same Wal-Mart customer buys more than one dish. "Gifts," Fleck says.

Fleck loves his relationship with Wal-Mart. "Fabulous," he says. The back of a thirty-six-foot motor home that Fleck used for a while to tour Wal-Marts and check on his product has a license plate frame that says: "I'd rather be shopping at Wal-Mart."

It's not just consistency, it's a businesslike respect. "They pay perfectly," for instance. And unlike with many retailers, Fleck doesn't get mysterious charge-backs that are really retailers taking their own discounts. "Kmart, in the old days, took that to a high art," says Fleck. "I once had a purchase order from Kmart for eight dishes, for $30—and it came with $600 in charge-backs." Makin Bacon owed Kmart $570 for selling them eight dishes.

Fleck still journeys to Bentonville from White Bear Lake about once a year, sometimes on his motorcycle, to meet in person with the buyer in charge of his category. "It's 666 miles from my front door to their front door," he says. "They want things to run smoothly, and not have a reason for a vendor to be in their face," says Fleck. "I shouldn't have a 'close personal relationship' with their buyer. It's just not needed. Other retailers, it's a totally different deal. You have to stroke them."

For Makin Bacon as a company, and for the consumers who buy the Makin Bacon dish, Fleck's decade-long relationship to Wal-Mart is a model in miniature of the Wal-Mart effect's working for everyone. Wal-Mart's orders are large, steady, and predictable and—something not to be overlooked in that stability—Makin Bacon's sales at Wal-Mart are large, steady, and predictable. Fleck can plan his purchasing—not just of plastic, but of packaging—well in advance. He can dive deep into Wal-Mart's data to understand his own business. And Wal-Mart literally lays the foundation for the rest of Fleck's business: His relationships with Target, with Carol Wright Gifts, with the one-off customers whose orders arrive by mail are all better because of Wal-Mart.

There is one central mystery of Fleck's, and Makin Bacon's, relationship to Wal-Mart. Since that very first conversation with Cheryl Knight about bringing in Makin Bacon cheaper than the Armour offer—just 2 cents cheaper, as it turned out—the issue of price has never come up. Unlike thousands of other vendors, Fleck has never had a Wal-Mart buyer tell him that the price of Makin Bacon must come down next year. Many manufacturers report consistent, irresistible requests for yearly 5 percent cost cutting. Wal-Mart has a whole marketing campaign devoted to just that—the cheerful price chopper who bounces through the store in TV commercials chopping the prices of familiar products. Even such modest cuts—pennies a year—add up quickly. Over just five years (four such cuts), the Makin Bacon dish would be going out of Wal-Mart at $5.68 instead of $6.97. (If the cost of the dish had risen with inflation, it would now be $9.09—but that argument wouldn't carry any weight in Bentonville.)

Fleck does have "intellectual property"; that is, Makin Bacon is patented and trademarked. But so are many ordinary consumer products. Charmin Ultra toilet paper, for example, lists twenty-six patents on the package. Makin Bacon does not have a line of products—just the one—and it is pretty inexpensive already. But Wal-Mart actually stocks a simpler, competing bacon-cooking dish from Nordic Ware that sells for $3.27.

Fleck has gotten better at his job, but his ability to wring costs out of Makin Bacon is limited to his ability to negotiate the price of polymethylpentene; and with the cost of a barrel of oil having tripled, the cost of polymethylpentene is also rising. "We run a lean operation," he says. And not just personnelwise. His dish, for instance, is designed to use one third as much plastic as the Nordic Ware dish, and it weighs far less, keeping down not just materials costs but also shipping costs.

Whatever his advantages, his charm, and the charm of his product, there's no getting around the core fact that Fleck is a single SKU vendor to the largest store in history. In an eyeblink, for any reason or no reason at all, Wal-Mart could move on from Makin Bacon, and Fleck's business life would never be the same. Many larger companies struggle every day in the face of decisions made in Bentonville.

Indeed, the lack of price pressure on Fleck is not only mysterious, it's crucial to his success. "I was reflecting on that," he says. "I went on a motorcycle ride, and I considered that. Why is it they've never asked for a lower price? I just don't know."

FOUR

THE SQUEEZE

Every time you see the Wal-Mart smiley face, whistling and knocking down the prices, somewhere there's a factory worker being kicked in the stomach.

—*Sherrie Ford, factory owner and longtime manufacturing*
management expert

A GALLON-SIZED JAR of whole pickles is something to behold. The jar itself is the size of a small aquarium. The fat green pickles, floating in swampy juice, look reptilian, their shapes exaggerated by the glass of the jar. The jar weighs twelve pounds, too big to carry with one hand.

The gallon jar of pickles is a display of abundance and excess. It is entrancing, and also vaguely unsettling. Wal-Mart fell in love with Vlasic's gallon jar of pickles.

Wal-Mart priced it at $2.97—a year's supply of pickles for less than $3! "They were using it as a 'statement' item," says Pat Hunn, who calls himself the mad scientist of the gallon jar of pickles at Vlasic. "Wal-Mart was putting it before consumers, saying this represents what Wal-Mart's about: *You can buy a stinkin' gallon of pickles for $2.97.* And it's the nation's number-one brand."

Because of Wal-Mart's scale, the Wal-Mart effect isn't just about delivering "always low prices." It's also about how Wal-Mart gets those low prices, and what impact the low prices have far beyond Wal-Mart's shelves, and beyond our own wallets: the cost of low prices to the companies that supply Wal-Mart, and to the people who work for those companies. That story can be found floating in Vlasic's gallon jar of pickles, the tale of how that gallon jar came to be sold at Wal-Mart.

Back in the late 1990s, Vlasic wasn't looking to build its brand on a gallon of whole pickles. Pickle companies make money on "the cut," slicing cucumbers into specialty items like spears and hamburger chips. "Cucumbers in the jar, you don't make a whole lot of money there," says Steve Young, who was then vice president of marketing for pickles at Vlasic, but has since left the company. But a Wal-Mart buyer saw the gallon jar at some point in the late 1990s, and started talking to Pat Hunn about it. Hunn, who has also since left Vlasic, was then head of Vlasic's Wal-Mart sales team, based in Dallas.

The gallon intrigued the buyer. For Vlasic, it was a niche product aimed at small businesses and people having large events. Still, in sales tests in Wal-Mart stores, priced somewhere over $3, "the gallon sold like crazy," says Hunn, "surprising us all." The Wal-Mart pickle buyer had a brainstorm: What would happen to the gallon if they offered it nationwide, and got it below $3? Hunn was skeptical, but his job was to look for ways to sell pickles at Wal-Mart. Why not?

And so in 1998, Vlasic's gallon jar of pickles went into every Wal-Mart, 2,500 stores, at $2.97, a price so low that Vlasic and Wal-Mart were only making a penny or two on a jar, if that. The gallon was showcased on a big, freestanding pallet display near the front of stores. It was an abundance of abundance.

"They went through the roof," says Hunn.

Says Young, "It was selling eighty jars a week, on average, in every store." Doesn't sound like much until you do the math: That's 200,000 gallons of pickles, just in gallon jars, just at Wal-Mart, every week. Whole fields of cucumbers were heading out the door.

The gallon jar of pickles became what you might call a "devastating success" for Vlasic. "Quickly, it started cannibalizing our non-Wal-Mart business," says Young. "We saw consumers who used to buy the spears and the chips in supermarkets"—where a small quart jar of Vlasic pickles cost $2.49—"buying the Wal-Mart gallons. They'd eat a quarter of a jar and throw the thing away when they got moldy. A family can't eat them fast enough."

The gallon jar reshaped Vlasic's pickle business: It chewed up the profit margin of the business with Wal-Mart, and of pickles generally; procurement had to scramble to find enough pickles to fill the gallons. The volume also gave Vlasic strong sales numbers, strong growth numbers, and a powerful place in the world of pickles at Wal-Mart.

The gallon was hoisting Vlasic and hurting it at the same time. Indeed, Steve Young, Vlasic's marketing guy, and Pat Hunn, Vlasic's Wal-Mart sales guy, agree on the details of the gallon, but years later they disagree over whether it was good or bad for Vlasic.

Hunn remembers cutting a deal with Wal-Mart whereby the retailer could only increase its sales of gallons if it increased its sales of the more profitable spears and chips in lockstep. The gallon was good.

Young remembers begging Wal-Mart for relief. "They said, 'No way,'" says Young. "We said we'll increase the price"—even $3.49 would have helped tremendously—"and they said, 'If you do that, all the other products of yours we buy, we'll stop buying.' It was a clear threat."

Hunn remembers the conversations differently. Things were more complicated, more subtle. "They did not put a gun to our head and say, 'It's $2.97 or you're out of here,'" says Hunn. "They said, 'We want the $2.97 gallon of pickles. If you don't do it, we'll see if some-one else might.' I knew our competitors were saying to Wal-Mart, 'We'll do the $2.97 gallons if you give us your other business.'

"We're all big boys," Hunn says. "We all make decisions."

Wal-Mart's business was so indispensable to Vlasic, and the gallon so central to the Wal-Mart relationship, that decisions about the fu-ture of the gallon were made at the CEO level. "One option was to call their bluff," says Young. But Vlasic was struggling as an indepen-dent spin-off of Campbell Soup Company, and couldn't afford to risk the Wal-Mart business. The pain didn't continue for weeks or months—the $2.97 gallon of Vlasic dills was on the shelves at Wal-Mart for two and a half years.

Finally, Wal-Mart let Vlasic up for air. "The Wal-Mart guy's re-sponse was classic," says Young. "He said, 'Well, we've done to pickles what we did to orange juice. We've killed it. We can back off.'"

Vlasic got to take the product down to half a gallon of pickles, for $2.49. By that point, Young says, profits in pickles had been cut by 50 percent—millions of dollars in lost profit, even as the business itself grew. Devastating success, indeed.

The meaning of the Vlasic story is complicated, but it cuts to the heart of how Wal-Mart does business. It shows the impact of Wal-Mart's scale and power in what we all think is a market economy. Wal-Mart's focus on pricing, and its ability to hold a supplier's business hostage to its own agenda, distorts markets in ways that consumers don't see, and ways the suppliers can't effectively counter. Wal-Mart is so large that it can often defy the laws of supply, demand, and compe-tition.

That's the scary part of the Vlasic story: The market didn't create the $2.97 gallon of pickles, nor did waning consumer demand or a wild abundance of cucumbers. Wal-Mart created the $2.97 gallon jar of pickles. The price—a number that is a critical piece of information to buyers, sellers, and competitors about the state of the pickle market—the price was a lie. It was unrelated to either the supply of cucumbers or the demand for pickles. The price was a fiction imposed on the pickle market in Bentonville. Consumers saw a bargain; Vlasic saw no way out. Both were responding not to real market forces, but to a pickle price gimmick imposed by Wal-Mart as a way of making a statement.

In the summer of 2004, Rob Walton, the chairman of the board of Wal-Mart, made an extraordinary appearance at an annual meeting of a group of lawyers in Washington, D.C. The meeting was for antitrust attorneys, and the topic of the event was "Buyer Power"—whether some companies are so big not as sellers of goods but as buyers of goods that they constitute a threat to the free market. The term for suppliers who are big enough to control prices and markets is familiar—that's *monopoly,* and anyone who has played the board game understands that if you control the available real estate, you get to charge not what the market will bear, but what you want. There is a parallel economic concept for a company that is such a large buyer— of pickles, say—that it holds an equivalent kind of price-control power. The term is *monopsony.*

Rob Walton gave an aw-shucks performance that Tuesday morning, one of which his daddy would have been proud. Walton said he was "initially hesitant" to address the group of antitrust lawyers. "Wal-Mart doesn't have much experience making public statements about anything as lofty as monopsony theory," he said. "But we talked about it, and decided to accept. Given the conference's subject matter"—buyer power—"we figured someone would say something about Wal-Mart." In the course of his speech, Walton said this about the company's suppliers: "Our supplier relationships are special. We do not consider ourselves customers of our suppliers; instead, we are partners." At the conclusion of his speech, Walton said, "We need healthy suppliers *at least* as much as they need us, if not more."

The papers presented by scholars at the conference weren't quite so optimistic that suppliers could depend on benevolence in doing business with customers as large and powerful as Wal-Mart. But real-world analysis of buyer power is not very advanced and remains shrouded in secrecy.

It's easy, of course, to point out that Vlasic walked into the gallon voluntarily, with years of experience doing business with Wal-Mart. But a product at a price isn't some kind of unbreakable vow. Right after the gallon was pulled out of the stores, in January 2001, Vlasic filed for bankruptcy. And while the gallon jar of pickles wasn't by any means the cause, Wal-Mart's behavior during Vlasic's struggle certainly wasn't that of a "partner" concerned about Vlasic's financial health.

IN LATE JULY 2003, FedEx Corporation announced that Wal-Mart had named FedEx "carrier of the year," among the companies providing transportation services to the retailer. The press release included a media contact, and it seemed a good opportunity to get some insight on the Wal-Mart effect. FedEx itself has reshaped the way people do business every day. It was surprising to learn that Wal-Mart uses FedEx—Wal-Mart operates its own trucks, the largest private trucking fleet in the country. Wal-Mart's "carrier of the year" would shed light on the good Wal-Mart does—how Wal-Mart eliminates inefficiency, irons kinks out of the supply chain, sweats out unnecessary costs. And there are few companies with the media savvy, or the accessibility, of FedEx.

The FedEx media contact was a man named Steve. He was thrilled to set up a story about how FedEx services Wal-Mart, about what it takes to be a vendor of the year to what was already the largest company in the world, and one of the most legendarily demanding customers. Steve even called back to ask a few clarifying questions: Would the story be just about FedEx's relationship with Wal-Mart at the white-collar sales level, or also about how FedEx actually provided on-the-ground movement of goods? Everything was important: truck drivers, warehouse people, computer support, white-collar FedEx Wal-Mart team members. The whole landscape of FedEx as transportation provider to Wal-Mart. Steve was psyched. He did mention in an e-mail message, "I've also let my contact at Wal-Mart know we are working with you."

The weekend passed and just after nine on Monday morning, Steve called. No e-mail this time. His tone of voice was somber. "I hate to make calls like this," he said. "We've spoken to our friends in Bentonville, and they've asked us not to say anything more than what was in the press release." No story? No rides in FedEx eighteen-wheelers racing across the nation with goods for Wal-Mart? "We can't participate," Steve said. "I'm sorry."

FedEx, of course, was then a huge global company on its own—nothing like Wal-Mart, but still: $22 billion in sales, 191,000 employees, a fleet of 643 planes. Perhaps, having graciously consulted "our friends in Bentonville," Steve could see the value and the fun in the story anyway, and move forward with confidence. FedEx was, after all, a grown-up company of its own, capable of speaking for itself. This suggestion elicited a long silence from Steve, followed by a strangled chuckle. "Oh, I'm afraid decisions like this at FedEx aren't made at the Steve level," he said. And that was it. Wal-Mart had ordered FedEx to remain silent, and FedEx, in the person of Steve, had instantly complied—even in a case where there were nothing but good things to say.

One of the reasons our picture of Wal-Mart is so incomplete, so one-dimensional, is that the people who do business with Wal-Mart won't talk about how Wal-Mart does what it does. Indeed, the stories in this chapter—the Vlasic story and those that follow—are unusual not because they are extraordinary, but for exactly the opposite reason: They paint a vivid, even harrowing, picture of what it's like to do business with Wal-Mart every day. Such stories almost never get told about Wal-Mart, even among insiders. Businesspeople on airplanes traveling to and from Bentonville, and staying in hotels around Wal-Mart's headquarters, are leery of one another. There is no sharing of Wal-Mart war stories. And while every story in this chapter comes from people who have worked for companies that do business with Wal-Mart, they no longer work for those companies; for the most part, they no longer work for any company where Wal-Mart could have a direct impact.

Wal-Mart has imposed a wall of silence around its operations, its relationships with its suppliers, even around the operations of its suppliers. The silence isn't a matter of business etiquette or courtesy—it is policy, chillingly absolute. The silence is backed by muscle, the threat of losing the business of Wal-Mart.

The silence runs up and down the range of companies, and up and down the organizational chart. It is one of the reasons that Wal-Mart chairman Rob Walton can say publicly, without fear of contradiction, "our supplier relationships are special" and "we treat our suppliers fairly." Many of the people who know Wal-Mart most intimately, who do business with the company every day, are terrified of Wal-Mart.

A media relations person, speaking on behalf of the division at IBM that provides computer hardware and software to big retailers, was eager to talk about IBM's 2005 analysis of "the ideal retail shopping experience"—which would surely include history's largest retailer. Asked about Wal-Mart, for which IBM is a supplier, the man said, "Wal-Mart has asked IBM not to use Wal-Mart as an example when we talk to the media about retailing, ever. We will never again, hopefully, comment on Wal-Mart directly."

Dial, the soap maker, does almost 30 percent of its business with Wal-Mart, equal to the business of its next ten customers combined. Said an executive at Dial: "We are one of Wal-Mart's biggest suppliers, and they are our biggest customer, by far. We have a great relationship. That's all I can say. Are we done now?" Goaded a bit, the executive responded with an almost hysterical edge: "Are you meshuga? Why in the world would we talk about Wal-Mart? Ask me about anything else, we'll talk. But not Wal-Mart."

One company that has never done business with Wal-Mart, but has considered it, offered to explain the business considerations that go into the decision to take on Wal-Mart as a customer. But after some internal conversations, a company official said they had changed their minds about talking about the fact that they do no business with Wal-Mart. They might do business with Wal-Mart at some point in the future, and there was no point making anyone at Wal-Mart angry now.

The CEO of an instantly recognizable consumer products company kept an appointment for a telephone interview about Wal-Mart's impact on business, on the way factories are run, on the quality of products that get designed and made, then spent forty-five minutes talking about why he couldn't talk about Wal-Mart. "You *know* they have a tremendous impact on innovation, on the development of new products. You know they are enormously damaging in that arena. I applaud you trying to get people to talk about it. People need to know. At the same time, I can't be connected to it at all. They wield so much power. If I talk at all, I am putting this whole company in extreme jeopardy. I'll have to lay off hundreds of people."

Another man, with decades of experience making consumer products and servicing Wal-Mart, had owned his company and been its

CEO. He sold the company years ago, and offered to talk about making and supplying Wal-Mart with a line of products that are also instantly recognizable. Before he could talk, he said, he had to first get permission from the current owners of the company. He called back to say he couldn't talk after all. "They've put the handcuffs on me," he said regretfully. "I understand. If I say something Wal-Mart doesn't like, and they lose Wal-Mart as a customer, who the hell do you get to replace them? What would I have said about Wal-Mart? I think Wal-Mart sucks. Excuse me, that's not a very nice word."

WAL-MART LIKES to convey a cheery, avuncular persona. There's the greeter as you enter the stores. There's the aura of Sam Walton, who tried to visit every store every year, who knew hundreds of employees by name. There's the yellow, smiling-faced price slasher bouncing through the store in Wal-Mart TV commercials, slashing prices with a rapier. Sometimes, the price slasher is dressed like Robin Hood—an audacious costume for the mascot of the world's most powerful company.

But there is nothing genial about the process by which Wal-Mart gets its suppliers to provide everything from tires to contact lenses, guns to underarm deodorant, at everyday low prices. Wal-Mart forces its suppliers to do everything from redesigning packaging to redesigning their computer systems if they want to sell to Wal-Mart. Wal-Mart will, quite straightforwardly, tell those suppliers what it will pay for their goods.

Wal-Mart wields its power for just one purpose: to bring the lowest possible prices to its customers. At Wal-Mart, that's a goal that is never met. For basic consumer products that don't change year after year, Wal-Mart is well known for insisting that the price drop 5 percent a year. Gib Carey is a partner at Bain & Company and helps lead the global consultant's consumer products practice. He has years of experience advising Bain clients who are also Wal-Mart suppliers. "Year after year," says Carey, "for any product that is the same as what you sold them last year, Wal-Mart is going to say, here's the price you gave me last year. Here's what I can get a competitor product for; here's what I can get a private-label version for. I want to see a better value that I can bring to my shopper this year. Or else I'm going to use that shelf space differently."

While the kind of pressure Wal-Mart can bring to bear is, at this point, well publicized, what almost no one outside the world of Wal-Mart and its suppliers sees and understands is the high cost of those low prices. Wal-Mart has the power to squeeze profit-killing concessions from suppliers, many of whom are willing to do almost anything to keep the retailer happy, in part because Wal-Mart now dominates consumer markets so thoroughly that they have no choice. The results can be dramatic or subtle, immediate or insidiously corrosive. Decisions made in Bentonville routinely close factories as well as open them. Wal-Mart's way of doing business can hollow out companies, gradually transforming full-fledged consumer products companies who design and manufacture their own products into little more than importers. Wal-Mart's price pressure can leave so little profit that there is little left for innovation. The Wal-Mart effect is unrelenting; even the demands for performance that may initially help a company get in shape, as would happen with an athlete working with an Olympic-level coach, can ultimately leave the same company gaunt and malnourished. What does the squeeze look like up close at Wal-Mart? It is usually thoroughly rational, sometimes devastatingly so.

John Mariotti is a veteran of the consumer products world—he spent nine years as president of the Huffy Bicycles division of the Huffy Corporation, and was a group president at Rubbermaid during its difficult years in the early 1990s. He now sits on the board of directors of World Kitchen, the company that sells Ekco, Pyrex, Corningware, and Revere brands of kitchen products.

He could not be clearer on his opinion about Wal-Mart: It's a great company and a great company to do business with. "Wal-Mart has done more good for America by several thousand orders of magnitude than they've done bad," Mariotti says. "They have raised the bar, and raised the bar for everybody in business."

When Mariotti was at Huffy, one of his early relationships at Wal-Mart was with a bicycle buyer, now deceased, named Bill Durflinger. Says Mariotti, "He said something to me which I've always remembered. 'We have a simple philosophy at Wal-Mart. We buy. You ship. You don't ship, we don't buy. You're feeling good because you have a great opportunity with us. But you are also assuming a great responsibility to us and our customers: to have the merchandise we've agreed on, where we need it, when we need it.'" Durflinger issued that warning to Mariotti in 1980, the year Wal-Mart first reported $1 billion in sales.

Indeed, says Mariotti, a lot of the grumbling about Wal-Mart has to do with a failure to grasp this fundamental principle: "They demand you do what you say you are going to do."

Huffy sold a range of bikes to Wal-Mart, twenty or so models, in a spread of prices and profitability. (Wal-Mart today sells more bikes than any other retailer.) "One year," says Mariotti, "we had a home run in our low-end product at Wal-Mart. It just took off, it ran like hell. I woke up May 1"—the heart of the bike-production cycle for the summer—"and I needed 900,000 bikes. My factories could only run 450,000."

Mariotti had committed to supply Wal-Mart with as many of that entry-level, low-price, thin-profit bike as they needed. As it happened, that same year, Huffy's fancier, more profitable bikes were doing well too, at Wal-Mart and other places. "I made the deal up front with them," says Mariotti. "I knew how high was up. I was duty-bound to supply my customer."

To get Wal-Mart its cheap bikes, Mariotti did something astounding. "I gave four of my SKUs [designs] to my competitors, and encouraged them, consented them, to make them, so I could supply Wal-Mart. I conceded business to my competitors because I just ran out of capacity." Mariotti, of course, knew the consequences of not fulfilling his Wal-Mart commitment. "Wal-Mart didn't tell me what to do," he says. "They didn't have to."

Still, it was a remarkable decision, really an incredible decision. Imagine Black & Decker giving power-tool designs to Craftsman; imagine Kodak giving digital camera designs to Canon; imagine Apple (now a supplier to Wal-Mart) giving iPod designs to Sony. And not just giving away the designs, but the very sales and profits of the business. In the case of Huffy, the Wal-Mart effect took hold without even a conversation about renegotiating the supply arrangement, the kind of conversation you might expect when marketplace circumstances take an unexpected turn, and bike maker and bike seller are partners.

Wal-Mart, says Mariotti, "is tough as nails. But they give you a chance to compete. If you can't compete, that's your problem." It turns out the legendary U.S. bike maker could not compete. The company made its last bike in the United States in 1999, becoming an Asian importer. Huffy did 18 percent of its sales to Wal-Mart in 2003, the last year it reported financial results, before being delisted from the New York Stock Exchange in August 2004 and filing for Chapter 11 bankruptcy protection in October. These days, 95 percent of the bikes sold in the United States are imported from China.

John Fitzgerald has decades of experience in the consumer goods world working with Wal-Mart, including nineteen years at Nabisco.

"I've spent a lot of time in Bentonville," he says. Fitzgerald, too, says, "Wal-Mart makes everyone better."

When Fitzgerald left Nabisco, he went to the French yarn company DMC as head of its U.S. operations. He got the job in 1998, at a critical moment for DMC, the market leader in embroidery thread. "We had more than four hundred SKUs [colors] of thread at Wal-Mart, they were our biggest customer, and they had just reduced, by 60 percent, the amount of shelf space allocated to the thread."

It was simple: Wal-Mart has benchmarks for how much revenue, and profit, every product on every foot of shelf space must generate. DMC's rainbow of 454 colors of miniature skeins of embroidery floss wasn't selling enough. Wal-Mart's crafts buyer simply reduced the amount of shelf space, so the thread's sales would hit the sales-per-foot benchmark.

There was just one problem. "The thread was compressed to the point that our sales dropped 30 percent, almost overnight," says Fitzgerald. "It was almost unshoppable in that space."

It was something of a crisis, to say the least. The Wal-Mart buyer realized it was a big problem too. "Wal-Mart said, we're not going to increase your square footage, but we're amenable to some other solution."

DMC, a 250-year-old company, scrambled to come up with a better way to display the thread in the small space. In just a few weeks, consultants were hired, ideas developed, prototype displays designed and produced. In the end, DMC created a multilevel lazy Susan, nicknamed the Rainbow Carousel, in which to display the small skeins of thread. For $1 million in manufacturing costs—a dramatic cost to display skeins of thread that sell for about 25 cents each—DMC could put the fixtures in every Wal-Mart in America, and rescue one third of its business.

Fitzgerald was worried that no sooner would DMC invest in the new fixtures than Wal-Mart would stop carrying crafts. "I had access to the top of the house," says Fitzgerald, "the executive vice president of merchandising. He said, 'We have no intention of getting out of crafts.' One thing I found with Wal-Mart, particularly, as much as people say they can be unreasonable, they do understand the ramifications. They can open and close plants. They can put companies in and out of business."

The new fixtures worked great—DMC thread is still sold on them in the crafts departments of Wal-Mart. Sales not only rebounded, but the carousels produced an 8 percent bump. These days Wal-Mart has decided that not all colors of the thread are selling fast enough, so the Rainbow Carousel does not have all 454 shades, giving the lazy Susan compartments an oddly gap-toothed appearance on the shelves at Wal-Mart.

But the challenges were not over for Fitzgerald. Wal-Mart didn't like DMC packing twenty-four items to a case. "One case, twenty-four SKUs, was just more days of supply than they felt they needed in stores," says Fitzgerald. "They demanded we take it down to twelve." Twelve items per case meant Wal-Mart was holding less inventory. It also meant twice as many orders for DMC, twice as many cases packed, twice as many packages shipped—all for the same amount of business.

"It was good for Wal-Mart," says Fitzgerald. "But we had to retool the factory in France to pack boxes in twelves." DMC didn't fight; it switched all its customers around the world to cases of twelve.

Just as Fitzgerald was leaving DMC, the yarn company was retooling again, in response to Wal-Mart's latest dictate: DMC was to pack yarn not for thirteen Wal-Mart distribution centers, but into boxes ready for twenty-seven hundred individual stores.

"Are you kidding me?" says Fitzgerald. "It doubled our cost of distribution. It was scary." Wal-Mart gave Fitzgerald a manual to read about how to gear up to pack for individual stores. They told him when to be ready. They didn't mention cost.

"They are price adverse," says Fitzgerald. "You cannot pass price increases on there." But Fitzgerald turned rationality back on Wal-Mart. "I went to senior management. I said, 'We're on board for this direct-store distribution. But we have to double the labor in our distribution center, we have to invest in new racks. You've simply transferred costs from your center to mine. I have to split that with you. I'm not asking you to take it all, but I have to split it with you. I need a price increase.'" Remarkably, Wal-Mart buckled to tiny DMC. DMC's total cost, 1 cent per box; Fitzgerald muscled Wal-Mart into paying half: half a penny per box.

Wal-Mart is, in fact, a genius at shifting work, and costs, that have traditionally been handled by retailers back to manufacturers. The company's own administrative costs and overhead are parsimonious compared to its competitors', a discipline reflected in its quarterly income statements and a discipline that is, in fact, admirable, and that gives Wal-Mart a real competitive advantage and, increasingly, a small image boost as well. However stingy it is with its own frontline workers, Wal-Mart chairman Rob Walton was able to tap that very stinginess to point out a striking contrast in his speech to the lawyers' group in the summer of 2004: "There is no Wal-Mart Tower to rival the Sears Tower in Chicago." (Sears, in fact, had to move its offices to the Chicago suburbs and sell the Sears Tower to save money just twenty years after moving in.)

But a significant reason Wal-Mart is able to keep its own costs down is not just basic frugality, but a strategic cost shifting to suppliers that is built into the way Wal-Mart manages its business. All retailers look to shift burdens to their suppliers for promotions, for stocking, for logistics. At Wal-Mart, however, there is nothing haphazard about the cost shifting. It is continuous and systematic. The

Wal-Mart effect means suppliers manage a chunk of Wal-Mart's business for Wal-Mart; it also means doing it smartly, and without self-interest, because Wal-Mart retains the power in the relationship. So Wal-Mart charges many of its vendors with keeping product in stock on its shelves; Wal-Mart cascades data about its sales out to its vendors—giving companies a remarkable window on the preferences of their own customers—but it gives those vendors the responsibility of analyzing those waves of data and reporting the insights back to Wal-Mart. That's what most of the thousands of Wal-Mart team members in hundreds of vendor offices in Bentonville are doing: poring over data, trying to understand why something is or isn't selling, and how to help it sell better.

More than that, in every major category of merchandise from lawn sprinklers to condoms, Wal-Mart designates a category captain, a company whose job is to analyze the performance for all the products in the category and recommend different mixes or displays or arrangements that will increase sales, even if it means increasing sales for competitors. The work of category captains, which have become common at competing retailers, doesn't actually determine how the toothpaste shelves are laid out, but it certainly influences it. More than that, the job provides Wal-Mart with a continual, deep, sometimes creative analysis of consumer product marketing, an analysis that Wal-Mart doesn't pay for, and that has traditionally been the province of the consumer products companies and their research firms. And although being a category captain provides some prestige and insight for suppliers, Wal-Mart is stringent about not allowing it to confer undeserved advantage. In that sense, it's just another cost of doing business with the retailer.

Starting in 1985, Michael Roth worked for three consumer products companies: Playtex, Revlon, and Warner Lambert (WL), respectively. He witnessed the growth of Wal-Mart's impact from his days at

Playtex, where, Roth says, "We set the rules, and the retailers played by the rules we set." A few years later, in the mid-1990s at Revlon, Roth says, "Whatever Wal-Mart wanted, we did." At Warner Lambert, Roth was head of trade marketing for the confections division, which then included a fleet of familiar products: Trident, Dentyne, and Halls. (Warner Lambert was subsequently taken over by Pfizer, and those three product lines were sold to Cadbury Schweppes.) The WL brands were the designated category captains for confections, and for the front-end checkout area of Wal-Mart.

"When you're a category captain, you get past the sanctum of sanctums," says Roth, "to the real back room. We had to sign our children's lives away. Our job was to come back with suggestions for confection, and for the design of the whole front end." The WL group invested $1.5 million in data, market research, analytical software, and the time of three or four people to handle the category-captain responsibility. The WL group came up with recommendations for both confectionary, and for reworking the somewhat chaotic displays at Wal-Mart's checkout stands. "We assumed all along that they would give us the benefit of the doubt on placement of new items," says Roth, who is now an independent retail consultant. "We knew that we had to be responsible with whatever we were recommending. We thought we were. We thought the research bore out that we were deserving of some incremental activity and space and placement." WL's candy and gum group wanted more display slots, and better display slots, at the prime space on the checkout stand.

Wal-Mart disagreed. Despite the investment and the work, "We got zippo out of the deal. Management was pulling their hair, and pulling my hair, because we weren't getting any incremental placements."

What's more, despite talk of partnerships with its suppliers, Wal-Mart does not let the length of a relationship, or sentiment, cloud its business decisions. The Lovable Company was founded in 1926 by the grandfather of Frank Garson II, who was Lovable's last president. Lovable made bras and lingerie, supplying retailers from Sears to Victoria's Secret; at one point, the company was the sixth largest U.S. maker of intimate apparel, with seven hundred employees in the United States and another two thousand at eight factories in Central America.

"We did business with Wal-Mart from the day they opened," says Garson. "We were one of their first suppliers." Eventually, Wal-Mart became Lovable's biggest customer. "Wal-Mart has a big pencil," says Garson. "They have such awesome purchasing power that they write their own ticket. If they don't like your prices, they'll go vertical and do it themselves—or they'll find someone that will meet their terms."

In the fall of 1996, says Garson, "Wal-Mart reneged on their contract with us. They had awarded us a contract [for sales], and in their wisdom, they changed the terms so dramatically that they really reneged." Garson, still worried about litigation years later, won't provide any more details. "But when you lose a customer that size, they are irreplaceable."

Lovable was already feeling intense cost pressure from Asian competitors when it lost Wal-Mart's business. Garson says for the wages of a single U.S. factory worker, competitors could hire seventy people in Indonesia.

Sixteen months after Wal-Mart pulled its business, in its seventy-second year, Lovable closed. "They leave a lot to be desired in the way they treat people," says Garson. "Their actions to pulverize people are unnecessary. . . . Wal-Mart chewed us up and spit us out."

As RARE AS it is to get any window on the impact Wal-Mart has in the sales, marketing, and senior management offices of America's companies, it is all but unheard of to glimpse the effect Wal-Mart's needs have on the factory floor, or on the way products are designed and made. In 1997, Sherrie Ford was hired to help improve the morale and the performance of the Welch's juice and jellies factory in Lawton, Michigan. "Welch's. The grape juice. Everybody has it in their refrigerator or sees it in their grocery store," says Ford. "Good product, good reputation." Ford is a consultant who specializes in factory management, in helping factories and their frontline workers adapt to the demands of a low-cost, just-in-time global manufacturing economy. Ford also owns, with a business partner, a factory of her own in Athens, Georgia, that makes electrical transformers, a five-hundred-person facility they bought from global electrical giant ABB in 2003.

Ford had plenty of experience working in consumer products factories, including a Johnson & Johnson factory in Georgia, before being hired by Welch's. She was surprised by what she found at Welch's Michigan facility. "Morale was terrible," she says. "The guard at the front gate was very biting, very hostile. The day I arrived, one employee had literally socked a manager in the jaw." Ford digs into the culture of a factory before guiding the workers in a carefully calibrated process of reinventing and restructuring their own work and priorities.

That first day at Welch's she said to a group of workers, "Pretend I'm your biggest customer, and let's toss a Koosh ball from person to person in the order of the production process." For a while, she got no response. "Finally, they say, 'Wal-Mart is our biggest customer.' It was said with loathing. It was said with despair, just despair."

At that Welch's facility in 1997, Ford says, the workers hated their most important customer. There were plenty of issues that fed into that, some of which had nothing to do with Wal-Mart. But Ford says the hostility to Wal-Mart was easy to understand from the point of view of the people making juice every day: "No matter how hard they work, how fast they get it done, how much improved the quality is, it's never good enough with Wal-Mart. The idea of a 'satisfied customer' was, for them, an oxymoron. It just doesn't happen. It doesn't compute."

That's why Ford says, "When you see the Wal-Mart smiley face, whistling and knocking down prices, somewhere there's a factory worker being kicked in the stomach." Ford has a sophisticated appreciation of the value of Wal-Mart in improving the efficiency of the supply chain around the world, even for its competitors. That impact just shows the range of Wal-Mart's influence and the potential for Wal-Mart's influence on the lives of factory workers. "I hold Wal-Mart accountable for some of this because of the phenomenon they've become," she says. "Wal-Mart says, 'How you do this is up to you.' But how people produce what they make for you does matter."

Mark Ingersoll comes to Wal-Mart's impact on the factory floor, and on product design, as a participant. Ingersoll, a design engineer, worked for the consumer division of Dutch electronics giant Philips for ten years, in two separate periods of his career. Starting in 1992, he and his family lived in El Paso, Texas, and Ingersoll traveled across the border to Juárez, Mexico, every day to the Philips TV factory there. "We were making ten thousand TVs every day," he says. "Magnavox, Sylvania, Philco, Philips. Color TVs, thirteen-inch up to twenty-seven-inch."

Ingersoll was the design engineer liaison between the Philips TV design group then based in Knoxville, Tennessee, and the Juárez factory floor. "I was right in the middle," he says. And acutely aware that hang-ups were costly. "If there was a problem and we shut down the production line, we were losing $250 per second, something like that."

Electronics makers, like apparel makers, started migrating their factories in search of lower costs well before Wal-Mart was a driving force. "We started out manufacturing in the northeast United States, and then moved that to Tennessee, and then to Mexico," says Ingersoll. By the time Philips had moved to Juárez, Wal-Mart was a significant customer, and a demanding one. "There was tremendous pressure to reduce costs," says Ingersoll. Products and processes were routinely redesigned to take out costs—TV cabinets made thinner, remote controls offered in a single color scheme instead of five different designs. "The first thing we took away were the extras they decided someone didn't need. My impression of the cost pressure was negative. It was simply: Lower the price. Find some way to lower the price."

The plant in Juárez is still in Philips's hands, but as Ingersoll was leaving, much of the production of typical TVs had moved to Asia. "They've lowered the price of the TVs to the point where they can't afford to pay $1 or $2 an hour they have to pay in Mexico." (Most recently, the Juárez plant has been revived to meet demand for high-end flat-screen TVs.)

Ingersoll, who has moved back with his family to New York State and no longer works for Philips, collects radios from the 1930s and 1940s, and especially appreciates the craftsmanship and design flourishes of their cabinets. He says there is a fundamental misunderstanding among Americans about offshore manufacturing, a confusion between the quality of the products and the people who produce them.

"The people in the factories are first class, really," he says. The production isn't poor quality, the products are. "They are reducing the costs of the product by compromising the design," he says. "They are designing the costs out by making poorer designs."

This unappealing element of the Wal-Mart effect has one virtue: It is egalitarian. It strikes the beloved giants of the U.S. economy with the same certainty and impact as everyone else.

For anyone who doubts that Wal-Mart prices can require products of inferior quality, the best examples are sometimes startlingly obvious. In July 2003, with fanfare befitting a royal wedding, Levi Strauss rolled blue jeans into every Wal-Mart doorway in the United States—2,864 stores that summer. Wal-Mart, seeking to expand its clothing business with more fashionable brands, promoted the clothes on its in-store TV network and with banners slipped over the security-tag detectors at exit doors.

Levi's launch into Wal-Mart came the year the company celebrated its 150th birthday. For a century and a half, one of the most recognizable, beloved, and durable names in American commerce had survived without Wal-Mart. But in October 2002, when Levi and Wal-Mart first announced their engagement, Levi Strauss was shrinking rapidly. Sales for Levi peaked in 1996 at $7.1 billion. By 2002, sales had spiraled down six years in a row, to $4.1 billion. The pressure on Levi goes back twenty-five years—well before Wal-Mart was an influence. In the decade of the 1980s alone, Levi Strauss closed fifty-eight U.S. manufacturing plants, and sent 25 percent of its sewing overseas. But by 2002, Wal-Mart's own, inexpensive house brand of jeans, Faded Glory, was estimated to do $3 billion in sales a year—a house brand nearly the size of Levi Strauss—and Wal-Mart sold more jeans than any other retailer. The value of Wal-Mart to Levi was clear: This one account could almost instantly revive the company's business.

But Levi had a problem. As it began negotiating with Wal-Mart, it didn't actually have any clothes it could sell the retailer. Everything was too expensive. In 2002, the year Levi announced it would start selling through Wal-Mart, half the jeans sold in the United States cost less than $20 a pair. In 2002, Levi didn't offer a single pair of jeans for less than $30.

To roll out a full array of clothes at Wal-Mart in the summer of 2003—kids', men's, women's—Levi Strauss had to assemble a fifty-person design and sourcing team, whose job was to develop a "value" line of Levi-branded products, jeans made of cheaper denim, with simpler designs, that were easier and less expensive to manufacture. Adult Levi Signature jeans now sell at Wal-Mart (and Target and Kmart) for $20 or $23—a real value, 25 to 30 percent less than the lowest priced Levi jeans elsewhere. To the touch, in everyday wear, Levi Signature jeans are perfectly serviceable, but utterly undistinguished. The only thing truly "Levi" about them is the name.

The excitement of Wal-Mart and Levi notwithstanding—the new products have sold well, although Levi's overall business continues to struggle—the whole exercise was disheartening, a confirmation of the discouraging aspects of the Wal-Mart effect, and the creeping irresistibility of the Wal-Mart economy. The "value" line of Levi jeans are both inexpensive and cheap; they also turn completely inside out exactly what, for 150 years, has made Levi's jeans so valued.

To survive in the face of the sort of pricing demands Wal-Mart made of Vlasic, Huffy, Lovable, and Levi Strauss, some consumer products companies have had to lay off employees and close U.S. plants in favor of outsourcing products overseas. Of course U.S. companies have been moving jobs offshore for decades, long before Wal-Mart was a retailing power, and Wal-Mart is hardly the only source of that kind of cost pressure. But there is no question that the chain is accelerating the loss of American jobs to low-wage countries such as China. Wal-Mart, which in the early 1990s trumpeted its claim to "Buy American," doubled its imports from China between 1997 and

2002 to $12 billion. In the next two years, Wal-Mart increased Chinese imports again by 50 percent, so that in 2004 the company and its suppliers landed Chinese-made goods in the United States with a wholesale value of $18 billion—almost 10 percent of everything imported to the United States from China.

Steve Dobbins is president of Carolina Mills, a seventy-five-year-old Maiden, North Carolina, company that supplies thread, yarn, and textile finishing to clothing makers, about half of whom supply Wal-Mart. Carolina Mills fabrics go into college sweatshirts, sleepers for babies, hardware-store work gloves. Carolina Mills grew steadily for decades, until 2000. In the last five years, as its customers have gone overseas, or gone out of business, Carolina Mills has shrunk from seventeen factories to five, and from twenty-six hundred employees to eight hundred. Dobbins's customers have begun to face imported clothing sold so cheaply to Wal-Mart that U.S. companies could not compete even if they didn't have to pay their U.S. workers any wages at all.

"People say, how can it be bad for things to come into the United States cheaply? How can it be bad to have a bargain at Wal-Mart? Sure, it's held inflation down, it's great to have bargains," says Dobbins. "But you can't buy anything if you're not employed. We are shopping ourselves out of jobs." More than that, says Dobbins, the manufactured goods coming to the United States so cheaply are made under factory conditions that would not only not be tolerated in the United States, they likely wouldn't even be legal.

"We want clean air, clear water, good living conditions, the best health care in the world," says Dobbins. "Yet we aren't willing to pay for anything manufactured under those restrictions."

Black & Decker, the Maryland-based power-tool maker that supplies Wal-Mart, among others, no longer operates any factories in the state where it was founded in 1910, although it does operate plants in

Mexico, the Czech Republic, and China. Barbara Lucas, senior vice president for public affairs at Black & Decker, without directly commenting on Wal-Mart, says simply, "The cost structure of operating manufacturing plants in the United States is just enormously out of sync with what people want to pay. Dramatically."

The L. R. Nelson sprinkler company is based in Peoria, Illinois; its founder, Lewen R. Nelson, introduced his first lawn sprinkler in 1911. The company, which is privately held, now makes more than a thousand different kinds of lawn-watering implements. In May 2005, Nelson announced it was laying off 80 full-time factory workers, bringing the company's U.S. hourly employment down to 120. At its peak employment in 1998, Nelson had 450 full-time U.S. employees, a number that swelled to 1,000 during the height of lawn-sprinkler production season. Now, although it has a state-of-the-art 315,000-square-foot factory in Peoria, the company makes no consumer lawn equipment there, just some highly technical commercial irrigation systems.

Dave Eglinton, the president of L. R. Nelson, explained the latest round of firings to the Peoria newspaper this way: "Wal-Mart said they would love to buy from us because some of the production is done in the United States, but the cost differential is so great that they told us that unless we supply them out of China, we couldn't do business."

Wal-Mart and Home Depot, said Eglinton, "are two of our biggest customers. Both of them have begun buying directly out of other factories located in China. If we didn't make the move we did, we would have lost the business completely."

A trip to the sprinkler shelves at any Wal-Mart reveals exactly how hard it's going to be for Nelson to compete, even using Chinese factories. Nelson's Easy Clik six-pattern garden hose nozzle is hefty; it feels solid in your hand. Price: $6.72. The Wal-Mart Mainstays house brand nozzle is in a display right next to Nelson's. Wal-Mart's nozzle is light as a feather—not flimsy, but certainly not robust. Price: $1.74. Buy the

Wal-Mart nozzle and you get to keep an extra five-dollar bill in your wallet. Both are labeled "Made in China." The two hose nozzles make Nelson's dilemma stark. Indeed, it's hard to see how the ninety-five-year-old Peoria company is going to compete with its own best customer long enough to stay in business—even making sturdy Nelson products in China.

Eglinton, a twenty-five-year veteran of Nelson, was quite clear in talking to the *Peoria Journal Star*: The sprinkler company had ceased domestic production of virtually all its products, and reduced employment by three hundred people over seven years, because Wal-Mart told it to.

What was striking about the Nelson layoffs wasn't their steadiness or scale, even in Peoria, a metro area of about 350,000 people. Global heavy-equipment maker Caterpillar, with $30 billion in sales and 80,000 employees in twenty-two countries, has its world headquarters in Peoria, and employs 16,000 people there. The city can absorb a few hundred layoffs.

No, what was truly incredible about the Nelson layoffs was Dave Eglinton's candor. It is unheard of for a company making consumer products to accompany its layoff or offshoring announcement with the most direct explanation: Wal-Mart made us do it. It's not just a breach of the Wal-Mart wall of silence; it's publicly blaming your most important customer for your own unpleasant business choices.

At least in part because of Peoria's relative isolation, even in the digital age, the unprecedented direct cause and effect between the Nelson layoffs, cheap Chinese factories, and pressure from Wal-Mart got virtually no other media mention or notice, even on the Internet, not anywhere. In a subsequent interview, Eglinton would say only, "Wal-Mart is a very, very good customer to us," and "What they've done for the consumer is really very good."

What's happening at Carolina Mills, Black & Decker, and L. R.

Nelson is, quite literally, the flip side of the Wal-Mart effect—the high costs of low prices. Eventually, there are no more efficiencies to be wrung out of the supply chain; there are no more pennies to be saved with smarter distribution or reduced packaging or cheaper plastic. Eventually, the only way to lower costs is to manufacture products outside the United States, in countries with lower labor costs, fewer regulations, less overhead. This element of the Wal-Mart effect remains largely hidden from public view. There is much public discussion of the shriveling U.S. manufacturing sector; there is much public discussion about the global economy, the shifts of jobs, about offshore competition, but outside of antiglobalization protesters, that discussion is often conducted as if it were a graduate seminar in astrophysics, with only glancing reference to causes or motive forces. It is as if the factory owners, the factory workers, their Chinese competitors, the governments and trade agreements, the stores, and even the customers (us) were all just bodies responding to the immutable laws of the physical universe, gravity, force, momentum, conservation of energy.

Wal-Mart's business relies on its own ceaseless hunger to reduce price a few more pennies (and its ability to transmit that hunger to its suppliers), whether through distribution efficiencies, or cheaper product design, or cheaper labor. Wal-Mart benefits from the impression that globalization is some kind of unmanageable economic weather system out of the control of everyone, affecting all players with indifference, benefiting those who happened to be properly prepared. That posture avoids any of the challenging discussion about *why* the world is suddenly so flat economically and what role a globe-straddling company like Wal-Mart plays in the flattening. Wal-Mart enhances its own image as just another economic planetary body with an impermeable barrier about how it gets its merchandise, and the impact of its needs on the companies that supply it.

Wal-Mart has taken to aggressively defending its own business practices by pointing out the number of jobs it creates. As part of Wal-Mart's new outspokenness in 2005, CEO Lee Scott said again and again that the company expected to create one hundred thousand new jobs in the United States that year, on top of the eighty-three thousand new jobs it created in 2004. But as in other examples, Wal-Mart's job-creation facts lack crucial context.

Most of what Wal-Mart sells us are consumables, things we use up in the course of daily life and need to replace: toothpaste, paper towels, laundry detergent, medicine, groceries. When Wal-Mart opens a new supercenter, people don't buy more Tylenol or Tide or Special K just because it's cheaper at Wal-Mart. They just shift where they buy those staples; much of Wal-Mart's growing U.S. business comes at the expense of other retailers.

The question then becomes, Does the opening of new Wal-Marts across the country really increase the number of jobs, or does it just increase the number of Wal-Mart jobs? From 1997 to 2004, the U.S. population grew 7.7 percent. If jobs in retailing had grown at the rate of the population, the country would have added 1.1 million retailing jobs during those seven years. In fact, the country added just over half that number—670,000 new retail jobs. That makes some sense; most stores can add shoppers without adding staff.

But here's the striking thing, and a completely unaccounted-for facet of the Wal-Mart effect: While the entire country was adding 670,000 new retail jobs, Wal-Mart was adding 480,000 jobs in the United States. More than 70 percent of all new retailing jobs in the United States in the last seven years came just from the growth of Wal-Mart. The remaining new retail jobs—190,000 in the entire nation spread over seven years—amount to just 540 new retail jobs in each state, each year, no more than the opening of a handful of new competitors' stores across the entire state during an entire year. While the number of Wal-Mart jobs grew 67 percent, the number of jobs in the rest of U.S. retail grew 1.3 percent. Wal-Mart, it turns out, created new retail jobs for itself, while its scale and vaunted efficiency were sucking the oxygen away from job creation in the rest of the retail trade.

The connection to the elimination of manufacturing jobs is less direct, but equally striking. While Wal-Mart was adding 480,000 jobs between 1997 and 2004, U.S. manufacturing jobs during those years fell by 3.1 million jobs, a loss of 37,000 factory jobs a month, on average, for eighty-four straight months.

Indeed, during the last seven years, a remarkable milestone has passed all but unnoticed: In 2003, for the first time in modern U.S. history, the number of Americans working in retail (14.9 million) was greater than the number of Americans working in factories (14.5 million). We have more people working in stores than we do making the merchandise to put in them. What's more, the number of Americans working in manufacturing is lower now than at any time in the last six decades, going all the way back to World War II, when the consumer economy hardly existed, and the population of the United States was half what it is now.

Wal-Mart, of course, can't be charged single-handedly with driving manufacturing jobs overseas. That is, in fact, the American dilemma: We find the abandonment of U.S. factories from Georgia to Michigan unnerving; we find cheaper stuff on store shelves addictive. And we don't connect the two. Consumer spending, however, accounts for two thirds of the U.S. economy, and Wal-Mart's influence across the consumer economy is unrivaled, unprecedented, and Wal-Mart's priorities are unwavering. During the same period that the number of U.S. manufacturing jobs fell by almost 20 percent, Wal-Mart's imports of inexpensive products from China alone increased 200 percent. Many elements are feeding the wave of inexpensive imports: complicated trade agreements, surprisingly quick industrialization in Asia, U.S. health-care costs, lax enforcement even of existing workplace safety and environmental laws in developing nations. But Wal-Mart does not hesitate to use its power; and Wal-Mart's single-minded obsession magnifies the Darwinian forces already at work in modern global capitalism and often brings them into laserlike focus on U.S. companies and U.S. factories. Just ask the residents of Peoria who used to make lawn sprinklers for L. R. Nelson.

FIVE

THE MAN WHO SAID NO TO WAL-MART

They had the lure of the Wal-Mart volume. Once you get hooked on the volume, it's like getting hooked on cocaine. You've created a monster for yourself.

—*Jim Wier, former CEO, Snapper, Inc.*

M CDONOUGH, GEORGIA, is a pretty, picture-book American town, with a beautifully manicured town square at its center—immaculate green grass, new light posts and benches, and fluttering pennants that describe McDonough as "a city of character."

Facing the square are four blocks of storefronts, most of which are occupied by active businesses. You can walk to four antique stores, a fresh produce stand, and even a day spa.

McDonough's town center is an almost perfect echo of a town square six hundred miles away in Bentonville, Arkansas. Even the dimensions of the two town squares are the same. In Bentonville, the nearest Wal-Mart is just a mile west; in McDonough, the nearest Wal-Mart is two and a half miles west—in both cases, less than five minutes' driving time. One square is the epicenter from which town squares have been shattered across the continent, and the other is one whose cheerful prosperity is a puzzle. Does downtown McDonough, Georgia, succeed in spite of Wal-Mart? Does it support Wal-Mart's more benign view that its stores do not in fact suck all the retail vibrancy out of small downtowns?

A mile south of McDonough's town square is an old, nondescript factory that is energetically trying to defy most of the conventional wisdom about manufacturing in the current global economy, a factory that is surfing the wave of the Wal-Mart effect—trying to ride it without being drowned by it.

The Snapper lawn-mower factory has been in McDonough for fifty years, and every Snapper lawn mower sold anywhere in the world—tens of thousands of mowers a year—is made in this factory. Coils of raw steel arrive on flatbed trucks every day, and brand-new, fire-engine-red lawn mowers leave every day, loaded in eighteen-wheelers.

The Snapper factory has had an aerobic, an invigorating, decade. Ten years ago it produced perhaps 40 models of outdoor equipment; now it makes 145 models. Ten years ago there were no robots or lasers or computer-controlled equipment at the factory; now robots do the welding, lasers cut parts, and computers control the steel-stamping presses. The productivity of the factory is three times what it was ten years ago, and the number of people working here is half what it was. Six hundred fifty factory workers make more outdoor equipment—more lawn mowers, leaf blowers, and snowblowers—than twelve hundred used to make.

These days the productivity of every factory worker is measured "every hour, every day, every month, every year," says Snapper president Shane Sumners, who walks the sprawling factory floor with comfort and familiarity. "And everybody's performance is posted, publicly, every day for everyone to see." It's a lot like Wal-Mart measuring the number of items every checker at every store scans every hour—except in the case of Sumners, it is one notch more demanding. Wal-Mart doesn't post everyone's performance for all to see.

Production at the Snapper factory is rescheduled every week, according to the pace at which mowers sell across the nation. A computer is required to juggle work assignments and balance the various parts of the assembly line. A daily 4:00 P.M. meeting monitors production and assigns work to a second shift, in case parts need to be made overnight for the next day's manufacturing.

Toward the southern end of the factory is one of several small "focus factories," this one dedicated to making and assembling Snapper's walk-behind mowers, the "push" mowers, although most of Snapper's are self-propelled. The main walk-behind manufacturing line—with twenty-eight people, including quality control—was recently charged with producing 265 lawn mowers in an 8-hour shift. Each hour's production was recorded on a white board as the hours ticked past, and the group hit the mark exactly. That's a new lawn mower, from loose parts to sealed box, every 109 seconds.

"It's all a matter of seconds," says Sumners with quiet matter-of-factness.

The Snapper lawn-mower factory hums with discipline and focus and urgency. It operates, literally, in Wal-Mart time. It must. It lives in the Wal-Mart ecosystem. But it does so—much like McDonough's town square—in defiance of Wal-Mart. Because three years ago the then CEO of Snapper's parent company politely but firmly pulled all Snapper products from Wal-Mart. That CEO, Jim Wier, is far too judicious to describe it this way, but he looked into a future of supplying Snapper lawn mowers and snowblowers to Wal-Mart, and saw a whirlpool of lower prices, collapsing profitability, offshore manufacturing, and the gradual but irresistible corrosion of the very qualities for which Snapper was known—the erosion of the very reasons Wal-Mart wanted Snapper to be its flagship lawn-mower brand. Jim Wier looked into the future and saw a death spiral. So he pulled out.

It's one reason every Snapper product continues to be made in the factory in McDonough, Georgia, one reason Snapper products are still made in the United States. But Shane Sumners has to spur his factory on with the same tirelessness as if it were supplying Wal-Mart—the efficiency of every factory worker measured every hour of every day—because Wal-Mart is setting the pace, even if you're not working for them.

A LAWN MOWER IS not a blender or a clock radio—a lawn mower doesn't seem like the kind of item you should buy without guidance. Even a simple, engine-powered lawn mower is a serious machine—gas, oil, spark plug, whirling blade. Understanding which one to buy, understanding how to run it and maintain it, especially for novices, might go better with an actual salesperson than as self-service.

Indeed, retail self-service is relatively new in the history of human commerce. Just one hundred years ago, American stores didn't allow customers to pick their own products; you came into a store and told a clerk what you wanted. (Until 1846, almost no stores even had fixed prices—you not only asked the clerk for what you wanted, you also haggled over the price of each item.) The first real self-service store of any kind is credited to Clarence Saunders, who opened a fully self-service grocery in 1916 in Memphis called Piggly Wiggly. In an early foreshadow of criticism that would be aimed at Wal-Mart, Saunders's stores—you had to shop for yourself!—were mocked, but Piggly Wiggly's dramatically lower costs, and lower prices, drove great business. Within seven years, by 1923, there were thirteen hundred franchised Piggly Wiggly stores in forty states.

The history of consumer culture in America in the last century has, in some ways, been powered by self-service, an idea Wal-Mart has continually bet on. In the last thirty years, self-service has swept through even the most complicated and delicate shopping experiences—stereo equipment, computers, fashionable clothing, new cars, and lawn mowers. Americans now buy more than 8.5 million push and riding lawn mowers a year—and they buy 70 percent of them at Wal-Mart, Home Depot, and Lowe's. Just twenty years ago, 80 percent of lawn mowers were sold at independent dealers.

The power of self-service is often in the price. You can buy a lawn mower at Wal-Mart for $99.96, and depending on the size and location of the store, there are slightly better models for every additional twenty-dollar bill you're willing to put down—priced at $122, $138, $154, $163, and $188. That's six models of lawn mower below $200. Mind you, in some Wal-Marts, you literally cannot see what you are buying; there are no display models, just lawn mowers in huge cardboard boxes.

But the least expensive Snapper lawn mower—a nineteen-inch push mower with a 5.5-horsepower engine—sells for $349.99 at full list price. Even finding it discounted to $299, you can easily buy two or three lawn mowers at Wal-Mart for the cost of a single Snapper. And Wal-Mart is aggressive about pricing, even compared to the home improvement superstores. Wal-Mart has three models of lawn mowers cheaper than the cheapest model at most Home Depot and Lowe's stores. A classic manual push-reel mower at Home Depot—at $129—is more expensive than the first two models with engines at Wal-Mart. In that way, Wal-Mart, and its home improvement colleagues, have not just changed the price of lawn mowers, they've changed the lawn-mower business completely. Wal-Mart—just a place where lawn mowers are sold—has reached deep into the way lawn-mower companies think about products, customers, service, pricing, and marketing; and it has changed how they do their work.

If you know nothing about maintaining a mower, Wal-Mart has helped make that ignorance irrelevant: At $99.96, $122.00, or even $138.00, the lawn mowers at Wal-Mart are cheap enough to be dis-posable. Use one for a season, store it, and if you can't start it the next spring (Wal-Mart won't help you out with that), put it at the curb and go buy another one. That kind of pricing changes not just the eco-nomics at the low end of the lawn-mower market, it changes expecta-tions of customers throughout the market. Why would you buy a walk-behind mower from Snapper that costs $519.00? What could it possibly have to justify spending $300.00 or $400.00 more?

That's exactly the question that motivated Jim Wier to stop doing business with Wal-Mart. It's a question Snapper president Shane Sum-ners answers with his own question: "Why does someone buy a Viking range?"

JIM WIER IS sixty-two years old, with a youthful twinkle despite a thatch of white hair. Wier is a solidly built man who dresses casually. He is comfortable with himself. He looks like a guy who might own the local garden- and power-equipment dealership, and who might have come to own it by starting work there after school as a fourteen-year-old boy. Wier, who until the summer of 2005 ran a group of lawn-equipment businesses that approach half a billion dollars a year in sales, is confident, direct, and unprepossessing. He mows his own lawn. "I don't want to hire a service," he says. "I still love to cut my grass."

Snapper was already selling lawn mowers through Wal-Mart when

Wier's company, Simplicity, bought Snapper in November 2002. Almost immediately on taking over, Wier stopped shipping Snapper mowers to Wal-Mart, a move that instantly cut Snapper's sales by almost 20 percent.

In a moment of unguarded candor not long after that decision, Wier told a local reporter near Simplicity's corporate headquarters in Port Washington, Wisconsin, what he thought of the decision of Snapper's previous senior management to sell through Wal-Mart. "They had the lure of the Wal-Mart volume," Wier said. "Once you get hooked on the volume, it's like getting hooked on cocaine. You've created a monster for yourself."

It is a more extreme assessment than Wier would give publicly now, but it was not a casually chosen comparison. Companies addicted to the Wal-Mart volume, like people addicted to cocaine, are always looking for the next hit, the next rush. They reorganize their business lives to sustain the ever-increasing need for more volume; their priorities end up skewed to support that single obsession; in the end, a lot of rationalization and self-justification can't disguise the fact that the need to pursue the volume, the addiction, changes the very character of the company—and of the addict. The difference between the company selling its products to Wal-Mart and the cocaine addict, of course, is that in important ways, the lure of Wal-Mart is not always bad. No one thinks being a cocaine addict is a reasonable career goal. But a company's main job is to sell its products—why wouldn't it sell through the most effective, ambitious outlet available?

"As our economic world unfolds," says Wier, "I don't think everybody is going to want to buy everything from big-box stores." Wier sometimes buys men's clothing at Jos. A. Bank Clothiers, a hundred-year-old national men's clothing store chain that sells well-made dress clothes at reasonable prices and has a low-key sales staff that helps men find clothes that fit well and look good. "When I go to Jos. Bank, they remember my name," says Wier. "Now imagine I go to Jos. Bank and look at the sweaters, and I'm looking at the prices." Sweaters at Jos. Bank cost $40, $50, $80, and up.

"Visualize we're making Snapper-brand sweaters. We sell them at Jos. Bank and at Wal-Mart, but at very different prices. Now, as a customer, you buy a sweater at Jos. Bank and later you're waltzing through Wal-Mart, and there's that damn Snapper sweater. The stitching is a little different, the color is a little different, but it's $20. And you go back to Jos. Bank and say, 'Hey, you screwed me. You overcharged me. I could have bought that sweater for 20 percent less at Wal-Mart!'

"And the man at Jos. Bank might say, 'Well, I took care of you, I helped you try it on, I gave you some pointers on what it would look good with, I found some socks that matched.' As a customer you might say, 'Yeah, well, maybe that was worth 5 percent. But 20 percent?'"

The problem gets worse with time because of the way Wal-Mart works with suppliers. "If you sell the sweater that first year for $20.00 at Wal-Mart," says Wier, "that first year of life is good. The manufacturer is happy, and Wal-Mart is happy. But in year two, what's Wal-Mart going to sell that sweater for? It's not going to be $20.00. Wal-Mart will say, 'How well did we do last year? This year we're going to double that volume. We sold two hundred thousand sweaters, and now we're going to sell four hundred fifty thousand. But it's going to be at $14.97.'" And if you're the sweater company, says Wier, you swallow hard, you do the math, "and you say, that's going to work out all right. But what's happening to those Snapper sweaters back at Jos. Bank?" And what's going to happen in year three?

As it is with clothing, so it is with lawn mowers. It's not just that Wier wants his products sold by stores where the staff understands the equipment, can explain the differences between models and brands, can teach customers to use a mower, can service it when something goes wrong. Wier wants customers who want that kind of help—customers who are unlikely to be happy buying a lawn mower at Wal-Mart, and who might connect a bum experience doing so not with Wal-Mart, but with Snapper.

In fact, Jim Wier doesn't really think that a $99 lawn mower from Wal-Mart and Snapper's lawn mowers are the same product, any more than a paper cup of 50-cent vending machine coffee is the same as a Starbucks nonfat venti latte. "We're not obsessed with volume," says Wier. "We're obsessed with having differentiated, high-end, quality products."

Even some of Snapper's walk-behind lawn mowers come with cup holders. The fire-engine-red cutting deck—to which the engine is bolted, beneath which the blade whirls, to which the wheels are attached—feels like a piece of steel, and not like a husky version of an aluminum foil roasting pan.

It's hard to believe, says Wier, "but when we do surveys of our customers, they like to cut their grass. They get personal satisfaction out of cutting their grass. And they want a good piece of equipment to do it. We're designed to give you the best quality of cut. We have full rollers on the riding mowers, to give that nice striped look on your grass, like on the baseball fields. It makes you feel proud of the home you own. Proud of your lawn. The neighbors walk by, they say, look how good the yard looks."

Snapper's products are sold by independent dealers of lawn equipment, some ten thousand across the United States (which is more than twice the number of Wal-Mart stores). "The person who goes to the independent retailer wants something a little different," says Wier. "A little better. Yes, it's the product. But it's also the buying experience, a level of comfort. You walk into that local retailer, he's a family man, the business has been passed down a couple generations. Some-one says, 'Hi, how are you?' They work with you to make sure you buy the right piece of equipment, the right mower. They show you how to operate it, they set it up, if need be, they deliver it. Many wives like to cut the grass, they'll show your wife how to use it.

"And if for some reason it requires maintenance, for a reasonable fee they'll come back, pick it up, service it, and return it to your garage."

Wal-Mart's lawn-mower priorities are clear: On most of the boxes in which its lawn mowers are packed, the largest thing by far on the outside of the box, far larger than the name of the brand, is the price: an enormous, black "$138" or "$154."

The question that Snapper and Jim Wier confronted is why you can't sell your products through a variety of outlets. Wal-Mart for years has had an informal rule that it doesn't want to own more than about 30 percent of a supplier company's business, because it doesn't want to be perceived to control the fate of a company. That means that even companies that do an incredible one third of their business through Wal-Mart still reach 70 percent of their customers through other outlets.

You can buy Fruit of the Loom T-shirts or a Sony Walkman, Pampers or a Sharp microwave oven or a LEGO Star Wars kit at Wal-Mart—and you can buy all those things at all kinds of other places too, from competing chains to individual specialty shops. Why not Snapper walk-behind lawn mowers?

One reason is simply perception. Wal-Mart has done such a good job portraying itself as a deep discounter, it's not a place people expect to find premium products. "If a brand is going to stand for being high end, with special features, catering to a particular kind of customer," says Wier, "that wasn't compatible with selling through Wal-Mart. The person who goes to an independent retailer wants something a little different, a little better. If you allow that same product to be in Wal-Mart, it will be priced and perceived—both those things—to be of a very different quality."

Wier was worried that simply keeping Snapper products in the Wal-Mart setting would tarnish their reputation—from Snapper at always low prices to Snapper being simply cheap. Because Wal-Mart insists on being lower priced than its rivals—and because its volume typically justifies lower pricing—Snapper products would also end up in the sweater conundrum. Loyal customers get angry when they buy a product at one price and then stumble on it sharply discounted somewhere else. It also leaves the independent dealers at a competitive disadvantage: They can't afford to educate wave after wave of customers who shop at their stores and then buy their products at Wal-Mart.

More important, Wal-Mart's pricing drives a completely different and sometimes corrosive phenomenon, one in which Wal-Mart slowly but insistently resets our expectations about what a product should cost, and about what it's worth. The process often proceeds at a speed not much greater than continental drift—but with the same kind of bulldozing power. Why shouldn't you be able to buy a cordless electric screwdriver for $9.99? Why shouldn't a twenty-four-inch color TV cost $145.00?

And so the standard Snapper mower—which lists for $349.99, sells at dealers for $299.00, and turns up at Wal-Mart for $289.00 or $277.00—ends up over time being not a $350.00 lawn mower for a good price but becomes a $277.00 lawn mower. When we see it for $299.00 at a dealer, we chuckle at the suckers who fall for that price. When we see it at a list price of $349.99, we shake our heads in wonder at the presumption of lawn-mower makers. But it's not really a $277.00 lawn mower—there's no profit in that price, no room for reinvestment, for innovation, for rising health-care costs, or a sudden spike in world steel prices.

When you sell something through Wal-Mart, you take on Wal-Mart as a partner in your business whether you want to or not. "Do you have to change the quality of your product to accommodate Wal-Mart?" asks Wier. "Of course. It happened. What they did was, they continue to drive the price down. They wanted to do the same thing with our products that they do with everyone's. They want more product at a lesser price. To achieve that, after a while, you do start taking some of the quality and the features out. And we just weren't willing to do that.

"We concluded we really couldn't serve two masters."

Quality and price can become very slippery concepts. If you can get a perfectly good DVD player at Wal-Mart for $39, you might actually be suspicious of a $129 DVD player. It's not better, it's just a rip-off. Sometimes cheap is inexpensive; sometimes it's cheap.

Jim Wier has spent most of his career in the world of outdoor equipment. Before he became president of Simplicity, he spent twenty-five years at Briggs & Stratton, the manufacturer of small engines. When he moved to Simplicity in 1999—the company was a customer of Briggs & Stratton's—he was taking over from a twenty-three-year veteran named Warner Frazier. Wier and Frazier shared the same barber, Ron.

One day Wier was getting a haircut, and Ron told him that Warner was trying to sell him on a Simplicity riding mower. "It's so much more expensive than an MTD," Ron the barber said to Wier. "What makes it different?" MTD makes a range of lower-end lawn tractors, including the Yard-Man and Yard Machines brands.

"First," says Wier, "I said, do you care what your lawn looks like? Ron said, 'Oh yeah, I do.' I said, that's important. Because if you want to buy something that just makes tall grass short, buy a Murray at Wal-Mart, or buy an MTD. If you want something to make a lawn look good, buy a Simplicity."

Still, Ron the barber wasn't convinced.

"I said to him, okay, Ron, you give haircuts, right? You cut my hair, right? Well, we could trade places. I could cut your hair. They'd both be haircuts, right?

"He said, 'Okay. I know what you mean.' "

IT'S NOT HARD to make a cheap lawn mower, and it's not hard to tell when you're using one. A cheap lawn mower feels flimsy, sounds louder than it needs to, and even when new requires a mysterious, frustrating combination of choke, priming, and pulling to get the engine to start. The cutting deck is stamped out of a piece of thin sheet metal. As time goes on, getting the motor to start seems more and more like an act of sorcery, the engine tends to belch more ugly exhaust when it's running, and various fittings rattle themselves loose and need to be tightened. (Toro, a brand that competes with Snapper, has a brilliant "guaranteed to start promise," in which some of its mowers are guaranteed to start on the first or second pull for several years. The only problem is that on the third pull, a Toro service-person genie does not magically appear; you have to load up your balky mower and take it to a local lawn-mower shop along with all your records showing proof of proper maintenance.)

Making a high-quality lawn mower requires a tireless attention to detail and constant improvement, which seems surprising for a machine that doesn't evolve that much.

All Snapper mowers, from the simplest walk-behind to the most elaborate riding mower that operates with the touch of a joystick, are painted one color: what Shane Sumners calls Snapper red. In the Snapper factory in McDonough, the finished chassis of riding mowers coast along slowly, dangling from an overhead conveyor as they approach a twenty-foot-long pool of red paint. The conveyor track dips low, and the mowers glide down into the pool and completely disappear beneath the surface, then rise up, gleaming red, before heading for a pass through a curing oven. It's not quite as simple as dip and bake, however. Each mower is electrically grounded as it hangs from the overhead conveyor, and a slight positive electrical charge runs through the sixteen-thousand-gallon trench of paint. "So the paint is attracted to the metal, and builds up on the parts and sticks very effectively and evenly," says Sumners. A man with a clipboard walks through the painting area, taking notes. With typical understatement, Sumners explains, "The painting is a closely controlled process." The painting process is monitored every hour—from the speed of the conveyor and the temperature of the ovens to the pH of the paint—along 115 parameters. That's just to get the mowers painted with the right level of quality and consistency, even without ever changing colors. "If you control the process," says Sumners, "you will get a good paint job."

At the receiving dock, beneath a sign that reads "Snapper's customers expect *zero* defects," incoming parts are segregated based on the McDonough factory's history of satisfaction with those parts. The parts from suppliers with a history of sending components that aren't 100 percent perfect sit in staging areas, awaiting inspection; components from suppliers with a history of "zero defects" go straight to where they are needed.

On the assembly line where self-propelled walk-behind mowers are being put together, one of the twenty-eight people working the day shift is Steve Chadwick, a fifteen-year veteran of the McDonough facility. Chadwick's job is "audit"—he pulls a mower at random from the dozens moving off the line and checks it against fifty-four quality items, recording everything from the pitch of the blade to the proper application of the decals that say "Snapper." Chadwick does twelve audits in an eight-hour shift. Today, eight of twelve mowers are perfect; four have small problems. "They were getting bubbles in the name stickers," says Chadwick. "But I think they've got that problem fixed."

Over where the riding mowers are nearing the end of their journey, two workers stand on opposite sides of the line, and each mower stops between them. They use computer-controlled laser measuring devices to precisely level the cutting deck of every riding mower. "What's the purpose of a lawn mower?" asks Sumners. "It's to cut grass. If you're cutting grass, you want it cut level."

From the leveling station, each mower proceeds to a final stop on the line before going on the truck. Here, a man wearing ear protectors squirts gas into the fuel tank and oil into the crankcase, pulls the starter cord, and brings the machine to life. He runs through all the gears and checks speed, engine performance, the mounting of the seat. The engine is given just enough fuel for the "run in." If the mower passes all the tests, the man sucks the oil back out and sends the mower on to be boxed.

As Sumners looks on, one of the riding mowers takes two pulls to start, then comes to life with a rough growl. In the blink of an eye, the technician shuts it down. "Did you hear how that sounded?" asks Sumners. "It's not right. That's a bad one." The mower is shunted off to be inspected and properly tuned if possible. Snapper "hot starts" and tests every riding mower before it leaves McDonough. "If we didn't," says Sumners, "that mower would have gone to a customer."

The Snapper factory started making riding mowers in 1951. The outgrowth of a sawmill blade business that started in 1894, it now has nearly half a million square feet of manufacturing floor space—10.5 acres of factory under one roof. In the area of the factory nearest the offices is a roped-off lineup of vintage Snapper mowers; the earliest ones have the neck and head of a fierce-looking snapping turtle mounted on the front of the cutting deck.

The company still makes, stocks, and distributes parts for mowers that are twenty years old. From the Snapper Web site, you can download the full text of owners' manuals for Snapper mowers going all the way back to 1951. The factory itself is unadorned and old, but it is old in the sense of solidity and use. There is nothing tired about it. More significant, there is nothing sentimental about this factory. It's not still here out of some misplaced sense of economic loyalty to U.S. manufacturing. It's here because it makes Snapper-quality lawn mowers at a competitive price. Even to stay competitive outside the big-box arena, Sumners understands that a relentless focus on efficiency is as important as quality.

In the two-story area of the factory where enormous presses shape sheet metal into mower parts, one thousand-ton press is being disassembled, parts and bundles of wiring trailing from it as if it had been disemboweled. It is an old machine, decades old. But working with its manufacturer, Snapper's technicians are putting new electronic controls on the machine. When it's back in operation, it will be able to stamp out lawn-mower parts 25 to 30 percent more quickly.

Near the metal stamping presses is an area of lathes. Unlike many companies, Snapper doesn't simply assemble its lawn mowers from parts other companies make. It really manufactures its lawn mowers. It buys disks of steel larger than the palm of a man's hand, and precision-machines the teeth to make transmission gears. "That is a high quality-control process," says Sumners, hefting one of the gears. "It's easy to screw up, and it has a high cost to customers, and to our warranty costs, if you mess it up." In the lathing area, a technician takes long steel rods, cuts them to the proper length, then machines their tapered shape and cuts threading on each end. These become spindles that attach the motor to the cutting blade.

"It takes skill to produce these parts," says Sumners, nodding a silent greeting to the lathe operator. "We quoted the cost of outsourcing those spindles in the last year, we quoted them in China. Sure we did. We'd be fools not to. We were making them cheaper here than what they would have cost to produce and bring over. We're keeping 'em here.

"But you have to measure yourself against the rest of the world. There's no walls around Georgia, that's for sure."

Even with no products at Wal-Mart, a company like Snapper has to compete psychologically, has to keep the price gap between the big-box lawn mowers and its lawn mowers rational. If it did not, its potential slice of the market would get smaller and smaller. Some of Snapper's dramatic productivity improvements in the last decade, in fact, seem to come almost directly from the Wal-Mart playbook.

Ten years ago, at about the time Sumners came on board, Snapper had fifty-two regional distributors. Getting mowers to dealers was a cumbersome two-step process. Snapper uses no regional distributors now—the company runs four regional warehouses of its own and sells and distributes directly to ten thousand independent dealerships. Ten years ago, in part because of the complexity of the middleman distribution system, Snapper carried a huge quantity of inventory. It paid to manufacture and ship thousands of lawn mowers—worth tens of millions of dollars—without quite knowing when they would be sold. There was a lot of product idling along on the road between factory and front lawn. Now Snapper is constantly trying to fine-tune the number of lawn mowers sitting in its warehouses. Planners come up with an ideal level of inventory for every model, for every region of the country, based on things like historic demand and the weather. The goal is to make sure every customer can get the mower he wants—while making absolutely the fewest number of lawn mowers. A cushion of extra lawn mowers is just wasted effort and money.

Today a single computer system runs the entire company, which makes purchasing, marketing, planning, and analysis more efficient.

"Ten years ago," says Sumners, "every department in house was on a separate computer system."

Technology is applied where it makes sense. Robotic welders handle the routine welding tasks for most of Snapper's mowers now. Output for a single welding employee has basically doubled because one person tends a robotic welder, loading and unloading mower parts. "The robot is always welding," says Sumners. "It never has to stop to load or unload parts. The staff person does that while the welding robot is welding." Together, he says, "they never miss a beat." Ten years ago there were no robots in the plant.

The factory is not just more productive—650 people turn out 50 percent more machines than 1,200 used to—the employees do a much wider range of work. Ten years ago McDonough turned out 40 different models of power equipment. In 2006, it will make 145 different models.

One model not on the list is a cheap lawn mower. "We have no desire or game plan to make a $99 lawn mower," says Sumners. Nor is the factory in danger of being outcompeted by China. Sumners says that less than 10 percent of the cost of each mower is labor. In many areas of U.S. manufacturing, like textiles, that ratio is inverted, with labor much more of the cost of a garment than the fabric itself. Even if Snapper could cut labor costs by two thirds, that saves only 7 percent of the cost of the mower; then you have to put mowers on a ship and get them to the United States and from the port to the dealers.

"It comes on the boat with a long lead time," says Sumners. "If there is an uptick in business—if it rains like crazy in the spring in the Midwest, and the lawn mowers are selling like gangbusters—you couldn't take advantage of that the way we can."

In a factory where every production worker's efficiency and quality are recorded every hour, there is a fine line between running a place that feels like a well-tuned machine and running a place that feels henpecked. The McDonough factory isn't hectic, but it is focused. No one is standing around idly. In two hours of walking the floor, dozens of employees nod at Sumners, but not one stops what he or she is doing to talk to him.

During the spring and summer, the factory pays assembly-line workers to cut grass. They work a four-hour shift, and they get to know the mowers they are making, to understand what they are like to use. They cut the grass of nonprofit groups around McDonough.

"You can work here all day long, then go out and jump on what we make and cut grass," says Sumners. "We make an end-use product— we make it, and it goes directly to consumers. That's very rewarding for folks who work here. I love this company. Everyone here takes a lot of pride in what we're doing."

And then, in case you might have missed it, Sumners says, "We believe in a lot of attention to detail and in measurables. When you make a premium product, if you don't control quality and durability, you have nothing."

JIM WIER SAYS that the day he went to Bentonville, Arkansas, to tell Wal-Mart he was pulling his lawn mowers from their stores was "one of the most interesting days of my life."

Tens of thousands of executives make the pilgrimage to northwest Arkansas every year to woo Wal-Mart—to marshal whatever arguments, data, samples, presentations, and pure persuasive power they have in the hope of getting an order from Wal-Mart or increasing their current order. Almost no matter what you're selling, the gravitational force of Wal-Mart's 3,811 U.S. "doorways" is irresistible. Very few people fly into Northwest Arkansas Regional Airport thinking about telling Wal-Mart no, or no more. Almost no one has ever spoken about the experience.

Around the time Wier's company, Simplicity, was buying Snapper, in the fall of 2002, Wier had decided that continuing to sell Snapper mowers in Wal-Mart stores was "incompatible with our strategy. And I felt I owed them a visit to tell them why we weren't going to continue to sell to them."

Wier says that from his perspective, "I'm probably pro-Wal-Mart. I'm certainly not anti-Wal-Mart. I believe Wal-Mart has done a great service to the country in many ways. They offer reasonably good product, at very good prices, and they've streamlined the entire distribution system in a great way. And it may be that along the way, they've driven some people out of business who shouldn't have been driven out of business."

In considering Snapper's relationship to Wal-Mart, Wier had two things going for him. First, he had another way to get his lawn mowers to customers—the independent-dealer channel—which was more effective, albeit more complicated, than Wal-Mart. And Wier had the courage, the foresight, to take an unblinking view of where his Wal-Mart business was heading—not in year three, or year four, but in year five and year ten. Snapper was at the point where the quality of the product would have to be reduced to meet Wal-Mart's retail price demands. It seems like an obvious logical outcome: Incessant pressure to reduce the retail price of manufactured products, year after year, must eventually lead to cheaper materials or fewer features because at some point a company has taken the inefficiencies out of its operation, and has thinned its profit margin as much as it can bear. And yet it is virtually unheard of to hear any Wal-Mart supplier ever acknowledge that Wal-Mart's pressure reduced the quality of any product.

For his part, Wier went to Bentonville with a firm grasp of the values of Snapper, the dynamics of the lawn-mower business, the needs of the businesses that sold 80 percent of his product, the needs of the Snapper customer, and the needs of the Wal-Mart customer. He was not dazzled by the tens of millions of dollars' worth of lawn mowers Wal-Mart was already selling for Snapper, or could sell; he was not deluded about his ability to go to Bentonville and beat them at their own game, somehow resist the price pressure. He was not imagining that he could take the sales now, and figure out the profits later. Jim Wier believed that Snapper's health—indeed, it's very long-term survival—required that it not do business with Wal-Mart.

And so in October 2002, with a colleague, Wier kept an appointment with a merchandise vice president for Wal-Mart's outdoor product category.

"The whole visit to Wal-Mart headquarters is a great experience," says Wier. It really is a pilgrimage to the center of the retail universe. "It's so crowded, you have to drive around, waiting for a parking space, you have to follow someone who is leaving, walking back to their car, and get their spot.

"Then you go inside this building, you register for your appointment, they give you a badge, and then you wait in the pews with the rest of the peddlers. The guy with the bras draped over his shoulder."

Normally, meetings between Wal-Mart buyers and people from supplier companies take place in the legendary meeting rooms along hallways just off the vendor lobby. These cubicles are simple to the point of barren—a table and four chairs, and thirty minutes of time to make your case, whatever it is. "It's a little like going to see the principal, really," says Wier.

In this case, Wier says, both he and the Wal-Mart managers "had a feeling that this would be an important meeting." So Wier and his colleague were scheduled to visit the vice president, in his office.

"When your turn comes, they put you through security, just like at the airport," says Wier. "They check your computer for viruses, they check your bags. We got by the little booths, and we got into the inner sanctum, the vice president's office."

The vice president for outdoor products had a small but reasonable office. He had a desk, with a chair, and a table behind his desk. And he had a sitting area for visitors like Wier.

"What I'll never forget," says Wier, "is that the seating area for us—it was just some lawn chairs that some other peddler had left behind as samples." The vice president's office was furnished with one folding lawn chair and one chaise longue.

And so the CEO from Simplicity, dressed in a suit, took a seat on the chaise. "I sat forward, of course, with my legs off to the side. If you've ever sat in a lawn chair, well, they are lower than regular chairs. And I was on the chaise. It was a bit intimidating. It was uncomfortable, and it was going to be an uncomfortable meeting."

It was a Wal-Mart moment that couldn't be scripted, or perhaps even imagined. A vice president responsible for billions of dollars' worth of business in the largest company in history has his visitors sit in mismatched, cast-off lawn chairs that Wal-Mart quite likely never had to pay for.

"The meeting started with the vice president of the category saying how it was clear that Lowe's was going to build their outdoor power-equipment business with the Cub Cadet brand, and how Home Depot was going to build theirs with John Deere," says Wier. "Wal-Mart wanted to build their outdoor power-equipment business around the Snapper brand. Were we prepared to go large?"

Talk about coming to the table with different agendas. The vice president was dangling an even greater temptation: Let's join hands and go head to head against Lowe's and Home Depot. Let's sell lots of lawn mowers.

"Usually," says Wier, "I don't perspire easily." But perched on the edge of his chaise, "I felt my arms getting drippy. This really was not going to be an easy meeting."

Wier took a breath and said, "Let me tell you why it doesn't work. As I look at the three years Snapper has been with you, every year the price has come down. Every year the content of the product has gone up. We're at a position where, first, it's still priced where it doesn't meet the needs of your clientele. For Wal-Mart, it's still too high priced, I think you'd agree with that.

"Now, at the price I'm selling to you today, I'm not making any money on it. And if we do what you want next year, I'll lose money. I could do that and not go out of business.

"But we have this independent-dealer channel. And 80 percent of our business is over here with them. And I can't put them at a competitive disadvantage. If I do that, I lose everything. So this just isn't a compatible fit."

Wier says the meeting remained civilized from start to finish. "They were not boisterous, they were not condescending," he says. "To their credit, I would say, after a period of time they took it very well." Not, mind you, that they actually took it. They strategized and argued. Snapper is, in fact, the kind of high-quality nameplate, like Levi Strauss, that Wal-Mart hopes can ultimately make it more Target-like.

The vice president suggested finding a lower-cost manufacturer. The vice president suggested producing a whole separate, lesser-quality product line, with the Snapper nameplate, just for Wal-Mart. Just like Levi.

"My response was, we would take a look at that," says Wier. "The reason I gave that response was, it was a legitimate question. In my own mind, I knew where I'd go with that"—no thanks—"but at that kind of meeting you at least have to be willing to say, I'll investigate."

And that was it. "The tone at the end was, we're not going forward as a supplier."

No lightning bolt struck. Except that Snapper instantly gave up almost 20 percent of its business. "But when we told the dealers that they would no longer find Snapper in Wal-Mart, they were very pleased with that decision. And I think we got most of that business back by winning the hearts of the dealers."

Snapper was successfully integrated into Simplicity, the company of which Wier was CEO, and he took the title of CEO of Snapper as well. In 2004, Simplicity was itself bought by the publicly traded company Briggs & Stratton, the company where Wier built his career, the company that makes many of the engines in Snapper and Simplicity mowers. Simplicity and Snapper operate as independent divisions inside Briggs & Stratton, and Wier remained CEO of both until late summer of 2005, when he resigned to join the private equity firm Kohlberg & Company. In a bit of business irony that speaks to the wisdom of never underestimating Wal-Mart's reach, Snapper's parent company now counts as a large, if indirect, customer: Wal-Mart. Many of the lawn mowers on display at Wal-Mart are powered by engines made by Briggs & Stratton.

For a while after Wier's visit to Bentonville, Simplicity quietly made a virtue of pulling out of Wal-Mart. The company had an advertising campaign in the trade press that said it made "products that fit everywhere except in a 'big box.'" In McDonough business is strong. Shane Sumners has plans to add a second assembly line for both walk-behind and riding mowers.

One serious hazard to Wier's strategy is whether the independent lawn-equipment dealers can really survive all the same pressures that have, for instance, hurt small, independent hardware stores.

"That is a legitimate question and a legitimate concern," says Wier. "I think we have a part in that outcome. Can Snapper, as a major supplier, continue to supply [the independents] with great product, and a product different than you can buy at Wal-Mart?"

One of the ways to compete with Wal-Mart, in fact, is not head on but aisle by aisle, that is, category by category. Wier points to Best Buy and Circuit City as specialty retailers that have succeeded despite efforts by Wal-Mart in electronics. But when Wal-Mart is determined to master a line of business, it can be hard for even large, well-established specialty retailers to compete, as Wal-Mart's dominance of toys and groceries shows. Toys "R" Us and two dozen supermarket chains have wilted in the face of effective competition from Wal-Mart. To help his independent equipment dealers, Wier did things like appearing on a panel about how to outmaneuver the big-box stores. His advice included the obvious—know more about your products, display them well, have friendly salespeople—and also the not so obvious—have clean restrooms.

The other way to compete with Wal-Mart is to focus, even in the mass market, on things besides price: design, fashion, quality, cachet, the feel of the shopping experience. That's the approach of Wal-Mart's most astute big-box competitor, Target, and of one of its most effective grocery competitors, Whole Foods. It's a strategy with a smaller overall market, a smaller demographic, but it's also a strategy that ultimately has more maneuvering room than Wal-Mart allows itself. The growth of both Target and Whole Foods in fact shows the power of quality, even competing against low prices. Wal-Mart guarantees that price will always matter; the popular nicknames for Target, "Tarjay," and Whole Foods, "Whole Paycheck," while affectionate, are also a gentle mocking of the upscale pretensions of what are really a discounter and a supermarket. Still, competing on price can ultimately turn into a chore for Wal-Mart, for its suppliers, even for shoppers. Competing on quality, on design, on cachet leaves a little more room for fun, and for profit.

Snapper, of course, isn't a retailer. Its competition with Wal-Mart is oblique—Snapper needs to help its independent dealers be competitive. Snapper is tireless about its own efficiency, its own costs, its own innovation—as if it were supplying Wal-Mart—because it needs to keep its customers from drifting to Wal-Mart. Wier had determined to lead Snapper to focus on quality, and through quality, on cachet. Not every car is a Honda Accord or a Toyota Camry; there is more than enough business to support Audi and BMW and Lexus. And so it is with lawn mowers, Wier hoped. Still, perhaps the most remarkable thing is that the Wal-Mart effect is so pervasive that it sets the metabolism even of companies that purposefully do no business with Wal-Mart.

And the power and allure of Wal-Mart is such that even Jim Wier, the man who said no to Wal-Mart, a man who knows all the reasons that that was the right decision, even Jim Wier has slivers of doubt.

"I could go to my grave, and my tombstone could say, 'Here lies the dumbest CEO ever to live. He chose not to sell to Wal-Mart.'"

SIX

WHAT DO WE ACTUALLY *KNOW* ABOUT WAL-MART?

Given the level of public interest in Wal-Mart and other 'big box' retailers, there has been surprisingly little independent research on their impact. . . . Research into this question is hampered by paucity of data.

—*Emek Basker, assistant professor of economics, University of Missouri, "Job Creation or Destruction?"*

EMEK BASKER, an economist with a Ph.D. from MIT and an undergraduate degree from the University of North Carolina at Chapel Hill, wanted to answer two of the simplest questions you can ask about Wal-Mart:

What effect does the opening of a Wal-Mart store have on prices in the immediate area?

What effect does the opening of a Wal-Mart store have on the availability of jobs in the immediate area?

She didn't want to look in just a couple places in the country for an answer, or in just a state or two. She wanted to answer those two questions definitively, for the nation. Does Wal-Mart really lower prices? Does Wal-Mart create jobs or destroy jobs? One way or the other, she wanted to prove it, to a mathematical certainty.

It would be harder than Basker thought. Now just four years out of graduate school, Basker is an assistant professor of economics at the University of Missouri, and she has completed those two pioneering studies on Wal-Mart's impact on the economy of the United States. But she had to overcome a significant hurdle. Both studies are built on a single foundation of data, really a single column of data that she had to construct laboriously, meticulously, by hand, over the course of months. A key reference turned out to be the Rand McNally road atlas of the United States. Not some special academic version, but the kind you buy at Wal-Mart. In fact, Basker had to use the version published for Wal-Mart.

Because before she could isolate and analyze the impact of Wal-Mart stores on prices and jobs, she needed a list of every Wal-Mart in the nation, and the month it opened. If you know when a particular Wal-Mart opened, in a particular county, you can look at what the county was like before Wal-Mart, and what the county was like afterward. In terms of prices, in terms of jobs—in terms of all kinds of things.

At the home office in Bentonville, which houses one of the two or three largest private databases in the world, it is hard to imagine that such a list of store opening dates isn't readily available—indeed, most Wal-Mart stores are known by their numbers, and the numbers in the United States are assigned consecutively as stores are planned. And, of course, the opening and existence of a Wal-Mart store is hardly a secret.

But you can't begin to assess the impact of an event until you know when and where the event occurred. Basker asked Wal-Mart for that simple file: a list of stores, by number, and the date they opened.

In a footnote in one of her papers, she writes, "Requests for store-opening data from Wal-Mart corporation were denied."

In fact, building the list of stores turned out to be a Herculean undertaking that might have discouraged someone of less determination. Basker compiled a list of the locations and opening dates of 2,382 Wal-Mart stores, "collected primarily from Wal-Mart annual reports, Wal-Mart editions of Rand McNally road atlases and annual editions of the *Directory of Discount Department Stores.*" The Wal-Mart edition of the Rand McNally road atlas includes a special set of pages that list every Wal-Mart in the United States by state and location, including the store numbers. Basker would cross-check annual reports, to see how many stores opened in a particular year, with successive editions of the road atlas, to see which stores opened in which years, and with the not always reliable *Directory of Discount Department Stores.* Basker was going to use the list to do serious math—her study of Wal-Mart's impact on employment includes five pages of math written out using equations and sentences like "that the measurement error across the two variables is uncorrelated seems plausible."

One of Basker's problems is that mathematical economic proof requires precision. She didn't need to know when a Wal-Mart store opened *approximately,* she really wanted to know the quarter of the year in which it opened or, better yet, the month. For whole years of Wal-Marts, she did not have that information. So she developed a formula that analyzed when Wal-Mart typically opened stores, and she applied that to the stores she knew opened in a particular year, and since she knew the basic order they opened (from the store numbers), she could take a pretty good mathematical guess at when each store opened. Then, because Basker has a Ph.D. from MIT, she did a separate calculation of the probability that her opening date might be wrong for any given store. And she included the chance of error right along with all the other math.

Mind you, this wasn't the hard part. She was just making a list of stores and opening dates, and using math to make it as accurate as possible. It took one year. With characteristic understatement, Basker says, "It was very tedious." It is easy to understand why she now refers to this list in her own paper as "a unique data set containing the locations and opening dates of all U.S. Wal-Mart stores." Unique, indeed.

If there is one place to turn for an understanding of the impact of Wal-Mart, one place where the many variations of the Wal-Mart effect on the businesses, wallets, and behavior of Americans would be dissected with scholarly enthusiasm, it is the economics departments of the nation's universities. What better way to put the anecdotes about Wal-Mart's impact in context than to actually do some studies that capture the Wal-Mart effect with certainty and precision? And what greater target of scholarly opportunity could there be than the largest, most powerful company in history? In fact, we appear to know for certain more about the geology of the surface of Mars than we know about the Wal-Mart Supercenter down the street.

The canon of Wal-Mart scholarship is so modest that in a couple afternoons at the library, you can read every significant academic paper written about the company's impact. There are fewer than twenty. That so fertile a field is as yet so barren, the scholars themselves can't resist noting. "Despite the dramatic proliferation of supercenters, relatively little is known about the impact [they] have on the performance of a traditional grocery store or how [they] change consumer buying behavior" (Singh et al., 2004). "While there is much anecdotal evidence to suggest that existing businesses are harmed by the growth of supercenters, there has been little academic research in the field, owing to a general lack of reliable data" (Stone et al., 2002). Even in the area of Wal-Mart's impact on prices—the very essence of the Wal-Mart effect, the big bang from which all other effects originate—as recently as 2003, Basker writes, "Although these theories make consistent predictions about the price impact of [Wal-Mart] entry, very little empirical work has been done to quantify these effects" (Basker, 2003). The scholarship is so thin that the studies often cite articles from the *New York Times,* the *Wall Street Journal,* and *USA Today* alongside the few references from peer-reviewed academic journals or conference proceedings.

Although what we now know for certain about the Wal-Mart effect, thanks to a handful of researchers, is limited, it is fascinating, sometimes surprising, and often vitally important. A few of the most fundamental questions have been tackled, and the answers established. And each study suggests a fresh array of urgent questions worth their own studies.

In the case of Emek Basker, once she had compiled her list of Wal-Mart stores and their error-adjusted opening dates, she unleashed herself. In her first study, "Selling a Cheaper Mousetrap: Wal-Mart's Effect on Retail Prices," Basker proved—proved!—that Wal-Mart lowers prices. "I find price declines of 1.5 percent to 3 percent for many products in the short run," she writes. "Long run price declines tend to be much larger, and in some specifications range from 7 percent to 13 percent."

If it seems like a head-slappingly obvious conclusion, well, it may be because there is a big difference between proving something and presuming something. If you shop, and you shop at Wal-Mart, you can pretty well tell that much of what you buy is cheaper at Wal-Mart. But that's anecdotal—that's what you're buying, in your town, at that moment in time.

Here's what Basker did: She collected the prices for a few very specific, commonly used products (Bayer aspirin, Winston cigarettes, Cascade dishwasher powder, Kleenex, Johnson's baby shampoo, Alberto V05, Coke, Fruit of the Loom briefs) four times a year, for the twenty-one years from 1982 through 2002, in 165 cities across the United States. That's how she knows what the prices were for years before Wal-Mart arrived, and for years after Wal-Mart arrived. She controlled for the effects of things like inflation, and for things ordinary people might never consider, like differences between cities in labor costs or the cost of land on which stores sit.

Then she plugged all her data, and her caveats, into her algorithms. The paper, to be published in the *Journal of Urban Economics,* includes a detailed explanation of Basker's methodology. It runs to twenty-two pages of math, charts, and tables, but that is how Emek Basker can say with absolute confidence what seems obvious: Wal-Mart lowers prices. The largest declines came in aspirin, laundry detergent (she used data on Tide, Cheer, or Bold), toothpaste (Crest or Colgate), and shampoo. And Basker found that Wal-Mart's impact on prices was greater in smaller cities—"cities with a large number of retail establishments per capita," as she puts it. As an aside, she notes that it's quite possible that Wal-Mart's impact might "lower prices in communities not served by Wal-Mart," because Wal-Mart's own efficiencies ripple out to suppliers and competitors. But she hasn't proven it, so she doesn't say it; she just offers it as a possibility.

Basker's second study tackles a much more urgent, and much more politically contentious, question. As she puts it, "Has Wal-Mart created more jobs than it has destroyed?"

This is also a much more complicated question. Even at the level of a county, employment dynamics are complicated, swept by national and global waves of growth and recession and by local events such as factory closings or openings. Basker is, in essence, an economic scientist. She didn't just want to see what happened to jobs in counties where Wal-Mart stores exist—she wanted to prove that whatever happened to jobs in those counties was caused by Wal-Mart.

To start tackling this task, she zeroed in on Wal-Mart's effect on retail employment specifically. In the contiguous forty-eight states, there are 3,111 counties. Basker looked at a little more than half of those counties—1,749, which had more than 1,500 jobs in 1964, job growth from 1964 to 1977 (that is, they weren't dying counties), and no Wal-Mart yet in 1977, so she could gauge the impact of Wal-Mart's arrival. She looked at job data for each of those 1,749 counties across twenty-three years. Because she used data for such a huge chunk of the nation, and over such a long period, she writes, "I am able to examine the dynamics of county-level retail employment over a ten-year period surrounding Wal-Mart entry, separately estimating short- and long-run effects."

Basker also asks two important subsidiary questions: Does Wal-Mart help or hurt the other businesses in the county where it enters? And does it matter if those businesses compete with Wal-Mart, or are in unrelated areas, like restaurants and automobile dealerships?

These are classic Wal-Mart controversies: Does Wal-Mart put smaller retailers who carry similar merchandise out of business? Does Wal-Mart generate so much traffic that existing nearby stores actually do better with Wal-Mart's arrival, at least if they don't compete head on? Finally—and just for fun, presumably—Basker looked at whether the opening of a Wal-Mart had any measurable effect on retail jobs in neighboring counties.

Here's what her pages of calculations show: In the first year after a Wal-Mart store opens, it adds one hundred new jobs to the typical county. Basker immediately writes, "Recall that the typical Wal-Mart store employs 150 to 350 workers." So even as Wal-Mart is opening, it is putting other people out of business. Even at the low end of the range—150 people working in a new Wal-Mart—50 people who had retail jobs in that county before Wal-Mart arrived immediately lost their jobs (or went to work for Wal-Mart). So in that first year, Wal-Mart created a net increase of one hundred new jobs, but they were all Wal-Mart jobs, and other retailers immediately fired people in the face of Wal-Mart's arrival.

In the years after Wal-Mart arrives, retail employment falls gradually, so that five years after Wal-Mart's arrival, there are only a total of fifty new retail jobs, again despite the fact that the new Wal-Mart store typically employs hundreds.

What's happening? Well, there is method to Basker's madness. Her analysis of the number of retail establishments in each county—divided into small, medium, and large—shows that the number of small retailers (fewer than 20 employees) falls. Three retailers close within two years of Wal-Mart's arrival, four close within five years. So despite the burst of excitement about the arrival of a Wal-Mart, Wal-Mart's success comes largely at the expense of the retailers already in business in a county. Wal-Mart may employ 300 people in a new store, but after five years, 250 people working at nearby retailers have lost their jobs—and four stores have gone out of business altogether.

Basker also looked at jobs at wholesalers, companies that supply goods to retailers. Part of Wal-Mart's efficiency is that unlike small- and medium-sized stores, it does its own distribution. In fact, Basker found that on average, a county lost twenty wholesale jobs after five years. So in jobs across retail, five years after the opening of a new Wal-Mart, employing hundreds, a county had gained thirty jobs.

And Basker's study has controlled for things like routine growth in retail, or population changes in a county. Those are thirty real new jobs. But just thirty. Basker didn't find any spillover value to Wal-Mart in generating new jobs in restaurants or car dealerships, but those may not be the places most likely to see benefit from Wal-Mart. As for the impact on neighboring counties, she writes: "Unfortunately, estimating Wal-Mart's effect on neighboring counties with any precision is impossible, as the confidence intervals around the point estimates are very large." She couldn't tell, in other words.

Basker's study shows that Wal-Mart's job impact is not quite as neat, or as sweet, a story as everyone would like. Does Wal-Mart create jobs? Yes, it does. Does Wal-Mart destroy jobs? Yes, it does. The press coverage of the study has been equally muddled—including some stories that refer to Basker as a man. What Basker proved is that Wal-Mart does create jobs in the typical county it enters—but just thirty new jobs after five years. Most of the hundreds of new jobs at a typical Wal-Mart ultimately come at the expense of existing retail jobs. In conclusion, Basker has this to say: "The small magnitude of the estimated effect of Wal-Mart on retail employment is striking in light of the level of public discussion on this topic."

Wal-Mart, which could not be bothered to make public a list of its stores and their opening dates to facilitate this or any other research, was very pleased with Basker's results. The company has referred reporters to her study, and on its walmartfacts.com Web site, Wal-Mart cites the study as "the most definitive look at this issue," noting the creation of the fifty new store-based retail jobs after five years. In a bit of brazenness and outright distortion remarkable even for Wal-Mart, the very same *paragraph* that cites Basker's study approvingly also asserts, "Studies show that new businesses spring up near Wal-Marts and existing stores flourish as they take advantage of the increased customer flow to and from our stores." No other studies are referenced, and Basker's study, of course, doesn't show anything of the kind. Basker proved the opposite: that the arrival of Wal-Mart closes four existing businesses, and has little or no effect on at least some nearby businesses. She also established that with the collateral damage in the wholesale business, the total new jobs a regular Wal-Mart creates is thirty after five years. But it's hard to crow much about opening a vast store that creates an average of six fresh jobs a year.

FROM 1998 THROUGH 2001, inflation in the United States was calm. Something that cost $10.00 in 1998 cost just $10.87 in 2001. For food, inflation during those three years was even more modest. Groceries that cost $10.00 in 1998 would have cost $10.77 in 2001. For food, that's annual inflation of 2.5 percent, for everything together, just a bit higher, 2.8 percent.

Those numbers come from the U.S. government, from the much-watched and much-relied-on Consumer Price Index (CPI) issued each month.

But here's the thing: Modest as inflation was in those years, it may be overstated by 15 percent per year. Now 15 percent of 2.5 percent doesn't seem like much—it reduces the inflation rate for food to about 2.125 percent a year. The groceries that cost $10.00 in 1998 really cost $10.65 in 2001, or 12 cents less. But that 12 cents add up fast in a country as big as the United States. If a family spends $100.00 a week on groceries, that's $5,200.00 a year. The official inflation figure, three years later, would lead us to believe the family was spending $61.24 more on groceries a year than it was. With 108 million households in 2001, that miscalculation comes to $6.6 billion that someone thinks we're spending on inflation-adjusted groceries that we're not in fact spending. And that's just the groceries.

How could one of the federal government's core economic statistics be off by 15 percent? Wal-Mart.

In what is perhaps the most significant economic study of the Wal-

Mart effect, an economist from MIT and an economist from the U.S. Department of Agriculture have done a painstaking analysis of the government's procedure for calculating the U.S. inflation rate for groceries, and they've concluded that the government gets it wrong, and seriously wrong, because the CPI simply fails to take into account the impact of Wal-Mart's lower prices. It's hardly a trivial mistake—companies, stock markets, banks, Congress, and the White House all watch inflation figures obsessively. Everything from future purchases of factory machinery, to the size of Social Security checks, to the interest rate you pay for a new mortgage turn in large measure on what inflation is doing. The CPI isn't reality; it's a statistic. What we actually buy and what we pay for it—that's reality. But the CPI is so important that it influences reality, and sometimes becomes it.

The government's miscalculation has nothing to do with Wal-Mart itself, of course, and if you buy your groceries at Wal-Mart, you saved the $6.6 billion (or your share of it), no matter what the government said the inflation rate was. But such a striking and systematic failure to get a vital economic statistic correct shows two things. It shows the incredible hidden power of Wal-Mart across the entire economy: Not only did Wal-Mart help keep inflation down, it kept inflation 15 percent lower than anyone knew. It also shows how hard it is to keep up with the range of the Wal-Mart effect, even for people who spend all their time and energy trying to do just that.

Understanding how the government got itself into this fix—how hard is it to miss the most important price phenomenon in the last fifty years when your business is prices?—is complicated. The study by MIT's Jerry Hausman and the USDA's Ephraim Leibtag will help explain it, as will a CPI economist named Patrick Jackman. But that explanation has to begin with what, for ordinary people, will seem a stunning revelation. Although the rest of us will be amazed to learn what Hausman and Leibtag "discover" in their paper, one group that wasn't surprised at all were the people who work at the Bureau of Labor Statistics (BLS), the people who compile and calculate the CPI every month. They are fully aware of Wal-Mart, they know they ignore it, and they ignore it on purpose.

The whole thing makes Jerry Hausman spitting mad. "I'm just an academic at MIT," he says. "But the BLS should fix its problems." The intent of his paper was more than to bring the the issue to light, it was to embarrass the BLS into fixing it. "I'll tell you this, if I'm ever found dead in an alley, it won't be the mob. It will be the BLS." Hausman doesn't sound particularly worried, however.

How hard could calculating the Consumer Price Index be? You check the price of bananas this month; you check again next month. Repeat. The BLS staff does record eighty thousand individual prices a month (although not eighty thousand items—multiple prices on identical items across the country). The CPI contains 211 categories of items from fruit to new cars to breakfast cereals. The banana, in fact, is pretty easy, at least until you take Wal-Mart into consideration. Once you get beyond the banana, things get complicated quickly.

Consider a box of Rice Krispies. This month, it's eleven ounces for $3.79. Next month, it's still $3.79—but now it's thirteen ounces. Whoa. The price didn't stay the same—it went down. The box is the same price, but it contains 18 percent more Rice Krispies. Next, let's check in with Sprint on the price of phone service. This happens to be the month when Sprint offers to switch all its long-distance customers from 5 cents a minute for long-distance calls to $18 a month for all the long-distance calling you want. Anyone who talked more than six hours a month long distance is going to have a lower bill; anyone who talked fewer than six hours a month long distance is going to have a bigger bill. But really, the comparison isn't square: $18 for all the long-distance calling you can make isn't the same product as 5 cents a minute for long distance. Changing the price has literally changed the product itself because the new pricing is going to literally change some customers' behavior. If it suddenly doesn't matter how much I talk long distance—which is what all-you-can-talk pricing says—I might talk a lot more. How do you fold all that into this month's CPI? Did Sprint's long-distance service get cheaper or more expensive?

Finally, let's consider a new 2006 Japanese sedan. The car maker advises us that it sells for the same price as the 2005. But it has side-impact air bags, which it never had before. Hmm. That's a new feature, although not quite as snazzy as leather seats or a sunroof. Still, in the world of the CPI, that new feature is just like the bigger box of Rice Krispies. The car got "cheaper," because the same amount of money bought more car. It's a quality improvement.

The complexity goes up rapidly. Consider figuring out the monthly pricing for something like medical care. What's the cost of a chest X-ray? The price that appears on the bill? The amount the insurance company reimburses? Which insurance company?

Here's how the complexity relates to Wal-Mart, or to ignoring Wal-Mart. The pricing folks at the BLS look not only at what products and services are for sale, how those products are changing, and what they cost, they also look at where things are sold. Haircuts cost different prices at boutique salons and at Supercuts—they are both haircuts, but they are not really the same. The venue matters. If you only survey the cost of music bought at record stores, you miss all the music sold online. So the BLS pricing staff is constantly watching markets to see where people are buying things, and trying to adjust where the prices that go into the CPI come from so that they represent what people are really buying, and what they are really paying. As you can imagine, that process lags behind the real marketplace—the federal bureaucracy moves more slowly than Amazon.com.

One market where there have been dramatic changes in the last fifteen years is the supermarket. In 1990, Wal-Mart sold essentially no groceries. Today Wal-Mart is the number-one grocer in the land (and in the world). It owns roughly 16 percent of the grocery market nationally, or $124 billion of the $775 billion we spent in 2004 on groceries. In some cities, Wal-Mart owns 25 or 30 percent of the grocery business—literally one out of four, or one out of three, families do their grocery shopping at Wal-Mart supercenters.

To the CPI economists, Wal-Mart supercenters are a bit of a puzzling entity. They aren't really traditional grocery stores: the offerings aren't quite as sophisticated, the shopping experience isn't quite as pleasant, the service isn't quite the same, the atmosphere is a bit warehouselike. As Wal-Marts roll out in communities across the nation, they are added as places for the pricing staff to gather pricing information. In fact, they are substituted for other chain stores so that the market mix between Wal-Mart and competing supermarkets remains balanced city by city. But here's what happens when a Wal-Mart gets substituted as a pricing venue: The CPI doesn't take account of the lower prices at the moment of the substitution. Rice Krispies are $3.79 at Kroger; the very same box is $2.99 at Wal-Mart. But that 80-cent price difference is "linked out." It's ignored. The CPI assumes that all the difference in cost is owed to a lesser-quality shopping and service experience at Wal-Mart—the Rice Krispies aren't really cheaper because the shopping experience overall is shabbier.

The study by Hausman and Leibtag barely contains its contempt for this method. "Even though packaged food items are physically identical at the two stores, the BLS procedure does not recognize any price difference between the stores. This procedure is not based on any empirical study. Rather, it is based on mere assumption. The assumption is completely inconsistent with actual real world market outcomes where Wal-Mart has expanded very quickly in markets that it entered. . . . [O]bserved consumer behavior cannot be explained by the BLS assumption of a compensating 'quality differential.' "

In other words, if shopping at Wal-Mart is such a distasteful experience, overcome only by the low prices, why would Wal-Mart be gobbling up 25 or 30 percent of the customers within a year or two of arriving in a city? And how glorious is it to shop at Kroger or Safeway or Albertsons these days anyway?

This critique is, in fact, the starting point of Hausman and Leibtag's paper. They go on to do two things: to recommend a different approach to Wal-Mart and to supercenters of all kinds, a procedure that would have them accounted for as a new choice for consumers, not a substitute. That would account for the initial price differential, along with any changes in prices that follow as Wal-Mart rolls supercenters into new cities. And they painstakingly calculate how far off the CPI's index of grocery prices is for the years 1998 to 2001.

Their study looks at prices not just at Wal-Mart but at any supercenter or club store. They found, across the twenty categories of food they examined, that supercenter prices were on average 27 percent lower than at traditional groceries, an astonishing discount. It's like getting one week of groceries free every month, just for moving your shopping to Wal-Mart.

Patrick Jackman, an economist for the CPI, says that Hausman and Leibtag have a point. Hausman, he says, assumes that all the difference in price between a regular grocery store and a store like Wal-Mart is owed to business efficiencies. CPI assumes the opposite. "We are assuming the price difference is all because of a quality change," says Jackman. "Jerry is saying, we ought to go to one pole, and we're at the other pole. The truth lies somewhere in between. And we don't know how to assess where in between it should be."

Jackman goes on to make a subtle but important point: Even in cities where Wal-Mart is a great success, 70 percent of the people still buy their groceries elsewhere, and pay more. Because CPI staff are forbidden by confidentiality rules to mention specific stores or products, Jackman couches his point carefully. "There has to be a reason someone is still going to Outlet A," he says. "It would be hard to argue that they wouldn't know about Outlet B, given how, uh, large Outlet B is." Whatever their reasons for going to Outlet A, those reasons are powerful enough to justify spending more, so there must be some kind of quality difference, at least for those customers.

The CPI takes the Hausman and Leibtag critique seriously, Jackman says. "We are certainly aware of this issue, and we are certainly looking at ways of accommodating it. But we haven't made any changes yet." Jackman sighs almost inaudibly. Hausman is a regular critic of the BLS's methods, and he is not a favorite there. "If it were easy to fix, we would have implemented it," Jackman says.

Hausman and Leibtag conclude that the impact of ignoring Wal-Mart, for the years they studied, comes to overstating grocery inflation by 15 percent per year nationwide. Given the attention that gets paid to inflation, where a few tenths of a percentage point move markets and impel the Federal Reserve Bank, that's dramatic. As Hausman and Leibtag put it in their paper, with a kind of algebraic conclusiveness: "We find that the BLS does not know that Wal-Mart 'exists' in terms of the estimation of a CPI." Their study—which has gotten virtually no attention in the mainstream media, despite what it says about both Wal-Mart and inflation—is almost the opposite of Basker's work in one important way: It is not a definitive look at what we know about Wal-Mart; it is a dissection of one very important thing we don't know.

Here's the truly amazing thing: Hausman and Leibtag's study just looked at what's called the CPI for "food-at-home," that is, food bought for preparation and consumption at home, or groceries. But the BLS uses exactly the same procedure for everything else Wal-Mart sells too. It's not just groceries: The entire U.S. inflation rate doesn't know Wal-Mart exists.

THE DEAN OF WAL-MART scholars is a professor and economist named Kenneth E. Stone, now retired from Iowa State University's extension service. Back in 1988, when Wal-Mart was one fourteenth the size it is now, a mere $21 billion in sales, Stone authored the study "The Effect of Wal-Mart Stores on Businesses in Host Towns and Surrounding Towns in Iowa." The typescript of that paper is available for downloading at Stone's Web site—it actually appears to have been typed on a typewriter. When Stone set out to systematically analyze the impact of Wal-Mart on Iowa's small towns, no one had undertaken anything like such a study before. Stone was simply doing his job as an extension economist at Iowa State.

"This study was made in response to a number of calls from chambers of commerce and business people concerning the likely effects of proposed Wal-Mart stores on their businesses," he writes on the opening page. "In no way is this an attempt to berate the Wal-Mart company; its stellar national reputation speaks for itself." That caveat wasn't all that important for this first study, but it would turn out to be prescient.

In the 1988 study, Stone looked at a total of fifty-five Iowa towns with populations between five thousand and thirty thousand. Ten had Wal-Mart stores, and forty-five did not. Although Stone looked at only the first three years of impact of a Wal-Mart's arrival (Wal-Mart only opened its first Iowa store in 1983), the basic outline of the Wal-Mart effect was clear. In towns with a Wal-Mart, sales of general merchandise leaped dramatically compared to the state average, up 55 percent per capita after three years. In the forty-five small towns within twenty miles of a Wal-Mart, total sales dropped 13 percent after three years, nearly double the decline for similar Iowa towns that weren't near a Wal-Mart.

But even in the towns with Wal-Mart stores driving dramatic increases in the retail trade, there were losers. Grocery stores lost 5 percent of their sales after three years; specialty stores—drugstores, clothing stores, toy stores, and the like—lost 12 percent of their sales after three years. Even service businesses in Wal-Mart towns lost business—down 13 percent after three years. Here Stone gingerly offered a fascinating bit of speculative insight: "It is a mystery as to why service type businesses lost sales after Wal-Mart stores opened in their towns. Conventional wisdom would suggest that these types of businesses should have benefited from the customer 'spillover effect.' One possible explanation is that there may be a perception by many that it is more economical to purchase certain new items at Wal-Mart, rather than having old ones repaired."

What made Stone's study possible is that Iowa provided detailed sales tax data for all its 856 towns and cities, by retail category. Stone was able to use that data to calculate retail sales for the towns he studied, by category, and control for changes in population or retail trends. His study, he points out in a single sentence, "does not prove causation." But the study was built on the premise that in a state like Iowa, "where population is static or declining," the amount of consumer spending is relatively stable, and the arrival of a Wal-Mart necessarily takes business from other merchants.

"This study has pointed out the winners and losers in Iowa, based on the first few years of operation of Wal-Mart stores," concluded Stone. "The intent of this study is to document what actually happened in the past so that business people may make better operational decisions in the future."

In the tradition of university extension divisions, whose role has been to use state university resources to solve problems in the communities they serve, Stone goes on to give brief bullet points of advice—things like avoiding competing head to head with Wal-Mart's merchandise, offering better service, and appealing to more upscale shoppers.

Ken Stone's study caused a sensation. Wal-Mart was still building its business in small- and medium-sized towns, and this first Stone study crystallized and quantified the kind of cyclonic impact that the arrival of a Wal-Mart had on the businesses in those towns and in the adjacent towns. The study also changed Stone's life and career. In the next five years, dozens of towns across the country would invite Stone in to talk about his discoveries, and to dramatically expand on his advice to local merchants on how to survive the arrival of Wal-Mart. Within five years, Stone had given presentations in every state except Delaware. By virtue of the fact that he had done actual economic analysis—even if only on small, stagnant Iowa towns—Stone became an expert on Wal-Mart's impact on local communities, and a guru of ways it might be possible for local businesses to survive the arrival of a Wal-Mart in town. Modest and unassuming, Stone was also able to see Wal-Mart quite clearly. As early as 1993, he predicted to a reporter, "This company has a good chance of becoming the biggest business in the United States." That year, Wal-Mart was still smaller than the corporate giants GM, ExxonMobil, Ford, IBM, and GE—all of whom it would pass in the next nine years.

In 1993, Stone updated and expanded his original study into a piece of work that was ultimately published in the peer-reviewed journal *Economic Development Review*. This time, Stone looked at thirty-four Iowa towns that had a Wal-Mart, and was able to examine the impact up to five years after Wal-Mart's arrival in those towns, and in neighboring towns that didn't have a Wal-Mart. At least in the land-scape of Iowa, where in 1993 the largest city, Des Moines, had just two hundred thousand people, the effects of Wal-Mart's arrival were dramatic. Using an economic analysis technique that allowed him to control for both changes in population and changes in the state's retail sales, Stone found that in Iowa's Wal-Mart towns, general merchandise sales grew 44 percent five years after Wal-Mart's arrival, and restaurant sales, perhaps benefiting from the increased customer flow to Wal-Mart, were up 3 percent five years after Wal-Mart's arrival.

Across the rest of the retail landscape, the arrival of Wal-Mart co-incided with a swath of destruction. Grocery stores lost 5 percent of their business after five years, specialty stores lost 14 percent of their business, and clothing stores lost 18 percent of their business—all while total sales were rising 6 percent, mostly due to Wal-Mart.

In towns that were nearby but didn't have a Wal-Mart, Wal-Mart vacuumed customers away: Clothing stores lost 13 percent of their business after five years; specialty stores lost 21 percent. Two items in particular jump out of Stone's second paper. In the years from 1983 to 1993, small Iowa towns, with populations between five hundred and one thousand, lost 47 percent of their total retail sales, apparently as people simply drove to Wal-Marts to shop. And during that same period, as Wal-Mart grew from no stores to forty-five stores in the state, 43 percent of all stores selling men's and boys' clothing went out of business. Nearly half of an entire retail category in a state was wiped out.

It was in this study that Stone first offered his two "rules of thumb" about the winners and losers when Wal-Mart arrives: "Rule 1: Merchants selling goods or services different from what Wal-Mart sells become natural beneficiaries. . . . Rule 2: Merchants selling the same goods as Wal-Mart are in jeopardy."

Wal-Mart itself took a while to figure out how to deal with Stone.

He told the Des Moines newspaper in 2004 that early in his work, he received a series of unpleasant phone calls from Wal-Mart executives, including one from current Wal-Mart chairman Rob Walton. The calls, Stone said, "sounded real threatening," so much so that he consulted a law firm. The attorneys advised him to ignore the calls, Stone told the paper. But by 1993, Wal-Mart was taking a more moderate approach. A spokesman for the company, quoted in a 1993 *New York Times* profile of Stone, said, "As near as I can tell, Dr. Stone tells people facts about Wal-Mart, about retailing and about their business, and let the chips fall where they may."

Stone officially retired from Iowa State in 2004, but he has continued to offer advice. Just eight weeks before Hurricane Katrina roared ashore, he was in Baton Rouge to talk to merchants about the possibility of competing with Wal-Mart. "Wal-Mart is not the end of the world," he told them. "If you know the business, you can compete with them."

Iowa is, of course, a special case (Stone eventually repeated the work in Mississippi, a state similar to Iowa in its retail landscape). The confirmation of Stone's studies on a broader, more complicated landscape would await the kind of work that Emek Basker has done. But Stone's work pointed out that it was possible not to rely on anecdotes, impressions, and gut feelings about Wal-Mart; you could ascertain and measure the Wal-Mart effect. Stone's work also showed the competitive value of digging into a specific market and understanding it completely.

In that same tradition comes Vishal P. Singh, an assistant professor of marketing at Carnegie Mellon University, and two colleagues from Northwestern's Kellogg School of Management. Singh and his colleagues persuaded a single outlet of a regional grocery chain in a northeastern state to let them look at what the arrival of a nearby Wal-Mart did to the business of that one grocery store.

It's fine to drive up on scenes of car accidents after the fact and try to figure out what happened. But if you really want to understand the collision of Wal-Mart and another business, it's great to be able to record it in real time, and play it back in slow motion.

The trio begin their 2004 paper (to be published in the peer-reviewed journal *Marketing Science* in 2006) with the almost totemic sentence of academic astonishment: "Despite their unprecedented growth and the threat they pose to [the] traditional grocery industry, relatively little is known [about] how entry of a supercenter in a market changes consumer purchase behavior or what it does to the bottom-line of an incumbent supermarket."

Singh and his colleagues hit on a brilliant strategy. They used the data that their test supermarket gathered from the "loyalty" cards it issued to its customers. Those are the cards issued to regular shoppers by a supermarket that are scanned before each shopping cart of purchases is rung up. The loyalty cards have proliferated in the last five years, and they ostensibly provide regular shoppers with discounts. They also record, track, and archive every purchase that every shopper with a card makes, down to the minute of the day the purchases are made. It is the perfect window for watching not only what happens to the whole supermarket after Wal-Mart opens, but also for analyzing what kinds of shoppers change their behavior.

The researchers' store is a classic modern American regional supermarket. It is located in a suburb where 70 percent of the customers own their own homes. The store is open twenty-four hours a day and has postal services, banking, video rental, photo developing, a pharmacy, bakery, deli, a seafood department, and a custom-cut meat department. In some ways, such a store is positioned to compete with Wal-Mart—if such competition is possible.

The group got loyalty card data for the market's business for the twenty months from November 1999 to June 2001, an incredible amount of information for a store doing roughly $1.5 million in business a month. (Loyalty cards were used in 85 percent of purchases; the data itself was anonymous, and the researchers pledged not to reveal the location of the store, or the chain.) Smack in the middle of the data period, in August 2000, a Wal-Mart Supercenter opened 2.1 miles from the supermarket.

The most dramatic finding was that in the face of competition from Wal-Mart, the supermarket lost 17 percent of its sales. "The magnitude of the lost sales is quite alarming considering that supermarkets generally operate on a principle of low margins and high volume, with profit margins of only about 1 percent," the researchers write. As dramatic as that 17 percent loss is, of course, it's completely consistent with what other studies, including Hausman and Leibtag's, have found: If Wal-Mart is going to get 15 to 30 percent of a community's grocery business, it's going to get it a chunk at a time out of existing grocery stores. We don't buy more Rice Krispies or milk because it's cheaper at Wal-Mart—we just move our buying over there. Still, it is rare to see that impact up close, right at shopping cart level. The lost business is so dramatic, it's as if the existing store simply closed its doors every Wednesday at 8:00 A.M., and didn't reopen until noon Thursday.

More interesting, however, is the deconstruction that Singh and his colleagues did of what the lost business looked like—how traffic changed, and who defected. "The majority of the losses came due to fewer store visits with little impact on the basket size once consumers are in the store," the researchers write. In other words, shoppers either stayed, or they took their business elsewhere. They didn't double shop, splitting their purchases strategically between their familiar store and Wal-Mart.

A bit less surprising, but still fascinating to have proven, is who moved and who stayed. "Households that respond to Wal-Mart are likely to have an infant and pet in the family [the loyalty card data shows things like purchases of diapers and pet food], and are more likely to be weekend shoppers." The Wal-Mart shoppers, in other words, are busy and buy large volumes of stuff. A cheaper, one-stop shopping alternative is going to be very powerful. "Similarly, store-brand buyers have a higher likelihood of moving purchases to Wal-Mart"—they're buying cheap stuff anyway, how much worse could the quality be at Wal-Mart?—"while households that spend a large proportion of their grocery expenditures on fresh produce, seafood, and home meal replacement items are less likely to [do] so." Because, of course, you can't get high-quality fresh produce, seafood, or ready-to-eat meals at a supercenter.

One grocery shopping myth that Singh and his colleagues do damage to is the idea that people want to grocery shop near their homes. Their study found that the distance to their store, or to Wal-Mart, explained little about which families chose to shop where. And without making too much of it, the researchers note that although grocery chains have struggled to figure out how to actually use all the data they collect with their loyalty shopping cards, their study shows one important idea: Figure out how to fight back.

It is hardly a trivial idea. As the study points out, "In the past decade, twenty-nine [supermarket] chains have sought bankruptcy court protection, with Wal-Mart as the catalyst in twenty-five of those cases." And that was before the bankruptcy filing of Winn-Dixie.

IN 2001, the *Journal of Retailing* published a paper titled "Retailer Power and Supplier Welfare: The Case of Wal-Mart." In an ambitious undertaking, UNC-Chapel Hill professor Paul Bloom and then graduate student Vanessa Perry set out to answer a big question: Does being a supplier to Wal-Mart help your business or hurt it? "We ask whether Wal-Mart has squeezed its suppliers into making concessions that have hurt their financial performance." What a great question.

Unfortunately, despite an enormous amount of work on the part of Bloom and Perry gathering and analyzing data on the profitability of hundreds of companies, both Wal-Mart suppliers and their competitors, the question turned out to be far more incisive than the answer. "Our results show that it is not possible to identify the impact of Wal-Mart upon supplier profits unambiguously," they write. "Ceteris paribus [all things being equal], we find that suppliers that identify Wal-Mart as a primary customer perform more poorly financially than those that do not identify themselves in this way. But these results do not suggest that suppliers 'should just say no to Wal-Mart.' While Wal-Mart may be using its power to squeeze suppliers, it is also possible that suppliers are willing to make concessions in the hope that a Wal-Mart relationship will help them expand their market share."

It's a complicated question, but for businesspeople, it is the essential question about Wal-Mart: Will doing business with Wal-Mart help my business or hurt it? It's an important question for consumers too. Reasonable profitability is what allows companies to hire talented people, pay them well, do research and development, and roll out wave after wave of innovations.

Unfortunately, not only was Bloom and Perry's study inconclusive, by the time it was published, the newest data they analyzed was seven years old, and the oldest data was thirteen years old. During the years it took to get the data, do the analysis, and get the paper into print, Wal-Mart more than doubled in size. No one has repeated the work, at least in part because the company that supplied the data for that original study no longer collects it in a way that allows looking for Wal-Mart suppliers.

Indeed, perhaps the most revealing bit of information from the

"Retail Power" study is one Bloom and Perry provide only indirectly. Appendix II of the study lists the largest twenty-five suppliers to Wal-Mart, in 1994, by dollar volume. Of the top ten companies, four subsequently went bankrupt and a fifth was taken private as it was failing. While utterly unscientific, a 50 percent failure rate is hardly an endorsement of Rob Walton's "healthy suppliers" pledge.

But there has been another ambitious effort to get at the answer to the same question. Gib Carey, the partner at Bain & Company who heads the company's consumer products consulting business, led a yearlong internal study of what it takes to be a successful Wal-Mart supplier. "The fact of the matter is, the way Wal-Mart is continuing to grow means that our clients cannot grow their business without finding a way to be successful with Wal-Mart," says Carey. "We have clients out there who would like that not to be true, clients who say, let's figure out a way to focus on selling through other outlets. . . . But we think Wal-Mart is an essential retailer, in a way that no other retailer is."

To understand the effect of "the essential retailer," Bain staffers did a probing financial analysis of thirty-eight publicly traded companies, some Bain clients and some not, that did more than 10 percent of their business with Wal-Mart. Bain also analyzed the performance of twenty companies in similar industries that weren't significant Wal-Mart suppliers, as a control group.

The analysis produced a consistent, vivid pattern. "For every percentage point of increased business these companies were doing with Wal-Mart," says Carey, "their operating margin declined to some extent." That is, the more business a company does with Wal-Mart, the less profitable each sale is. "It may be pressure," says Carey, "or it may be that companies are intentionally letting some [profit] margin decline to aggressively grow their business with Wal-Mart."

Whatever the reason, the numbers are striking, and they are a vivid warning about letting business with Wal-Mart grow at the expense of the rest of a company's business. As Wal-Mart consumes a greater chunk of a company's sales, it simultaneously offers a smaller slice of profitability. Companies doing 10 percent or less of their business with Wal-Mart had operating profit margins of 12.7 percent. Companies that become what Carey calls "captive suppliers" to Wal-Mart—selling more than 25 percent of their goods to Wal-Mart—see their profit margin cut almost in half, to 7.3 percent. "What we've found as we've continued to work with clients," says Carey, "is that Wal-Mart is really forcing companies to either get their act together, or get crushed."

THE MOST SURPRISING, and in some ways the most disturbing, conclusion from an academic study of the Wal-Mart effect was the result of little more than idle curiosity on the part of Penn State University professor Stephan Goetz and a postdoctoral student working with him. Even now, with the work about to be published, Goetz himself is amazed by what they uncovered.

Goetz is an economist with a particular interest in poverty, and the long-term causes of poverty. While he was finishing a project analyzing poverty rates, he was hearing more and more about the battles between the people who think Wal-Mart damages communities and those who think its low prices bring irresistible benefits. The conversation in local communities often includes not just whether to allow a particular store in, but also whether to actively woo Wal-Mart with road improvements or tax breaks. That is, whether to give tax money to Wal-Mart to encourage it to build a store.

Having already looked at a whole range of things linked to

poverty—education level, age, employment growth, single heads of households—Goetz decided to see if there was any connection between Wal-Mart and poverty. The question certainly has public policy implications for local governments. If Wal-Mart somehow *causes* poverty, then counties and cities certainly need to think hard before giving the company tax money to help it build new stores.

Still, Goetz thought the question was just a curiosity, almost an afterthought. "I was sure that after we controlled for all those other long lists of factors that cause poverty, there would be nothing left to explain, no poverty left over." Goetz and his colleague found, naturally, that "there are no academic studies that examine the impact of Wal-Mart on county-wide family poverty rates."

Goetz and his colleague examined changes in family poverty rates in every U.S. county from 1989 to 1999, a period, the study notes, that "coincides with the booming 'New Economy' decade." They controlled for a whole spectrum of known causes of poverty, and they applied the same kind of demanding statistical analysis that Basker does. The New Economy had a great impact on reducing poverty nationwide. According to Goetz's study, family poverty rates at the county level fell from 13.1 percent to 10.7 percent. The New Economy lifted nearly one in five poor families out of poverty.

What the study discovered is so startling, it's hard to absorb: They found that once you control for everything else, U.S. counties that had a Wal-Mart just before 1989, or that added one during the decade, had higher poverty rates than counties that were Wal-Mart free. In a county with at least one Wal-Mart, poverty fell not to 10.7 percent but to 11 percent. The difference—three tenths of a percentage point—looks trivial; it is almost a rounding error. But it is not. In counties with a Wal-Mart, the rate of poverty fell 10 percent more slowly than it would have without a Wal-Mart during that decade.

"We were surprised," says Goetz. As the study puts it, "We find that the presence of Wal-Mart unequivocally raised family poverty rates in U.S. counties during the 1990s." The question, of course, is how Goetz can be certain that the poverty is *caused* by Wal-Mart, rather than simply coincidentally correlated with it. "That's a very important question," Goetz says. "We're not looking at the poverty rate, really, we're looking at the change in the poverty rate over time. We're not explaining the poverty rate, we're explaining the change." And looking at Wal-Mart as a factor just as they would look at education level or whether a family with children had two parents present or one. After accounting for all the other things that cause poverty rates to change, then plugging Wal-Mart into the statistical equations, says Goetz, "There is an effect that we can only explain by Wal-Mart's presence."

As small as the number seems, Goetz says it comes to roughly twenty thousand American families in poverty because of Wal-Mart, or about seven families per county. The remarkable thing is how well that number matches up, at least in scale, with the results of Emek Basker's research. She found that the arrival of a Wal-Mart store caused four small businesses to close within five years; the employees left jobless when those businesses closed might well have seen their families slip into poverty.

The poverty study, too, has gotten only modest attention in the media. But one reporter asked Wal-Mart for a reaction, and Wal-Mart spokeswoman Mia Masten offered a glib defense: "Oftentimes, a study can say what you want it to say." Marketing studies commissioned by corporations, of course, do sometimes say what the companies want them to say. But peer-reviewed academic studies don't work like that. For those who think the poverty study says what Goetz wants it to say, he offers the method, the data, and the algorithms so they can take their own run at it.

" 'You can show anything with the numbers,' that was the response," says Goetz. "Is that what they do when they tell us about their stores? About what their workers are earning? That's really offensive to someone who spends a lifetime doing scholarly work. We're actually trying to get at the truth of what's going on in society."

SEVEN

SALMON, SHIRTS, AND THE
MEANING OF LOW PRICES

I wouldn't think American parents would want to feed themselves or their children with something being produced by a
worker who is miserable, and who works in terrible conditions.
And I don't think Wal-Mart should tolerate that.

—*Rodrigo Pizarro, executive director, Terram Foundation*

THE GLASS SEAFOOD display case in Wal-Mart Supercenter #2641
near Allentown, Pennsylvania, is small, but it is a mouthwatering
testament to the power of global sourcing. From Thailand—sea scallops and three kinds of shrimp. From Namibia—orange roughy. From
the United States—swordfish steaks and fresh shrimp. From China—
squid, scallops, tilapia, and crawfish. From Russia—Alaskan king
crab. From the Faeroe Islands—cod. (The Faeroe Islands are an archi-
pelago in the North Atlantic, halfway between Iceland and Norway,
population forty-seven thousand—no Wal-Mart, but some Wal-Mart
effect.)

Every item for sale is meticulously labeled—kind of fish and country of origin—but also whether the seafood is farm raised or wild

caught, and whether it has been previously frozen. The signs them-selves conjure exotic images. The squid are a "wild-caught product of China." Wild, indeed.

Right down front in the display case, with fillets thick and long enough that they run from the front of the case all the way to the back, is a platter of Atlantic salmon. Each fillet, the flank of big fish, is gleaming and vivid pink-orange. The salmon is a "farm-raised product of Chile," according to the sign, and it's fresh. It managed to get from southern Chile to a small town seventy miles outside Philadelphia—more than five thousand miles—without even being frozen. The salmon fillets are priced at $4.84 a pound. Almost any American over thirty is old enough to remember a time when you could hardly buy a quarter of a pound of salmon for $5.00. Any American over forty can recall an era when salmon was a delicacy. A half pound of smoked salmon, the kind you'd put on a bagel, might have cost $16.00 or $20.00. But there it is, in the Wal-Mart display case—pink, oily, and alluring—salmon fillets for $4.84 a pound. That's not a special; it's the everyday low price, and available in most supercenters from one end of the country to the other. It's a couple of dollars a pound cheaper than farm-raised salmon at a typical supermarket. It's less than half the price of the farm-raised salmon sold by Whole Foods.

Salmon for $4.84 a pound is a grocery-store showstopper. If prices contain information, if prices are not just a way of judging whether something is expensive or affordable but contain all kinds of other signals about supply, demand, prestige, and even the conditions under which products are made (bad freeze in Florida, expensive orange juice; hurricane on the Gulf Coast, expensive gasoline), then salmon for $4.84 a pound is a new, unintended Wal-Mart effect. It is a price so low that it inspires not happiness but wariness. If you were so inclined, you couldn't mail a pound of salmon back to Chile for

$4.84. It's a price so low, it doesn't seem to make sense if you think about it for even a moment. Salmon at $4.84 a pound is a deal that looks a lot like a gallon jar of Vlasic dill pickles for $2.97—it's a deal too good to be true, if not for us as the customers, then for someone, somewhere. What exactly did Wal-Mart have to do to get salmon so cheaply?

In the last fifteen years, the salmon is the fish that has conquered America. In 1990, across the United States we ate half a million pounds of salmon a day. Today, we eat more than 1.75 million pounds of salmon a day. In many homes, salmon is one of the dinner menu items served once a week, in the lineup alongside chicken and pasta and beef. Per capita consumption of salmon has tripled since 1990. In terms of growth, no other fish comes close. (Americans still eat more shrimp and more canned tuna fish than salmon.)

All you have to do is pick up a menu at any midpriced U.S. hotel to see it: Salmon is the one protein you can make the centerpiece of all three meals a day, almost without noticing: bagel with smoked salmon, sliced tomatoes, onions, and capers for breakfast; Caesar salad topped with a piece of grilled salmon for lunch; and a nice pan-sautéed fillet of salmon with a sweet corn and avocado salsa, on a bed of garlic mashed potatoes, for dinner.

Most of the salmon served in the United States is Atlantic salmon—a species found wild in the Atlantic ocean, but also the species of choice for salmon farmers because it is relatively mild man-nered and grows quickly. Ninety-five percent of farm-raised salmon is Atlantic salmon. There are also five kinds of wild Pacific salmon, of the sort available in summer during salmon runs—chinook, chum, coho, pink, and sockeye. But wild salmon is not just seasonal, it's pricey; if you're eating wild salmon, you didn't just stumble into it. (Wild Atlantic salmon is endangered and can't be caught in North America.)

The Atlantic salmon fillet in grocery display cases and on restaurant menus is, as one expert in the business says, "a factory product"—hatched from eggs, raised to adolescence in freshwater hatcheries, grown to maturity over two years in open-topped ocean cages of thousands of fish suspended in cold coastal waters. And most of the farm-raised salmon we eat comes from Chile—65 percent of the farmed salmon sold in the United States is imported from Chile; most of the rest comes from Canada. As bemusing as it is to see how salmon has found a place on American menus and plates as a kind of affordable luxury, salmon really has conquered the economy of southern Chile. The area around Puerto Montt, six hundred miles south of Santiago, now has eight hundred salmon farms, and the salmon business provides nearly one in ten of the area's jobs. In 2005, Chile expected to export $1.5 billion worth of fresh-packed salmon, with 40 percent of it coming to the United States. Salmon is the second largest export in Chile now, behind copper, ahead of fruit.

"Five years ago," says Rodrigo Pizarro, "salmon wasn't on the list of exports. Chile didn't have any salmon twelve years ago." Pizarro is an economist who heads Terram, a Chilean foundation dedicated to promoting sustainable development in Chile. Understanding the impact of salmon farming is one of Pizarro's most urgent projects. When he says that twelve years ago Chile didn't have any salmon, he's not exaggerating for effect. He means it literally.

Not only is the Atlantic salmon not native to Chile—the Chilean coastline, of course, runs along the Pacific—but as Pizarro puts it, "Atlantic salmon is an exotic species in the whole Southern Hemisphere." The Atlantic salmon doesn't appear naturally anywhere south of the equator. Farming salmon in Chile is a bit like farming penguins in the Rocky Mountains. Now, however, not only are there far more Atlantic salmon in Chile than people, there are ten times as many, maybe even one hundred times as many. More salmon are harvested in Chile now than anywhere else in the world, including Norway. Even as the price has drifted down, the value of Chile's salmon exports has risen nearly 70 percent in five years. Chile wants to increase the amount of salmon it exports by 50 percent again by 2010.

In just a decade, salmon farming has transformed the economy and the daily life of southern Chile, ushering in an industrial revolution that has turned thousands of Chileans from subsistence farmers and fishermen into hourly paid salmon processing-plant workers. Salmon farming is starting to transform the ecology and environment of southern Chile too, with tens of millions of salmon living in vast ocean corrals, their excess food and feces settling to the ocean floor beneath the pens, and dozens of salmon processing plants dumping untreated salmon entrails directly into the ocean.

Pizarro is thoughtful, direct, and passionate about his country without being excitable. "Anyone who is working in a salmon plant, it's very much a factory-type system," he says. "It's an industrial-type system. If you were to see the factory, it's just like Charlie Chaplin's movie *Modern Times*. The plants are very clean, very modern, with proper apparel and gloves. The issue is not the health conditions of the fish. It's the labor conditions of the workers"—long hours, a demanding pace using razor-sharp filleting implements, low pay. As for the farms themselves, he says, "All the information we have indicates that the environmental impact is considerable."

Wal-Mart is not just another customer of farm-raised Chilean salmon. Wal-Mart is either the number-one or number two seller of salmon in the United States (the other top seller is Costco), and Wal-Mart buys all its salmon from Chile. Wal-Mart, in fact, may well buy one third of the annual harvest of salmon that Chile sells to the

United States. That kind of focused purchasing in an arena of surging production is one part of how Wal-Mart delivers salmon for $4.84 a pound to supercenters around America. Chilean salmon needs markets; Wal-Mart has 1,906 supercenters. That kind of focused purchasing also gives Wal-Mart and its customers a unique window on the impact all that salmon raising, salmon buying, and salmon selling is having far away from Bentonville, in southern Chile. Does it matter that salmon for $4.84 a pound leaves a layer of toxic sludge on the ocean bottoms of the Pacific fjords of southern Chile?

Wal-Mart's ability to reach in and remake the operations of its suppliers is unchallenged. And Wal-Mart's single-minded focus on using that power to reduce price has sent waves of change across the U.S. economy and around the globe. But what if Wal-Mart imposed conditions on its suppliers that went beyond cost, efficiency, and on-time delivery? What would the ripples from that look like?

Rodrigo Pizarro has a calm appreciation for both the impact of the salmon industry in Chile and the opportunity. He also has a sophisticated appreciation for American business and consumer culture. "I know what kind of story Wal-Mart has," he says. "I am not naive about Wal-Mart." Pizarro's undergraduate degree is from the London School of Economics, his Ph.D. is from the University of North Carolina at Chapel Hill. How does he think Americans should think about that salmon in the seafood display case at Wal-Mart, selling for $4.84 a pound?

"I remember when I was in the United States, you had a debate about Kathie Lee Gifford promoting clothes which were produced in an offshore factory with awful labor," says Pizarro. In 1996, at a congressional hearing, a well-known labor rights activist revealed that the workers in a Honduran factory making a line of clothes under the TV personality's name were children. The Kathie Lee Gifford line was sold exclusively at Wal-Mart. By the time the use of child labor became public, Wal-Mart had stopped using the factory. But the ensuing scandal took Gifford and Wal-Mart by surprise, and the publicity was scorching. Forbidding child labor is one of the absolutes of the global economy. But the larger issue of the overseas factory conditions where products sold in the United States are made is still being navigated gingerly by multinationals. They don't necessarily want to assume the responsibility, and the cost, for monitoring everything that goes on in workplaces in countries that have their own laws, cultures, and enforcement mechanisms; they also don't want to have to explain dramatic, unsettling revelations about how the familiar products they sell manage to have such low prices.

Pizarro is thinking not of child labor in particular, but of the widespread public outrage when American shoppers connected clothing they were familiar with, a well-known personality, and sweatshop factory conditions.

Says Pizarro, "Increasingly, the American consumer is aware of these types of working conditions, and the salmon is the same as the clothes. The only difference is, what is being produced by these workers is something the American consumer is feeding to his children."

IF YOU LOOK AT the growth of three things between 1990 and 2005, the graphs are near perfect shadows of one another: farmed-salmon production in the world, farmed-salmon production in Chile, and Wal-Mart's grocery business. They all start low on the scale, and go almost vertical after a few years. Wal-Mart did not create the farmed-salmon business; Wal-Mart did not plant the salmon farms in southern Chile. But the dramatic growth of domesticated salmon drove down prices for salmon and fed Wal-Mart's ability to deliver salmon to the fish counter; and the dramatic growth of Wal-Mart's grocery business created a huge opportunity, and a huge appetite, for salmon that has fed the salmon-farming industry.

The reason salmon was an expensive delicacy, a special-occasion food, in the United States in the seventies and eighties was because all that salmon was wild caught, almost all in Alaska. The supply was sharply limited. The summer season was short, the salmon poured in, and it was either eaten, canned, smoked, or frozen. Good-quality salmon wasn't just a delicacy in the United States—it was a rarity, it was seasonal, available when the ocean made the salmon available.

James Anderson is a professor at the University of Rhode Island and chairman of the Department of Environmental and Natural Resource Economics. He is an expert on fisheries, with a specialty in worldwide salmon and shrimp fisheries. Wild salmon used to be common in New England's rivers, as they are in the Pacific Northwest. "Wild Atlantic salmon has been decimated for sixty or seventy years," he says. "The largest run for Atlantic salmon used to be the Connecticut River—and we destroyed that by 1890. Since salmon aggregate to swim upriver to spawn, it's easy to catch the fish with traps. You can catch 100 percent of a run going up a river—then you get no salmon run at all the next year." Human activity forced the Atlantic salmon into an endangered state. "It was overfishing, it was dams, it was habitat destruction," says Anderson.

The Norwegians, with their own natural salmon stock, a culture of small farmers, and a coastline rich in protected fjords, started experimenting with raising salmon in pens in the late 1960s. In the United States, a company called Domsea started a salmon farm in Washington State in 1969. Domsea was started by Union Carbide, then owned for a while by Campbell's, and according to Anderson, it first sold modest amounts of farm-raised salmon commercially in 1971.

Some oddities of the economy kept salmon farming in check commercially for a while. In the Northwest, there was resistance from existing salmon businesses and from potential neighbors of salmon farms. There were also transportation problems. "Back in the 1980s," says Anderson, "jetliners wouldn't allow fresh fish on the airplanes. It may seem silly, but there weren't appropriate boxes. In the late 1970s and early 1980s, all they had was a kind of wax box lined with a plastic bag and some ice. It would leak and drip a bit. In the back of a truck, who cares? But in a jet, that matters a lot. All you need is a little salt water dripping down into things . . ."

By the mid-1980s, the Norwegians were not only successfully raising commercial quantities of salmon—Anderson visited Norwegian salmon farms in 1984—they were also interested in selling it internationally. "They came to the East Coast of the United States," says Anderson. "They targeted the white-tablecloth restaurants. They would fly it in in these Styrofoam boxes, they were selling it for $5 or $6 or $7 a pound wholesale."

The chefs loved it. "The salmon that was here was crap, to put it mildly," says Anderson. "A lot of the salmon they sent [from Alaska] to the eastern United States would be last year's frozen steaks. It had been frozen six months. 'The idiots in Philadelphia will eat it'—that was sort of the attitude. The farmed salmon was much better." Not only was the farmed salmon better quality, but the Norwegians offered it all year round. "The Norwegians kept the price high," he says. "They just kept expanding their market. They would hit thirty restaurants in Boston, Chicago, Cleveland."

The worldwide salmon aquaculture business was in its infancy, but the dimensions of the market were becoming clear. The total harvest in 1985 was fifty thousand metric tons. It doubled in two years. By 1990, it was three hundred thousand metric tons. As the 1990s dawned, the Canadians and the Chileans started aggressively farming salmon, and the price started to drop dramatically as the worldwide supply surged.

Salmon farming in Chile was spurred by a business incubator called Fundación Chile, according to Rodrigo Pizarro. "A lot of young businessmen, in the late 1980s and early 1990s, men who were the sons of families with historical business ties, found out about salmon and went to the south to find out what was happening," says Pizarro. "They went to a sort of frontier area—and they stayed in those places and built this industry. It took five or ten years." Among other things, Chile's rugged coastline is much like Norway's, dotted with inlets and fjords that provide the kind of protection that pens of farmed fish in the ocean need.

Anderson has visited the salmon farms of Chile as part of his academic work. "They had no history of aquaculture in Chile," he says. "None at all. But there is a real entrepreneurial spirit in Chile. And they had cheap labor, and a cheap environment." Salmon farming flourished.

There was one more impediment to making salmon a real mass-market product in the United States. "At first," says Anderson, "farmed salmon was sold whole, head on, in the United States." That might have worked for premium restaurants, but supermarkets weren't interested in filleting salmon on a mass scale, and American consumers were no more interested in buying head-on salmon than they are in buying head-on chicken.

The marketing and technology innovation came in part from Chile, says Anderson. "In 1994 or 1995, the Chileans said this is stupid. Why ship all those heads and bones and stuff up to the United States?" The innovation was what Anderson calls the "pin-bone-out fillet." The pin bones are the line of sharp, stubborn bones running along a salmon fillet. "Through some technological innovation and cheap labor, the Chileans started pulling the pin bones out, really semimanually," says Anderson. "Then they would portion the fillet, and send it up skin on or skin off." Head-off, pin-bone-out salmon made all the difference for the American market. "This is a major, major feature for supermarkets. They didn't want to hack the salmon themselves in the back," says Anderson. It also made salmon appealing to midmarket restaurants like Red Lobster.

Salmon production grew dramatically. The Norwegians, in fact, have largely been squeezed out of the U.S. market by the Chileans and the Canadians, and the price has dropped steadily, sometimes dramatically.

Now, says Anderson, you can get salmon from farms in Chile up to the United States faster than you can get it down from Alaska. "In Chile," he says, "they harvest the fish early, early in the morning, when it's still dark. They get it to the processing plants near the farms right in the morning. Then it's on a truck or a plane to Santiago, and then on a plane to Miami. There's fish killed in southern Chile that is in Miami or New York in under forty-eight hours."

In 1985, the total world farmed-salmon harvest for the year was fifty thousand metric tons. Twenty years later, in 2005, Chile sent ten thousand metric tons, just to the United States, just in January.

SALMON FARMING ON a commercial scale is really only twenty years old, and on a mass scale, it's more like ten years old. Aquaculture is an industry growing much more quickly than its impact can be measured, understood, and managed.

"Have you ever seen a hog farm?" asks Gerry Leape, vice president of marine conservation for the National Environmental Trust, a Washington-based environmental nonprofit group. "These fish are the hogs of the sea. They live in the same sort of conditions, it's just in water. They pack them really closely together, they use a lot of prophylactic antibiotics, not to treat disease, but to prevent it. There's lots of concentrated fish waste, it creates dead zones in the ocean around the pens."

Jennifer Lash is executive director of the Living Oceans Society, a marine conservation group in British Columbia, which is one of two centers of salmon farming in Canada. "Salmon are generally raised in open-net pens," she says. "There is a metal cage on the surface, with nets hanging down to a netted bottom.

"The density of fish depends on the nation, but they grow tens of thousands of fish per net, 1 million or 1.5 million per farm. Then they all go poo. There is a huge amount of waste going into the ocean. People say, oh, that's natural, all fish go poo in the ocean. But not in that kind of concentration. It just smothers the seabed." One million salmon produce the same sewage, says Leape, as sixty-five thousand people.

The ocean pens suffer from another source of pollution—excess feed. Any food that isn't consumed settles to the ocean floor, adding to the layer of feces. The waste itself contains residues of antibiotics and other chemicals used to keep the fish healthy during the two years it takes them to grow to harvestable size.

All those problems are manageable; it's just that managing them costs money, and if there is no reason to spend that money, no incentive, then no one does.

In southern Chile, says Pizarro, the impact on the daily lives of the local people comes not so much from the pens of fish as from the processing plants built to prepare them for export. "What salmon farming has done is move the people from subsistence agriculture to factory work," says Pizarro. "Salmon farming for the people is about the processing plants, it's not about the farms."

The plants themselves are modern and hygienic, in part because

American companies fear nothing so much as importing tainted food that sickens their customers. Despite the cleanliness, the processing plants suffer by most accounts from the kinds of sweatshop issues more commonly associated with garment factories in developing nations.

"The hours worked are not respected," says Pizarro. "There are a lot of women working in the processing plants. There are a series of issues in terms of sexual harassment, in terms of hours worked standing up. They are not allowed to go to the bathroom. And there are antiunion practices."

Pizarro is quite careful in discussing the labor issues. "Much of this is denied by the companies," he says. "But currently, the labor standards are very weak, and they are very difficult to enforce. These plants are very far away from Santiago."

Part of the reason Wal-Mart can sell a salmon fillet for $4.84 is that, as Leape puts it, "they don't internalize all the costs." Pollution ultimately costs money—to clean up, to prevent, to recover from. But right now those costs aren't in the price of a pound of Chilean salmon. Salmon-processing facilities that are run with as much respect for the people as the hygiene of the fish also cost money—for reasonable wages, for proper equipment, for enough workers to permit breaks and days off. Right now those costs aren't in the price of a pound of Chilean salmon either.

Groups like Pizarro's and Leape's, concerned about salmon's impact in Chile and elsewhere, agree on two things. The salmon industry isn't going away—Chile has declared that it intends to increase production another 50 percent by 2010. And the key to managing the impact of salmon farming, to making the business sustainable for both Chileans and their environment in the long term, isn't self-regulation or government regulation. It's the customers, the big corporations who buy salmon by the ton. Even the corporations realize that.

"When the guys with the checkbooks talk," says Bill Herzig, "the producers listen." Herzig knows because he is one of the guys with the big checkbooks. He's senior vice president of purchasing for Darden Restaurants—Red Lobster, Olive Garden—for all proteins, including seafood. "We own thirteen hundred restaurants," says Herzig. "We have to have something to feed those customers, not just this year, but five years and ten years from now. We won't put something on our menu if we don't believe the supply is sustainable."

Darden is one of the companies that imposes standards on its seafood suppliers. "We go into processing plants, we audit the process, we want a U.S. approach to a manufacturing facility"—no matter where it is in the world. Darden has food inspection staff based in Singapore, India, Thailand, China, and Latin America. "We have a formal auditing process," says Herzig. "We audit the factories where food is processed, then we go back to see how it's being raised—with shrimp, with fish. We want to understand things like how the cold chain looks." The cold chain is the process by which fresh, raw seafood is kept cold during transportation and processing.

Herzig remembers a *60 Minutes* segment on how U.S. hog farms work—their waste is often untreated, and the pigs live in densely packed barns. "That's not good stuff," says Herzig. "That needs to be cleaned up. We don't like to see things done in a way that is not proper. And we do not hesitate to use our checkbook to encourage people to do the right thing."

That's why someone like Rodrigo Pizarro thinks a company like Wal-Mart could have such a rapid and positive effect on improving conditions in the salmon industry in Chile. Wal-Mart buys so much salmon that if it imposed and enforced a set of standards on how salmon was to be raised, and how salmon workers were to be treated, salmon farming and processing companies would need to comply, either to keep Wal-Mart's business or to stay competitive. And because the volume of purchasing is so high, and because Chile is driving to further expand the supply of farmed salmon, the improved conditions for both the salmon and the people would not cause much of an increase in the price of a pound of salmon in the seafood case.

"It wouldn't be considerably more," says Pizarro, who is working on just such a set of standards, backed by research, that he plans to present to Wal-Mart and other companies in early 2006. "The increase in cost is not something to pick a bone about. It would be 10 or 20 or 30 percent, a minor cost when you are making a long-term investment."

The result could be a completely new kind of Wal-Mart effect—Wal-Mart using its enormous purchasing power not just to raise the standard of living for its customers, but also for its suppliers.

IN WAL-MART #2194, in Alexandria, Virginia, just down the road from the Pentagon, there is a display of boys' clothes carrying the George label, one of Wal-Mart's house brands. One of the items is a blue Oxford-cloth button-down shirt. It has a pocket, lined and reinforced cuffs, with buttons. It has a little label on the shirttail that says, "Classic Oxford," with five tiny bear-paw prints embroidered on it. The blue shirt is a perfect miniature of Dad's, right down to the little loop sewn in place on the back between the shoulder blades. It's a Sunday-go-to-church shirt for a two-year-old boy. It is adorable. The label in the neck says, "Made in Bangladesh." And the price: $5.74. The price is an immediate alert—a Vlasic-pickle, Chilean-salmon alert. The price makes almost no sense.

How is it possible for Wal-Mart to produce such a lovely shirt—the fabric, the buttons, the sewing, the perfect stitching with nary a stray thread or raveled edge of fabric, the trip from Bangladesh—and sell it for less than the price of a child's movie ticket in the United States? If you could somehow see a video of the factory where the shirt was made, of the people who sewed it, would you still be able to button your two-year-old boy into it and smile?

In the global economy, the familiar stuff floods into stores: Levi's jeans, Ohio Art Etch A Sketches, Black & Decker cordless electric screwdrivers, Huffy bikes, Nelson sprinklers, and acres of clothing and accessories—stuff not just for Wal-Mart, but for the Gap and Abercrombie & Fitch and Home Depot and Disney. But more than ever, we have lost track of the places where the products come from, the factories where they are made, the people who make them. In this country, we have a social contract about what working in a factory should be like, and about what a factory should not do to the environment. It is a social contract that has taken a hundred years to develop and come to consensus on, a social contract that continues to evolve, that is codified in laws and rules at both the state and federal level. This isn't about wages; it's about things like work hours, safety, overtime, breaks and days off, proper equipment, health regulations, fire exits; it's about what a factory cannot emit into the water and air as it manufactures things, and how emissions must be treated in advance and handled. Even in the United States, the way that factories should operate, and the way they do operate, is a bumpy process. But there is rough agreement, and there is a whole apparatus for making sure the rules are followed.

But what happens when the clothing factory, or the toy factory, or the power-tool factory moves overseas? Often the machines themselves are unbolted from American factory floors, packed up, and shipped off to factories in Mexico or Asia. Again, setting aside the question of hourly pay itself, which necessarily varies according to the economy of the country, under what conditions are those clothes and toys and power tools manufactured? Clearly, one of the ways companies are saving money isn't simply in wages. Just as Chilean salmon is cheap because many of the costs of salmon farming aren't in the price, so the factories in developing countries are cheaper because the whole superstructure of rules around those factories in the United States—the workplace, safety and pollution rules—can be left behind. If you could wiggle your nose and transport a toy factory from China, or a tool factory from the Czech Republic, or a clothing factory from Bangladesh, and have it land in North Carolina, would that factory be legal here?

S. Prakash Sethi, an expert on global factory conditions, just laughs at the question. "No, of course they would not be legal here. They are not even legal in China"—or almost any country you would choose. In many countries, the factories don't even follow their own rules, let alone ours. "At the end of the day, the factories will do whatever reduces their cost," says Sethi. "You can save lots of money by not having pollution controls, by not paying workers correct overtime, by not giving workers a day off." Sethi is a university distinguished professor at Baruch College's Zicklin School of Business and has spent the last twenty years investigating the behavior of multinational corporations overseas, trying to find ways to persuade them to follow ethical business practices, going back to companies doing business in South Africa during apartheid. He now heads an unusual outside group he helped create that monitors the factories that produce toys for Mattel; in the last ten years he has been in dozens of factories around the world.

One of the dark bargains of the global economy is that while the familiar stuff continues to arrive without interruption, and often with prices steadily dropping, the way that stuff is made is less and less familiar, more and more remote, and perhaps less and less acceptable, all the time. The factories themselves would be illegal in the United

States because of the way those factories treat their workers and their communities; but the products of those factories are perfectly legal, indeed, the very unappealing manner in which they are produced makes them cheaper all the time, and so more appealing all the time.

"Because of the pressure of cost," says Sethi, "factories do everything possible to save on the third decimal of a penny. Wal-Mart is one of the primary, if not the most important, engines that pushes those costs down."

In a world long gone, we could step onto the fishing wharf, we could step into the dress shop, we could stop at the roadside vegetable stand and have some sense, however modest, of the conditions under which the food and products we bought were created. Today we rely on the laws, and on the companies themselves, sometimes to our disappointment and disgust. Nike, the Gap, Reebok, Disney, Wal-Mart have all had to face, explain, and recover from sweatshop problems in the last twenty years.

And every time the door of a factory in a developing country that makes stuff for Americans is cracked open, the view inside is unsettling. The prices suddenly make sense, and not in a reassuring way. Both Kathie Lee Gifford and Wal-Mart denied the allegations that a Honduran factory using children was making Kathie Lee Gifford clothes. The denials were both true and a lie. By the time of the congressional hearing, the clothes were no longer being made by children. But they had been.

In the fall of 2004, two women from Bangladesh spent a month touring college campuses, talking about their experiences working in clothing factories in Dhaka, the capital of Bangladesh. They were brought to the United States by a labor rights group, the National Labor Committee (NLC), which works to uncover and publicize inhumane factory conditions around the world. It was the NLC's executive director, Charles Kernaghan, who told Congress about the child labor that had been making Kathie Lee Gifford clothing. The two factory workers from Bangladesh speak no English; their translator for the tour was an NLC staffer who came over with the women from the NLC's Dhaka office. The details of the women's lives as Bangladeshi garment workers—lives they described again and again, at Yale, at Harvard, at the University of Iowa, at the University of Wisconsin—are like something not just from around the world, but from a different century.

As a sixteen-year-old junior sewing operator at the Western Dresses factory in Dhaka, Robina Akther's job was to sew pocket flaps on the back pockets of pants that Western Dresses was making for Wal-Mart. She says she earned 13 cents an hour—fourteen hours of work a day, $26.98 a month. If she didn't sew to the mandated pace, 120 pairs of pants per hour, here is what Akther said would happen: A supervisor would slap her across the face with the pants she was sewing. "If you made any mistakes or fell behind on your goal, they beat you," says Akther's translated account, which is posted on the NLC's Web site. "They slapped you and lashed you hard on the face with the pants. This happens very often. They hit you hard. It is no joke."

If what Akther says is true—Wal-Mart did not challenge the account as it was published in college newspapers, nor have they challenged the account that is posted on the NLC's Web site—then it is possible that Wal-Mart's customers were buying pants off the display racks that might literally have been used to beat the people who made them. Who is wearing those pants now?

As Akther describes it, life in the Western Dresses factory was an unending series of days making clothes, starting before 8:00 A.M., lasting until 10:00 P.M. or 11:00 P.M., seven days a week. Ten days off in a year—not even one a month. No talking at the sewing tables, no drinking water at the sewing tables. No going to the bathroom except at the moment when permission is given, and then, "the bathrooms are filthy with no toilet paper or soap."

Despite the relentless work, Akther told college audiences, "I clean my teeth with my finger, using ash. I can't afford a toothbrush or toothpaste." Do Americans need clothing to be so inexpensive that the people making it cannot afford a toothbrush?

At the wages she described—typical for garment workers in Bangladesh—if Robina Akther were to have worked for fifty years as she did for those twenty months at the Western Dresses factory, if she could have survived fifty years, her total wages for the half century would have been $16,200. Wal-Mart's profit in 2004—profit, not sales—is $19,597 per minute.

Robina Akther's account now appears in a new forum: In September 2005, she sued Wal-Mart in court in the United States, alleging that in a factory making clothing for Wal-Mart, to Wal-Mart's design and price and schedule demands, in a factory essentially controlled by Wal-Mart, she was not even provided with the basic wages, overtime pay, and protection from physical abuse that Bangladeshi law provides. Actually, in the lawsuit, Akther is identified only as Jane Doe III—she is anonymous, along with fourteen other workers from five countries who are plaintiffs against Wal-Mart. The fifteen factory workers—from China, Indonesia, Swaziland, and Nicaragua, as well as Bangladesh—all make or made merchandise for Wal-Mart, and all have nearly identical claims of sweatshop mistreatment. In the suit, Jane Doe III—Robina Akther—is arguing that Wal-Mart didn't just have a contract to buy clothes from the Western Dresses factory; Wal-Mart had a contract with her and her fellow factory workers, and that their systematic mistreatment is Wal-Mart's responsibility. Not Wal-Mart's ethical responsibility, Wal-Mart's legal responsibility. It is possible that Robina Akther is going to reach out from Dhaka and turn the Wal-Mart effect on its head.

WAL-MART'S MOST immediate defense to the sweatshop lawsuit is the same as its defense has been when such allegations have emerged in the media every few years over the last decade. The company has a code of conduct for its suppliers and how they must treat their workers, it takes the code of conduct seriously, and the code is backed not just by Wal-Mart's ability to pull its business, and by its unchallenged ability to enforce its will on suppliers, but by a global factory inspection staff that fans out every day to see what life is like in the factories that make products sold at Wal-Mart. "We are a global leader in monitoring supplier factory conditions," Wal-Mart says in a statement issued in response to the lawsuit filed by the factory workers, "and if we find that any of our suppliers' factories are unwilling to correct problems, we end our relationship with them." The preamble to the suppliers' standards document reminds factory owners exactly why Wal-Mart takes the standards so seriously, conjuring the memory of Kathie Lee Gifford in a single phrase without mentioning her. The standards matter precisely because "the conduct of Wal-Mart's suppliers can be attributed to Wal-Mart and its reputation." Wal-Mart now issues a report each year, accounting for its factory inspections, and the performance of what it calls its "ethical standards" team.

At first blush, the report, and the ethical standards team, seems both vigorous and reassuring. That is, in fact, part of Wal-Mart's point: Not only do we at Wal-Mart take the conditions under which products are made seriously, but we take them seriously so you don't have to. Buy the $4.84 salmon or the $5.74 toddler shirt without worry.

In 2004, Wal-Mart bought products directly from fifty-three hundred factories in sixty countries around the world, and Wal-Mart reports that every one of those factories was inspected at least once. Wal-Mart inspectors also audited twenty-three hundred factories of its vendors—factories producing goods technically for other companies, but whose merchandise ended up on the shelves of Wal-Mart's stores.

Wal-Mart has ethical standards offices in Shanghai, Shenzhen, Dubai, Singapore, Bangalore, and Cholomo, Honduras. In all, Wal-Mart's inspectors did more than 30 factory inspections a day—12,500 in 2004. It is an impressive effort.

And to encourage a sense of accountability and security for the workers in those factories, Wal-Mart's supplier standards code requires that the code itself be posted in any factory making goods for Wal-Mart. The code has been translated into twenty-five languages.

And the results? In 2004, violations were serious enough at 108 factories that they were banned from doing business with Wal-Mart. Another 1,211 factories had serious enough violations that they were disqualified from doing business for some period; 260 of those corrected their violations and were permitted to come back as suppliers.

The lawsuit that Robina Akther and her fellow factory workers have filed against Wal-Mart, in state court in California, is the work of another U.S. labor rights group, the International Labor Rights Fund. The viability of the suit turns on some novel legal theories, not least of which is that employees for foreign companies, working in factories in foreign countries, have the right to sue in a California state court. The forty-seven-page complaint in the suit is an inventory of allegations of mistreatment that range from the mundane to the medieval: systematic wage and overtime violations, but also locking workers inside factories, forcing them to work all night to complete orders, withholding months of pay to prevent workers from quitting.

Every one of the practices alleged would be forbidden by the Wal-Mart code of conduct. That is, in fact, the core argument of the lawsuit: What Wal-Mart's code of conduct says is one thing; what actually happens is something else.

In fact, the lawsuit goes a step further. The problem isn't callous, greedy, and inhumane factory managers. "Wal-Mart is itself the reason for the inhumane conditions," the suit alleges. "It uses its vast market power to insist on low unit prices that are possible only if workers are squeezed to such an extreme degree that they can barely survive the long hours and low wages they are forced to endure." Wal-Mart's insistence on low-cost merchandise, the lawsuit alleges, "makes it impossible for suppliers to comply with even the most basic laws where they operate, including wage and hour laws."

It seems hard to reconcile the allegations in the lawsuit with Wal-Mart's detailed accounting of its ethical-sourcing effort. But if you dig into Wal-Mart's own report, part of the answer becomes clear. Yes, the factory inspections team did 12,500 inspections, but only 8 percent of them were surprise inspections. That means 1,000 inspections were unannounced, and 11,500 were scheduled in advance. Still, Wal-Mart reports, 9,900 of the inspections resulted in violations serious enough to either suspend a factory or put it on notice. Even if you presume that the 9,900 number includes every single surprise inspection—that is, if you presume that every surprise inspection resulted in uncovering serious violations—that leads to a remarkable conclusion: 8,900 inspections of factories in 2004 revealed serious violations in factories that knew in advance that Wal-Mart inspectors were coming.

If the code of conduct has to be signed by the factory management, if it is posted on the factory wall, if the inspections are scheduled with advance notice, and still thousands of Wal-Mart supplier factories get a "yellow" or "red" rating, well, how seriously are the factories really taking Wal-Mart's code of conduct? And if those are the conditions in the factories on a day when managers know Wal-Mart is coming, what is life like on a typical day? If 90 percent of the factory inspections were unannounced, what would Wal-Mart find then?

In fact, Wal-Mart may say it takes its fourteen-year-old ethical-sourcing program seriously, but it is far from what experienced sourcing experts like Prakash Sethi consider the gold standard, in at least three important ways. The gold standard is unannounced inspections. The gold standard is off-site interviews with workers to permit maximum candor. Wal-Mart interviews workers privately, it says, but on-site managers know whom Wal-Mart talks to. The gold standard is to use independent third-party auditors to avoid a conflict of interest between factory performance and the production needs of the company. Wal-Mart writes its code of conduct, and Wal-Mart enforces its code of conduct. One outside group that measures corporate social responsibility, KLD & Company, compiles and maintains the Domini 400 Social Index of socially responsible publicly traded corporations. KLD in 2001 removed Wal-Mart from the list of responsible investments, saying in a white paper that Wal-Mart "has not done enough to ensure that its domestic and international vendors operate factories that meet adequate labor and human rights standards." The president of KLD, Peter D. Kinder, said at the time, "Wal-Mart's market dominance puts it in a unique position to lead retailers in a cleanup of sweatshop abuses. To date it has declined to do so."

In the larger context of Wal-Mart's global operations, the factory-inspections program could seem less like a diligent effort than a grudging one. The team in 2004 was increased to 202 full-time staff members from 114. But the typical Wal-Mart Supercenter, a new one of which opens five times a week, employs 500 or more people. The entire global ethical-standards and factory-inspections team has less than half the staff of a single supercenter.

A more vivid contrast would be to compare Wal-Mart's operations with those of another company that claims to take factory conditions seriously. The Gap, like Wal-Mart, has a public code of conduct and an in-house team of auditors based around the globe, and it issues an annual report on its own factory-inspection results. The Gap has a ninety-person factory-standards team. Although it operates in arenas very similar to Wal-Mart's for the products they source and sell, the Gap's annual sales are tiny compared to Wal-Mart's: $16.3 billion in sales in 2004 versus Wal-Mart's $288 billion. Even if you take out Wal-Mart's grocery sales—if you presume that salmon farms and beef-processing plants don't need to be inspected—if Wal-Mart were staffed the same way as the Gap, it would have nine hundred inspectors, not two hundred.

It is possible, in fact, both that Wal-Mart did 12,500 factory inspections and that Robina Akther was beaten with the clothes she was making for Wal-Mart. It is possible that as there is information in the price of a pound of salmon, so there is information in the price of a little boy's blue Oxford cloth shirt made in Bangladesh.

IN JULY 2005, four Wal-Mart staff members traveled quietly to Chile to look at conditions in the salmon industry. It wasn't a Wal-Mart trip; the Wal-Mart staff members were part of a larger group of twenty buyers, industry representatives, environmentalists, and others who spent four days talking to Chileans, looking at salmon farms, and touring processing plants.

Gerry Leape of the National Environmental Trust had two staff members on the trip, along with representatives from several marine conservation groups in British Columbia, where regulation of salmon farming and salmon processing is further along than it is in Chile. Rodrigo Pizarro met the group in Chile.

Part of the goal of the trip was to start developing a consensus on what needs to be done to make salmon farming sustainable in Chile, across a wide group of constituencies. The Wal-Mart staff members were in the group for a couple reasons, according to Leape, Pizarro, and others: to learn the dimensions of both the industry and the problems, and to hear for themselves what Chileans have to say.

Wal-Mart, according to Leape, realizes that issues around salmon farming in Chile are a potential flashpoint for it, a vulnerability, a food version of the Kathie Lee Gifford problem. Indeed, for most of 2005, Wal-Mart was in quiet but consistent conversations with several environmental groups to try to understand what kind of standards, and what kind of enforcement, would solve the salmon-sourcing problem. The conversations are a delicate dance, especially in a year when in the United States, the Sierra Club and two major unions joined forces to create an organization to publicly challenge Wal-Mart across a broad front of its practices.

The environmental groups in conversations with Wal-Mart want to bring along the big company toward a view that it can, that it must, use its power to solve some of the environmental and labor problems that the industries it relies on create. They think Wal-Mart could ultimately do for corporate environmental stewardship what it has done for corporate productivity and efficiency. Wal-Mart wants to be seen as taking criticism seriously, and it wants to be seen as a responsible citizen. But the environmental groups don't want to be duped, or co-opted, by a Wal-Mart campaign that turns out to be more public relations than substance. And Wal-Mart does not really know that much about taking "externalities" into consideration in managing where its products are coming from and how they are made. If salmon poo needs to be cleaned up and properly disposed of, well, that's not a way of making salmon cheaper—it's potentially a way of making salmon more expensive. And Wal-Mart must surely be worried that once you open the door to considerations other than what's required by law, to considerations other than what's required to improve efficiency and decrease cost—well, where will the demands end? What won't people ask of Wal-Mart?

Indeed, it is possible to argue that it's not Wal-Mart's job to worry about salmon farms in Chile. Protecting the waters of Chile, and the workers of Chile, is the responsibility of the government of Chile. Wal-Mart's job is to obey the law, and to deliver low prices. That, in fact, is pretty much how things have looked from Bentonville for forty years. But the global economy is turning out to be much more complicated.

In Chile, according to four people who were with the group, the Wal-Mart staffers were reserved, polite, and kept their own counsel. They listened, but revealed little.

At one meeting, Rodrigo Pizarro got to speak directly with the Wal-Mart representatives. "I was very insistent to them about the social conditions of the workers," says Pizarro. "My impression is, they were very impressed by the sanitation conditions of the processing plants they were taken to. But they were surprised by the claims of the labor issues. On the other hand, they were very polite and willing to understand the issues."

The Wal-Mart representatives got a potent illustration of the importance of the labor problems. The meeting was interrupted by labor unions coming into the building and holding a rally inside to protest the working conditions at the salmon-processing facilities. Pizarro says the concerns of the workers cannot be lightly brushed over.

"What I told the Wal-Mart representatives," Pizarro says, "is that I am convinced if the labor conditions are the way they are, it wouldn't be surprising to me if an American consumer found a nail or a knife in their fillets. Once Wal-Mart realizes that the same workers who are producing the food product may sabotage it, then surely, for their own self-interest, they will have an interest in seeing labor conditions improved.

"When I said that to them," says Pizarro, "clearly they were more interested."

Leape, of the National Environmental Trust, is not directly involved in Wal-Mart's conversations about the salmon standards, but he knows the people who are. "Wal-Mart will adopt standards. The question is how strong they will be," Leape says flatly. "They dictate terms to their suppliers all the time—how to produce it, what should be in it, what they'll pay for it. They've got a responsibility, if they want a sustainable product."

Pizarro, too, is optimistic. "We don't have to impose very high conditions to make a considerable improvement in people's lives," he says. "What I would say is, in a global economy, we're all globally responsible. I think Wal-Mart will make changes. It has to."

From the outside, the changes look easier to impose than they will be. For Wal-Mart, it's not simply about adding a few new bullet points to the existing list requiring companies to deliver products on time, on price, packaged the way Wal-Mart requires. Using Wal-Mart's purchasing power to improve the environmental and working conditions under which those products are produced requires a radical shift in thinking at the home office, a willingness to admit that not every cost squeezed out is good. But forty years of discipline and culture at Wal-Mart, from the buyers in Bentonville out to the pallets lined up in Action Alley of every store, runs counter to the hopes of Rodrigo Pizarro and Robina Akther.

Pizarro knows one point of leverage that Wal-Mart never ignores: shoppers. And he thinks if American consumers understand what's required to deliver salmon at $4.84 a pound, they won't think the price is worth the cost. "I wouldn't think American parents would want to feed themselves or their children with something being produced by a worker who is miserable, and who works in terrible conditions," says Pizarro. "And I don't think Wal-Mart should tolerate that."

EIGHT
THE POWER OF PENNIES

The customer is not a moron. She's your wife.

—*Kevin Roberts, worldwide CEO, Saatchi & Saatchi, speaking at*
the "Emerging Trends in Retailing" conference, Sam M. Walton
College of Business, University of Arkansas

I T ISN'T YET eight o'clock on a Thursday morning, and Wal-Mart #5229, the store in Wyncote, Pennsylvania, just north of Philadelphia, has been open less than an hour. It is a cool summer morning, much of the parking lot is still in shadow and much of it is empty. This is unusual. Wal-Mart #5229 is an urban Wal-Mart, opened in January 2004 in the shell of a failed Kmart store, and modest in size by Wal-Mart standards, just 112,500 square feet. If you pay close enough attention, most Wal-Marts have distinctive personalities. No. 5229 is often crowded to the point of chaos, and the toy department, the baby department, and the toothpaste aisle often look like they've been ransacked rather than stocked.

Customers at #5229 standing in line with full shopping carts to check out often have to wait so long that they form lines that curve out and block the main aisle along the front of the store. It often takes longer to pay for a cart full of stuff than it took to fill the cart in the first place.

This store has been known to run out of bags. Often there are no carts available to shoppers coming in the door, and this morning is no exception. A long line of dozens of nested carts snakes out the main entrance—the carts have clearly spent the night scattered in the parking lot, something that would make Sam Walton scowl. This morning, however, #5229 is uncharacteristically quiet, almost serene. The aisles are easy to navigate, the departments are neat and well stocked. For some reason, no one has activated the TV monitors that squawk, again and again, "What's new at Wal-Mart!"

The Wal-Mart effect begins, and ends, in the stores, with the shopping and the shoppers. Wal-Mart derives all its impact, all its power, from us, from our willingness to open our wallets, just a few dollars at a time. In categories of consumables—the half of Wal-Mart's sales that includes groceries, health and beauty, and general merchandise— the average product we buy from Wal-Mart costs something less than $3—indeed, none of the top fifteen most frequently purchased items cost even $3. That means a couple things. It means that the small stuff matters—the company that became the largest and most powerful in history isn't a military contractor or a car company; it isn't the result of savvy lobbyists in Washington or the happenstance of controlling the supply of petroleum, or some kind of cabal that is beyond the understanding of ordinary people. The largest and most powerful company in history is built by each of us handing over three single-dollar bills, over and over again.

In fact, the real power of Wal-Mart doesn't come from selling the average consumable at $3.00—the power comes from a much smaller sum, just $0.03. The magic of Wal-Mart has always been in selling the $3.00 item for $2.97—that's the genius of Sam Walton. He realized instinctively that Americans would change their habits to buy a $3.00 item for $2.97, especially if it was $2.97 every day. And he figured out how to run a business that could be profitable giving up those three pennies.

There is no better place to start appreciating the power of those pennies than to do some shopping, to look at a few products on the shelves of Wal-Mart #5229 in Wyncote. Consider first a bottle of ordinary bath oil, Alpha Keri Shower & Bath Moisture Rich Oil, found in the health and beauty section that Sam Walton himself considered critical to Wal-Mart's drawing power. It comes in a slim, clear plastic bottle, so the turquoise oil is visible. Alpha Keri is an indulgence. Per ounce, it costs more than a $24.00 bottle of Merlot. If gasoline—oil itself, that is—sold for what Alpha Keri bath oil sells for, a gallon of gas would cost $127.52. At Wal-Mart, the eight-ounce bottle of Alpha Keri costs $7.97. Everywhere else, the identical bottle is more than $8.00, often north of $9.00. Pulling a bottle of Alpha Keri from the shelf provides a sense of security. Wal-Mart is on our side: As expensive as each squirt of bath oil is, at Wal-Mart you're getting it as inexpensively as it is to be found. That is the very point of Wal-Mart, the core value of the whole company. For shoppers, that is the Wal-Mart effect: Whatever Wal-Mart is charging, it's a safe bet it's the best price you can find. You can pitch the Alpha Keri in the cart without a second thought.

But part of what is so interesting about shopping at Wal-Mart these days is that the experience is different from aisle to aisle; the very same promise that gives comfort in one department is unsettling in another. Although Wal-Mart #5229 is not a supercenter, like most regular Wal-Marts these days it has a half dozen aisles of basic, high-volume grocery items: milk, eggs, bread, pasta, breakfast cereal, soda, canned vegetables. Consider a can of cut green beans, no salt added. Canned vegetables are big business—only seven categories of consumables sell more individual units at Wal-Mart than canned vegetables. At a typical suburban grocery store, a can of Del Monte green beans—no salt added—costs $0.99. Store-brand green beans typically cost $0.79 a can. Catch a sale, and it's two cans of house-brand beans for $1.09, or $0.55 a can.

At Wal-Mart, a can of private-label no-brand no-salt-added cut green beans is 44 cents. That's the everyday low price. The beans are 20 percent cheaper off the shelf at Wal-Mart than they are anywhere else, even on sale. Every day they are less than half the price of a can of name-brand beans at the grocery store.

Two steps from the beans are Snow's minced clams, also in the can. If you're making linguine with white clam sauce, you're likely using Snow's minced clams. At the supermarket, they run from $1.20 to $1.40 a can; anything below $1.20 is cheap. At Wal-Mart #5229, they are never more than $1.12. Occasionally—as at Wal-Mart #1348, in Wilmington, North Carolina, one day—they are dramatically cheaper, $0.98 a can.

But buying green beans for half what they typically cost, buying clams 10 or 20 or 30 percent cheaper, that doesn't provide a feeling of comfort. If you notice the price difference in the beans or the clams, you can't help but wonder how they do it. If you think about how they do it, you may get a tickle of uneasiness.

What do the fields look like where those green beans are raised (in Canada, the can says), who's picking them, and what's left behind? And what's the quality of 44 cent green beans, anyway?

It's easy to imagine the ocean bottom off New Jersey scoured clean of all life as Snow's fishing boats struggle to land enough clams to satisfy Wal-Mart's monstrous appetite.

Shopping at Wal-Mart isn't an innocent experience now, if it ever was. It is a mix of satisfaction, wonder, puzzlement, and guilt. The nagging feeling, of course, is its own hidden cost, unaccounted for in the 44 cent cost of a can of green beans.

How much does Wal-Mart save us every year?

Let's start out simply, and just consider groceries, where the low estimate is that Wal-Mart saves its shoppers 15 percent on a typical shopping cart of food.

In 2004, Wal-Mart shoppers spent $124 billion on groceries. That food, purchased at other supermarkets, would have cost $146 billion. So Wal-Mart grocery shoppers alone saved $22 billion.

If the rest of the merchandise Wal-Mart sells is just 5 percent cheaper than at competing stores, that's another $8 billion.

So a conservative estimate is that the people who shopped at Wal-Mart last year saved $30 billion. That's the equivalent of a $270 Wal-Mart rebate check for every family in America every year.

But no one shops "on average," and the figures have more immediacy, more power, at the level of a family. Consider a family of two adults and two kids, with an annual income of $52,000. A family like that might easily spend $125 a week on groceries, or $500 a month. If Wal-Mart comes to town, and they can save 15 percent on their groceries, that comes to $75 a month. That $75 adds up to $900 over the course of a year—it's the equivalent of an extra weekly paycheck; it's more than seven weeks of free groceries. And that's just the groceries.

Why would you pay more? Who can afford to pay more? Who turns down an envelope filled with $900?

In purely economic terms, the $30 billion in savings directly from Wal-Mart—not accounting for the money saved as other retailers increase their efficiency and lower their prices to compete—that $30 billion even puts in some perspective the twenty thousand U.S. families that Stephan Goetz found Wal-Mart elbowed into poverty. Even if each of those families had an income of $52,000 before ending up impoverished (which is unlikely), and even if that meant they had no income and were on public assistance, their total lost income comes to $1 billion—one thirtieth the total direct savings. A market economy is always reallocating resources, and often those resources are actual people who lose jobs and have to find new ones. The problem, really, is that real people don't live in the "macro" economy; real people don't live in the long term. The problem is the contrast, the clarity that the Goetz study gives the larger trade-off: Should some people lose their livelihoods so everyone's power tools and underwear and laundry detergent can be cheaper? In a market economy, in a democracy, the answer is always an emphatic yes. That efficiency is the source of progress, the progress that creates new jobs and new opportunities that sweep up the people previously displaced. But the starkness of the trade-off—our shopping at Wal-Mart costs those people their jobs—is usually safely hidden in the complexity of the economy, unless your neighbor works at a factory that closes.

The wages of the people who work at Wal-Mart aren't obvious as you're shopping, nor are the stores Wal-Mart has put out of business or the kind of pressure Wal-Mart applies to its suppliers—or all the things those suppliers have to do, good and bad, to cope with that pressure. In the modern world, there is nothing unusual in that disconnection; the wages of the people who work at McDonald's aren't obvious either, and most of us have no idea how cows become Big Macs. But some of how Wal-Mart does what it does is vividly clear right there in the stores; as shoppers, we either overlook it, or we've become so accustomed to it that Wal-Mart has reset our expectations.

Shopping at Wal-Mart is not a delight; it is often work, and it can easily descend to drudgery and frustration. The parking lot is huge; just getting inside is a hike. The store is vast and so noisy—visually psychologically, literally—that it requires concentration and discipline and energy to stay on course, to find what you need and head for the next thing. If you need help, it is rarely at hand. If something is out of stock, you've invested so much time and effort to get to that particular shelf in that particular aisle that the gap is more than disappointing; it's aggravating. Buying clothes is its own trial—the apparel areas are often a mess; the racks are so jammed with merchandise it's hard to see or find anything; and space between racks is so narrow that if you attempt to steer a shopping cart between them, you can't help but knock blouses and pants to the floor. The clothing departments are almost unshoppable. Waiting to pay, you often have time to ponder whether the savings is worth the effort. If a product lacks a bar code sticker, or if the scanner won't take your coupons, the cashier will often bring the checkout process to a halt and call for help, standing with arms crossed while the minutes tick away and a supervisor arrives at her own pace. And it is all much more daunting if you're hauling a kid or two along with you. The only thing likely to make you smile at Wal-Mart is the price. In fact, it isn't really a place to shop, it's a place to buy things—bring a list, check the items off, get out. Getting what you need is a mission, and it often feels exactly like that.

One number, one ratio, perfectly captures and contrasts the shopping experience across stores: how much merchandise a store sells for every employee.

Wal-Mart sells $178,125 worth of stuff per employee.

Target sells $156,506 worth of stuff per employee.

Whole Foods sells $121,875 worth of stuff per employee.

As those numbers go down, the pleasurability of the shopping experience goes up, and that's no accident. Sure, Wal-Mart sells so much more per employee than everybody else because we buy more at Wal-Mart, and because of the frugality they apply to their headquarters operation and the magic they apply to their distribution system. But most of the workers are in the stores, and at Wal-Mart, there just aren't that many of them there. That's why you often can't find someone to open the jewelry cases if you want a watch that's locked up. That's why half the checkout lanes, or two thirds of the checkout lanes, are unstaffed, even as customers are waiting ten or fifteen minutes to pay. Wal-Mart is relentless at measuring its own costs; it isn't so interested in measuring its customers' costs.

Often, as a result, we get exactly what we pay for, and we don't even notice. A metal bar stool costs $24.87 at Wal-Mart; a Graco Pooh Harmony Highchair costs $72.44; an exercise bike costs $88.88; and a whole dining room set, table and four chairs, costs $174.86. But you don't get a bar stool, a high chair, an exercise bike, or a dining room set. You get a heavy box of parts, and you get to build the exercise bike or the dining room table in the factory of your family room. As it has so deftly and relentlessly pushed work back onto its suppliers, so Wal-Mart has outsourced the actual assembly of many but the simplest products to the customers. Wal-Mart is certainly not alone in this, but as in so many techniques pioneered elsewhere, Wal-Mart has adopted it with relentless enthusiasm. The stores are rapidly expanding their home furnishings offerings. Many Wal-Marts now have large displays of furniture—dressers, desks, shelves, grandfather clocks, beds—but the only assembled versions are chained in place. No wonder the products are so cheap. We're making them ourselves.

THE AMERICAN ATTITUDE about money is complicated. On the one hand, the homily often attributed to Ben Franklin, "A penny saved is a penny earned," is older than the nation itself. (Franklin actually wrote, "A penny sav'd is twopence clear," in 1737.) There is in the American character a deep strain of frugality, of penny-pinching, going back to colonial and frontier times and sharply refreshed during the Depression and the rationing during World War II. Making due has often been a necessity, a goad to resourcefulness and invention; when making due is not a necessity, it remains for some a source of pride, even smugness.

But we are also the country where the average credit card balances being carried by a family from month to month are more than $9,300— and that average includes the 40 percent of families who pay their balances off each month. Take those people out, and the average family is carrying $14,400 in credit card debt. Meanwhile, despite all the money we save shopping at Wal-Mart, we actually save almost nothing. The family savings rate in the last year is below 1 percent. The typical family with an income of $52,000 may be saving more than $900 a year at Wal-Mart, but they are putting away less than $500 a year for the future. Wal-Mart notwithstanding, our spending is growing faster than our income. And even as a desire to pay less has created the world's dominant company, a desire for indulgence has created the world's most popular café. Starbucks has nearly twice the worldwide coffee shops as Wal-Mart has stores. Starbucks is built on a customer philosophy exactly opposite to Wal-Mart's, charging more for a cup of coffee than anyone would have imagined twenty years ago. The price of half the drinks on the Starbucks menu board is more than $3.

The American attitude about how corporations present the frugality or indulgence they are selling is equally inconsistent. Southwest Airlines is the Wal-Mart of flying, and we love Southwest. Southwest's fares, much like Wal-Mart's prices, are often so low they are hard to believe. In markets from one side of the country to the other, Southwest offers nonstop flights that cost under $100—round trip. The cab fare to the airport often costs more than the one-way flight itself. Southwest is no frills. The company doesn't even bother assigning seats, resulting in a preboarding queue up and an onboard jockeying for seats that can take some getting used to. The staff of Southwest is legendarily cheerful and helpful. And Southwest is profitable, thirty-two straight years of profitability, despite an overcrowded market, rising fuel prices, and the 9/11 attacks.

But Southwest is also a brutal, unsentimental competitor. In May 2005, as a nearly crippled US Airways was struggling through its second stint in bankruptcy, Southwest inaugurated service in Pittsburgh, one of US Air's key hubs. A few months before that second bankruptcy filing in September 2004, Southwest had launched service in another key US Air market, Philadelphia. In fact, as 2005 wound down, four major U.S. airlines were in bankruptcy—United, US Airways, Delta, and Northwest—and only one major airline was profitable: Southwest. In 2004, Southwest made $6 million a week in profits; the rest of the major airlines lost more than $170 million a week. Southwest has never laid off an employee; since 2000, its competitors have fired 135,000. There are many reasons for the tumult and pain in the airline business. But one of those reasons is Southwest. The airline with a winsome red heart in the middle of its logo (the company's home airport is Love Field in Dallas) has revolutionized the economics, the cost structure, the customer experience, the pricing, and the competitive landscape of commercial aviation. Like Wal-Mart, Southwest has done more than deliver inexpensive airfares: It has reset our expectations about what it should cost to fly. A round-trip ticket from New York to Fort Lauderdale that costs $240 seems expensive. That is the Southwest effect, in fact.

Despite the destruction left in the wake of the soaring orange and blue Southwest 737s, though, no one protests the arrival of Southwest into a new city. Despite the tens of thousands of jobs obliterated at other airlines as pilots, mechanics, flight attendants, and gate agents lose good-paying jobs with benefits and pensions, no one petitions airport boards to deny Southwest boarding gates. Although Southwest manages to operate with roughly 25 percent fewer staff members per plane in its fleet than the major airlines, no one pickets Southwest check-in gates on the days Southwest starts flying. When Southwest enters a market, or adds flights in an existing one, the airline often promotes the service with the cheerful advertising tagline "You are now free to move about the country." And Americans agree.

In 2005, Southwest carried more passengers than any other U.S. airline. We love Southwest Airlines. We do not love Wal-Mart.

The difference is important, and it's no accident. It's partly just a matter of style, of Southwest's carefully constructed corporate personality. Southwest has a sense of humor, and invites us to have a sense of humor too. Southwest staff outfits include khaki shorts, gate agents manage the preboard cattle call with a wink that shows they realize it's not the most relaxing way to begin a flight, and flight attendants have the impertinence to mock the FAA's ridiculous pretakeoff safety announcement, most of which is still devoted to instructing passengers in the arcane art of fastening and unfastening their seat belts. In fact, by offering safety announcements in song or in Dr. Seuss couplets, the flight attendants often get people to listen to something they otherwise ignore. Southwest staff members are not just cheerful, they are fairly well paid. The airline's business model, the low prices they offer customers, doesn't require our silent complicity in exploiting the very people who are taking care of us. There is no hidden universe of squeezed suppliers; with Southwest we buy the product they produce. And for years airline passengers have had no love for the competing airlines that Southwest has all but hobbled. Southwest has managed to play the underdog role—the sense of humor helps—even as it has slowly grown to dominance. Meanwhile, the absurd, mysterious, and constantly shifting pricing structures of the major airlines, and a decade of utter indifference to customer service, makes it easy to cheer Southwest's success, and smile along with them.

Southwest Airlines isn't just cheap, it's fun. Wal-Mart isn't just cheap, it's joyless, when it's not downright vexing. Wal-Mart takes its duty to lower prices so seriously, there's no room for any other attitude, for them or us, except duty. Even without doubts about wages, suppliers, local businesses, American jobs, and quality, Wal-Mart has done such a superb job of austerity from start to finish that austerity is all that's left. This is, after all, the company that has made a brilliant marketing virtue of positioning the merchandise in the middle of the store aisles, still piled on the shipping pallets. Why even put the stuff on the shelves? We're selling it too fast to bother.

There is no playfulness. Wal-Mart is like the stern, authoritarian eighth-grade math teacher who suddenly tries to crack a joke the day before spring break—the humor rings hollow, and the effort itself seems odd and insincere. Wal-Mart has no sense of humor about itself, and we have no sense of humor about Wal-Mart.

But we respect Wal-Mart, and as with how we regard the eighth-grade math teacher, a great many of us clearly appreciate what Wal-Mart can do for us. And any individual Wal-Mart store does still have the capacity to surprise its customers, and those surprises sometimes move trailer loads of merchandise.

In the wide aisle running past sporting goods in #2247 is a pallet piled chest high with ammunition. Case upon case of 12-gauge Remington shotgun shells, 250 shells for $29.80. It seems odd to see so much firepower simply sitting out where you might find a pallet of Pampers.

In #2836, near the electronics section, is a pallet stacked with boxes of Cisco routers, for use setting up a home wireless Internet network. The mythic stature of Cisco Systems—the company's routers handle much of the traffic on the Internet—seems deflated a bit by seeing a mound of two hundred boxed Cisco routers, available to anyone with $69.69.

In #2198, as you walk in through the automatic doors, is a pallet with ready-to-buy bouquets of fresh flowers. The surprise: It's the middle of February, and #2198 is near Minneapolis, just down the road from the Mall of America. The parking lot is ringed with piles of snow; it's 25 degrees outside; and as you step inside, #2198 offers bouquets of fresh-cut flowers.

Sometimes the surprise is just a kind of head-shaking consistency about the dedication to low prices. Tucked way in the back of a Wal-Mart, a dramatic 14 percent price rollback: a 28-cent item cut to 24 cents. In the Reading Center, Sam Walton's own autobiography, *Made in America,* is for sale. Cover price: $7.99. Shelf price: $5.62.

And sometimes the surprise is a small window into what it must be like to work with and think like the people who make Wal-Mart go. In one store one afternoon, the men's clothing area is walled off with boxes of shirts and pants waiting to be unloaded. Printed on each cardboard box of clothing are instructions to the store staff, "Return for credit, Wal-Mart DC #16. Each box cost the company an average of $0.85." In another store, a single box awaiting unpacking in the infant department reads, "This box cost Wal-Mart $3.66. Return immediately to Wal-Mart DC." On another side of the box is printed, "Return with pride."

Many Wal-Marts now have skylights. Not a few scattered skylights, but enough so that no matter where you stand, if you look up, you can see the sky through at least three skylights. During the day, the skylights flood a Wal-Mart store with natural light; they give the store, and the shopping experience, a sense of calm. Tom Seay, who ran Wal-Mart's real estate operations from 1974 to 1996, that is, from 78 U.S. stores to 2,740 stores, chuckles about the skylights. Stores with skylights have their lights on computer-controlled dimmers. The skylights not only make the stores more appealing, they also save Wal-Mart money by reducing the electric bill.

The rollback of something that costs 28 cents to 24 cents, the discounting of Sam Walton's own wisdom by 30 percent, the reusable company-owned cardboard boxes, with their prices printed right on them, the lovely skylights in the service of lower operating costs— that is the DNA of Wal-Mart in all its purity and simplicity and power. And it is one reason that the business of Wal-Mart is in trouble.

Kevin Roberts, the worldwide CEO of the ad agency Saatchi & Saatchi, was the kickoff speaker in October 2004 of a retailing trends conference at the Center for Retailing Excellence at the University of Arkansas's business school, which is named for Sam Walton. The University of Arkansas is in Fayetteville, just thirty miles down the road from Bentonville, and the audience was filled with almost five hundred people, most of whom had the attentive, well-scrubbed air of Wal-Mart vendor-team members, from companies like Dial, J. M. Smucker, and 3M.

Roberts, whose company does work for Wal-Mart, gave a spirited but devastating analysis of the state of the company. "What is the current problem for retail, and for manufacturers?" he asked the audience. "Commodification. You can get the best deals ever. And Wal-Mart has been a big player in this. And is the consumer grateful for it? No! They expect it!"

Wal-Mart is exhausting to its customers. "Go into a Wal-Mart," Roberts said. "There's very little mystery left. Go into a Wal-Mart. It's not sensual at all." Without mentioning Target, he was conjuring it. Wal-Mart is enervating; Target is refreshing. "The consumer is tired of the transaction business," said Roberts. "Wal-Mart's current purpose is adding dollars to consumers. Saving them money. But Wal-Mart is not loved. And you don't marry someone you respect. Wal-Mart has become irreplaceable. It needs to become irresistible."

It is precisely the difference between Southwest and Wal-Mart. "To be loved," Roberts concluded, "you have to be lovable."

IN THE SEPTEMBER 2005 issue of *Vogue,* for the first time ever, Wal-Mart bought eight pages of advertising, right alongside Dior, Gucci, Bill Blass, and Prada. The Wal-Mart pages were as stylishly executed as they were astonishing. Each page displayed real Wal-Mart

customers—an actress, a mom, a college professor—artfully pho-
tographed wearing clothes mostly bought at Wal-Mart. Each page
listed the items and the prices, a George tweed blazer ($23.82), a Jor-
dache tunic ($12.88), a No Boundaries chemise ($9.87). In the Dior
and Prada ads, of course, it's not always clear what product is being
sold; there certainly are no prices.

In the same issue of *Vogue* is another company with prices in its
ads. Target's eight pages of ads are a little more in tune with the off-
kilter fashion-world spirit of *Vogue*—they include quotes from the de-
signer Isaac Mizrahi, and one of the eight pages is a picture of a white
horse (no price provided). But the appearance of Target-like fashion
ads from Wal-Mart—in *Vogue*, of all places—is a signal that Wal-Mart
sees the problem that "always low prices" has, finally, created for it.

If you're selling stuff based on price, and based on your ability to
offer a better deal all the time, eventually you run out of room to go
lower. It costs *something* to make anything. What's more, our appetite
for paper towels, toothpaste, diapers, toys, TVs, kitchen gadgets, groceries, and even budget apparel is naturally limited. It's limited by
what we need, with a little thrown in for the impulse purchase.

Style and design constitute the antidote to the cul de sac that price
represents. You can't just keep charging less, but you can give people
something with a spritz of fun and fashion, and charge more. That's
what Target does—in its products and in its stores as well. It's not just
fun; it's good business. The signature sign of the health of a retail
company is the growth in sales, not overall, but at stores open at least
a year. This "same store sales" figure measures the drawing power,
the appeal, and the growth power of existing stores.

Wal-Mart's same-store-sales figures show that, hard as it is to believe, the power of "always low prices" is waning. In the calendar year
1998, Wal-Mart's same-store sales rose 9 percent. In calendar 1999,
they rose 8 percent. In 2001, they rose 6 percent. Since then, it's been

5 percent (2002), 4 percent (2003), and 3.3 percent (2004). In the first half of 2005, same-store sales were up just 3.2 percent. There has not been a year of such anemic growth for Wal-Mart's stores, going back twenty years. (Although, considering how fiercely Wal-Mart pushes down prices on many products, 3.3 percent growth is itself an achievement, since a lot of merchandise is getting cheaper.)

Target, meanwhile, has been trouncing Wal-Mart in the same-store-sales measure. In 2004, Target was up 5.3 percent against Wal-Mart's 3.3 percent. In the first half of 2005, Target was up 6.5 percent—more than double the growth rate of Wal-Mart's stores.

The reason is simple: Style. Style, versus price.

Wal-Mart knows this. Hence the ads in *Vogue*—the first of 116 pages of Wal-Mart ads in *Vogue* through 2007. The same month the *Vogue* ads appeared, the *Wall Street Journal* ran a front-page story describing Wal-Mart's early efforts at a Target-like makeover for its apparel business: stores with clothing racks that are more widely spaced and easier to access; lower shelves; a reorganized apparel-buying staff. The company is slowly retrofitting many of its clothing departments with hardwood floors to give them a warmer, more inviting mood.

But recognizing the problem, even recognizing the solution, in the case of Wal-Mart may not matter. The *Vogue* ads, for instance, are nicely executed—the women look happy and fashionable, the clothes look cute and stylish, and the Wal-Mart logo appears in a different hue on each page. But the idea that you could, in a leisurely way, work the aisles in the local Wal-Mart women's wear department and assemble a style is completely at odds with the actual experience of clothing shopping day to day at Wal-Mart.

Wal-Mart has no way of thinking about style, of effectively adding fashion to the frugality equation. Style is just like salmon or factory working conditions abroad. It involves adding costs back into the system for something intangible, something almost immeasurable. In the case of style, it's adding costs back in to get something fashion-able. In the case of salmon or factory working conditions, it's adding costs into the system to make the lives of salmon or factory workers better in a way that also can't be quantified in Wal-Mart terms. Even if Wal-Mart's senior leadership agrees in principle that all these ideas are smart—smart business, smart image building, smart long-term strategy—it will be a struggle for them to take hold. It's like imagin-ing Southwest Airlines suddenly adding business class.

Wal-Mart's dramatically slowing same-store sales growth—half what it was just five years ago—is a sign of another problem. Long, long ago Wal-Mart put itself in a box. It was indeed a big box, it was bigger than anyone imagined. But Americans are clearly close to Wal-Mart saturation, not culturally or politically or morally, but literally. The nation simply doesn't need to buy much more from Wal-Mart than it already does.

As of the fall of 2005, Wal-Mart had 3,811 stores in the United States. That's one store for every 78,000 Americans. Here's one way of thinking about that: A U.S. member of Congress represents 680,000 citizens; a typical Wal-Mart store manager only answers to one ninth that many constituents.

America is nearly full up with Wal-Marts. There are some areas of growth potential—California has only 191 stores, and just based on population it could easily support 460. New York City, the largest city in the nation, has not a single Wal-Mart. Wal-Mart only has 16 percent of the national grocery market; it might one day have 30 percent. But for Wal-Mart, that's all fill-in growth.

The most startling numbers are these: 53 percent of the U.S. popu-lation lives within five miles of a Wal-Mart; 90 percent of the U.S. pop-ulation lives within fifteen miles of a Wal-Mart; 97 percent of the U.S. population lives within twenty-five miles of a Wal-Mart. Geographi-cally, the country really is full up with Wal-Mart stores.

The rest of the world, however, is mostly empty of Wal-Marts. So the company can continue to grow, and even grow dramatically, even if it doesn't master fashion in the U.S. The company has fewer stores in China (population 1.3 billion) than in Alabama (population 4.5 million). Wal-Mart has no stores at all in India (population 1 billion). If you look just at market size, Wal-Mart could easily be a half-trillion-dollar-a-year company by 2010. Indeed, $500 billion in sales in 2010 requires just 12 percent overall annual growth—more conservative in the next five years than Wal-Mart has averaged in the last five years. International expansion is driving Wal-Mart's overall growth already, but it hasn't been universally successful. Wal-Mart rapidly conquered the retail markets in both Canada and Mexico; but it has struggled in Germany and Japan, where its operations are not even profitable, let alone dominant.

Wal-Mart may well continue to dominate American retailing for years, or decades, to come. But it's likely that twenty years from now we'll look back on the early twenty-first century as the moment when Wal-Mart's real struggles began. Wal-Mart is as addicted to its low prices as its customers. The idea that Wal-Mart will somehow shake off its low-price soul, that it will gradually infuse style and other intangibles into a culture that measures how many items each cashier scans each hour—that kind of transformation runs counter to every instinct on which Wal-Mart has been built.

No company has more discipline or focus than Wal-Mart, but all that discipline and focus are designed to wring costs out and bring prices down. If cost isn't the ultimate question anymore, what are the important questions? How many of them are there, and which ones do you take into account on which occasions? It's like trying to teach a right-handed adult to write left-handed; it's like trying to force your three-dimensional mind to imagine a fourth dimension. All of Wal-Mart's instincts cry out against other considerations. There is no human adjustment harder to make than to abandon the very principles that have been the source of your success and adopt their opposites as the path to continued success.

And there's another hurdle, even if Wal-Mart were to somehow find within itself a way of setting cost aside as the ultimate arbiter of business decisions. There's us, the shoppers. Wal-Mart has spent forty years teaching us what things should cost, which way prices should go, and why cheaper is better. We have learned that lesson well.

NANCY RIDLEN SHOULD not be a Wal-Mart shopper. For years she and her husband, Don, ran a glue company called Ridlen Adhesives. Ridlen made glues for consumers: craft glues, wood glues, glue sticks. "Glue, glue, glue," says Nancy Ridlen. "We made the glue, we bottled it, we shipped it." Ridlen sold glue to Woolworth, to Target, to Kmart. And, of course, to Wal-Mart. "It was our biggest account," says Nancy Ridlen.

Don Ridlen went to Bentonville regularly, and Ridlen shipped pallets of glue sticks off to Wal-Mart. Often, says Nancy, an order would come in from Wal-Mart, "and we'd have forty-eight hours to turn it around. So we had to keep glue in stock for them. You have to be ready." The price pressure was constant.

At some point in 1991, Nancy Ridlen says, Wal-Mart said, "We don't want to pay 50 cents for these glue sticks. We'll pay 45 cents. Either you take it, or we'll go somewhere else."

"They didn't ask," says Nancy Ridlen. "That was a demand, honey." For Don Ridlen, that nickel was the last nickel. He couldn't sell Wal-Mart glue sticks for 45 cents, and Wal-Mart pulled its business. "Over a dispute about a nickel, they walked away," says Nancy Ridlen. "Exactly." She can barely restrain the tears as she recounts the story fifteen years later.

Ridlen was left with pallets of unsold glue sticks. Don Ridlen couldn't make the business work anymore, and Ridlen Adhesives went bankrupt. Nancy Ridlen says the canceled Wal-Mart order, on top of years of price pressure, was the cause. Don Ridlen has since died. But he told the same story to someone in the crafts industry; and Linda Harrison, the woman who ultimately bought the assets and the name of Ridlen Adhesives, and who does no business with Wal-Mart, had heard the same thing.

For purposes of this story, though, it doesn't matter whether Ridlen Adhesives went under because Wal-Mart pulled its business over a nickel per glue stick. Nancy Ridlen believes that Wal-Mart sent the family glue business into bankruptcy. And yet, she says, "I do shop at Wal-Mart." Even a woman who thinks Wal-Mart destroyed her family's livelihood—"It is a monster that must be fed at any cost," she says of Wal-Mart—even Nancy Ridlen still shops at Wal-Mart. She pauses. "I have to deal with it all the time," she says.

Randall Larrimore was just like Don Ridlen, on a much larger scale. Larrimore was the CEO of the company that included Master Lock in January 1997, when Master Lock announced that, after seventy-five years making locks of all kinds in Milwaukee, it would begin to import some products from Asia. Not too long after that, Master Lock opened a factory of its own in Nogales, Mexico; Master Lock no longer makes locks in Milwaukee. Its three hundred employees there just make parts, which are sent to Nogales, where eight hundred factory workers assemble the locks. Forty percent of the company's locks are now made by outsourced factories in China.

Larrimore left the company in 1997, but he knows well what happened to Master Lock: "I think 'every day low prices' is the start," he says.

For years, he says, as manufacturing costs in the United States rose, Master Lock was able to pass those costs along. At some point in the 1990s, though, Asian manufacturers started producing locks "for substantially less, and still making an adequate profit for themselves. When the difference is $1, retailers like Wal-Mart would prefer to have the brand-name padlock or faucet or hammer.

"But as the spread becomes greater, when our padlock was $9, and the import was $6, then they can offer the consumer a real discount by carrying two lines. Ultimately, they may only carry one line."

Larrimore did the first manufacturing layoffs at Master Lock. He negotiated with Master Lock's unions himself. He went to Bentonville. "I loved dealing with Wal-Mart, with Home Depot," he says. "They are all very rational people. There wasn't a whole lot of room for negotiation. And they had a good point. Everyone was willing to pay more for a Master Lock. But how much more can they justify? If they can buy a lock that has arguably similar quality, at a cheaper price, well, they can get their consumers a deal."

Larrimore is a shopper himself; he understands the psychology of consumers confronted with identical items with different prices. A two-time CEO of large companies, Larrimore still sometimes wrestles over the pennies.

"Just today," says Larrimore, "I bought gasoline at the local station in the center of our little town. I paid 6 or 8 cents a gallon more than if I had driven a mile out near the highway. As I was pumping, I was kicking myself, thinking, this is really stupid; I've spent $2.50 I didn't need spend. Then I thought, on the other hand, I really appreciate this guy being in town. I'm sure his costs are higher. And I'm going to spend $2.50 to help him stay in business."

The hundreds of Milwaukee employees of Master Lock who shopped at Wal-Mart to save money shopped their own jobs right to Nogales, and to China. Not consciously, not directly, but inevitably.

"Do we as consumers appreciate what we're doing?" says Larrimore. "I don't think so. But even if we do appreciate it, I think we say, here's a Master Lock for $9, here's another lock for $6—let the other guy pay $9."

In that sense, Sam Walton's insight about Americans could not have been more unerring. We will give up convenience and service and enjoyment, fashion and quality, to get a better deal. The reason price has such power for us can seem frustratingly elusive.

In fact, one of the most potent feelings that Wal-Mart inspires, the source of much of its gravitational force over consumers, goes all the way back to Ben Franklin's exhortations to frugality. Shopping at Wal-Mart means paying less for something than you otherwise have to. You can buy exactly the same product and spend less, and you know it. Shopping at Wal-Mart represents individual fiscal restraint. It represents prudence.

You can wheel the shopping cart filled with bags out into the parking lot knowing that, all things being equal, you are $5 or $10 or $20 richer simply because you were smart enough to shop at Wal-Mart. The low prices are a virtue, and they confer virtue on us. That, too, is the Wal-Mart effect. Wal-Mart doesn't just save us money; it makes us feel good about ourselves by doing so. Once you leave the store and the mission itself is behind you—the hike from one side of the big box to the other, the lack of anyone to answer questions, the momentary puzzlement at a price that seems just too low, the line at checkout—once you're hoisting the bags into your car, shopping at Wal-Mart feels good. You can feel proud of yourself. Shopping at Wal-Mart is, quite literally, a virtue. And the only way to crack the power of low prices—to change either Wal-Mart or us as shoppers—will be if those low prices no longer seem so virtuous.

NINE
WAL-MART AND THE
DECENT SOCIETY

The question of how to assure that American capitalism creates
a decent society is one that will engage all of us in the era ahead.

—*Wal-Mart CEO H. Lee Scott, February 2005*

I N THE SUMMER OF 2003, researchers for one of the world's largest
advertising agencies, Foote Cone & Belding, went to Oklahoma
City, Oklahoma, to try to better understand in a systematic way who
shopped at Wal-Mart, and why.

They chose Oklahoma City because it looked like America demo-
graphically, and because it had all four kinds of Wal-Mart stores (Supercenter, Wal-Mart, Sam's Club, Neighborhood Market). The
researchers studied a whole range of things: shopping habits, number
of trips to various kinds of stores, how competition changed as Wal-
Mart grew.

For those skeptical that Wal-Mart touches the lives of virtually
every American every day, the research found Wal-Mart owned 27
percent of the market for groceries in Oklahoma City, and that 93
percent of Oklahoma City residents had shopped at Wal-Mart in the

previous year. Whatever stores those other 7 percent were shopping in had surely reshaped their own business to compete with Wal-Mart.

Perhaps the most interesting thing the researchers did, though, was ask questions about how Oklahomans felt about Wal-Mart, and divide Wal-Mart shoppers into something they called attitudinal segments. They discovered four basic kinds of Wal-Mart shoppers: champions, enthusiasts, conflicted, and rejecters.

The champions, 29 percent of Oklahoma City shoppers, are Wal-Mart missionaries. They love Wal-mart; most weeks they visit the stores twice (7.3 times in four weeks), and they spend more than $100 a week there ($402 in 4 weeks).

The conflicted shoppers—15 percent in Oklahoma City—actively dislike Wal-Mart because of its impact on communities, wages, and jobs. But by a wide margin, they are the second most frequent shoppers at the store—they go more than once a week (5.6 visits in a month), and they spend nearly as much at Wal-Mart as the champions—$289 a month.

Conflicted Wal-Mart shoppers spend three times as much money at Wal-Mart as those the study called enthusiasts, and they go to Wal-Mart nearly six times as often. The conflicted folks, who were "very Wal-Mart negative," are actually more enthusiastic shoppers than the enthusiasts. (Even the Wal-Mart rejecters shop at Wal-Mart an average of nine times a year, and they spend more than $450 a year.)

The Foote Cone research, released in early 2004, got almost no attention. But it suggests two remarkable, related insights. The first is the depth of feeling Americans have about what is, fundamentally, just a place to shop.

Are there Circuit City "rejecters"? Are there Sears "champions"? Are there "conflicted" Super Target shoppers? Sure, people develop preferences—and companies like Whole Foods, with a distinctive lifestyle positioning, often have passionate followings. But the very categories of attitude Foote Cone sorted Wal-Mart shoppers into seem more appropriate for a politician, a divisive social issue, even an ideology, than they do for a store.

The other important point the research makes is that the Wal-Mart effect is so powerful, the gravitational force the company exerts on us is so irresistible, that the second most important group of customers for Wal-Mart actively dislikes the place. We've become so accustomed to a noisy public conflict about Wal-Mart that it may be easy to slide past the significance of this point.

How many companies can say that the amount of customers who use their services second most often, and spend the second most amount of money with them, are "very negative"? Does Old Navy have a large group of "very negative" customers? From the other end of the relationship, from the perspective of ourselves as customers, how many of us dislike a restaurant but eat there once a week anyway?

Wal-Mart doesn't just reshape the economics of business, the dynamics of global manufacturing, the traffic patterns of American cities—Wal-Mart reshapes our own behavior. Indeed, the Oklahoma City study found that 62 percent of people routinely inconvenience themselves to shop at Wal-Mart.

So even within ourselves, we struggle unsuccessfully to answer the question we started with: Is Wal-Mart good or bad? The answer is surprising for both its simplicity, its obviousness, and also for its power:

Wal-Mart is something utterly new.

Wal-Mart is carefully disguised as something ordinary, familiar, even prosaic. The business model is built on the shopping cart. But, in fact, Wal-Mart is a completely new kind of institution: modern, advanced, potent in ways we've never seen before. Yes, Wal-Mart plays by the rules, but perhaps the most important part of the Wal-Mart effect is that the rules are antiquated; they are from a different era that didn't anticipate anything like Wal-Mart.

That is the source of the company's sweeping ability to suffocate inflation across the entire U.S. economy. And it is the source of the company's ability single-handedly to drive manufacturing jobs overseas.

Wal-Mart has outgrown the rules—but no one noticed.

At the moment, we are incapable as a society of understanding Wal-Mart because we haven't equipped ourselves to manage it. That is the reason for our ambivalence, our appreciation and aversion, our awe and our nervousness, our confusion.

BEFORE THE INVENTION of machines powered by gasoline engines, there was no need to devise rules for cars. When there is one car for every twenty-five people (1917), you need rules of the road, but you don't need to worry about something as remote as the impact on the sky of a car engine's exhaust gases. But when there is one car for every two people in the country (1975), you very definitely need emission controls—they may in fact seem quite urgent. But between the time Ford started selling the Model T and the year catalytic converters were first required on cars, sixty-seven years passed.

The car—the car in America—is an instructive point of comparison to Wal-Mart. Is the car good for America? Absolutely. We love our cars—we love the freedom they have given us, the sense of control, the independence, the pleasure. Of course, cars have also given us air pollution, suburban sprawl, mindless mobility, the homogenization of regional culture, higher taxes, reliance on oil from foreign countries, the obliteration of the natural landscape, and violent death on an epic scale. Cars kill more than forty thousand Americans every year. But we do love our cars. (And most of us are now required by law to wear seat belts in them, but we took ninety years to agree on that.)

Of course, we did not go from being an agrarian society reliant on horses, carts, and the occasional train, directly to a society that is literally built around the demands of the car. It took decades—decades to appreciate the impact of the automobile, decades to appreciate the opportunity, the costs, the nature of the forces at work, and the scale. Putting the proper limits on cars—not just pollution and safety controls, but also speed limits, fuel economy, zoning, highway funding—has not been a quiet or easy process. It has been a series of battles, nationally and locally, involving information, priorities, profits, power, and accusations of bad faith on all sides. The effort to put the proper limits on cars, in fact, has often involved competing visions of what kind of country America is, and what kind of country it is going to be. And that's only appropriate: It would be hard to find a single element in the U.S. economy and landscape that has been more important in shaping our lives in the last hundred years than the car.

The national conversation about Wal-Mart is, in many ways, exactly the same kind of conversation. It is a conversation about priorities, about values, about what kind of country this is and what kind of country it's going to be. It is a conversation about power, and competing visions of the future.

Do we value cheap merchandise more than good factory jobs?

Do we value the convenience of buying everything from eggs and eyeglasses, Levi's and lawn mowers in a single place more than charming main streets with local shopkeepers?

Do we value the freedom of a business to decide where and how to serve its customers more than the responsibility of a local government to safeguard the shape and character of a town?

In a democracy, do we want a single company to have the reach and power that Wal-Mart has—a power that right now is accountable to no one?

But what could be more democratic than a company that is literally built up from the choices made every day by ordinary Americans voting with their debit cards, compelled by nothing but their own choice?

We feel so passionately about Wal-Mart, and Wal-Mart's corporate behavior—but how is Wal-Mart different from Target or Home Depot, Sears or Best Buy? Do we really think those companies are somehow "nicer" than Wal-Mart?

Wal-Mart is already the largest nonoil company in history, but it has a very bluntly stated goal of being twice its current size in 2010. Does that change the balance? What happens when Wal-Mart is twice the size it is now—and alongside it are a half dozen companies the size Wal-Mart is today?

Do we value the "rules" of economic fair play as they happen to be written right now more than our ability to recognize and manage a totally new kind of economic power?

Why don't we give Wal-Mart more credit for doing exactly what it has promised—always low prices? No company can claim greater fidelity to its core value—no company, in that sense, is more truly trustworthy than Wal-Mart. Wal-Mart has the scale of the early-twentieth-century trusts—Standard Oil, U.S. Steel—but those companies accumulated power on behalf of themselves and their executives and their priorities—ordinary people, and the rest of the country, be damned. That's why they weren't permitted to survive. Wal-Mart does exactly the opposite: It accumulates power on behalf of us, the ordinary people. And it has been as steadfast, as reliable, in that mission as AT&T was, for instance, in delivering dial tone when you picked up the telephone. Of course AT&T wasn't permitted to survive either.

SAM WALTON DID not set out to create the largest company in history, nor was Wal-Mart born with power and impact. Wal-Mart #2, in Harrison, Arkansas, ninety miles east of Bentonville, originally opened in a shaggy strip mall, set up in such a way that if the Wal-

Mart idea didn't work out that well, the store itself could be chopped back, and the unneeded selling space walled off and subleased to some other store. That was in 1964, when #2 started out at about eight thousand square feet. It has moved twice in Harrison, and today #2 is a supercenter twenty times the size of the original.

As hard as it sometimes is for people outside Bentonville to believe, the stories of Sam Walton's modesty, unpretentiousness, and frugality are authentic. You can be modest, unpretentious, frugal—and also driven, tireless, and determined to drive a hard bargain. Those are the values that Sam Walton infused into his company—into his stores, his managers, his staff, his way of doing business every day. And if you look at Wal-Mart today—at the peak of its power—it still embodies those values: modesty, unpretentiousness, frugality, drive, energy, determination to drive a hard bargain.

It is part of what is so confounding about Wal-Mart—how bad could a place be if the vice presidents furnish their headquarters offices with cast-off lawn chairs?

Those values are the source of Wal-Mart's success. It is no accident that the largest company in history grew up in rural Arkansas, far from the distractions, the noise, the competing priorities and muddled values of the big cities. It's easy to make fun of little ol' Bentonville, but only if you've never been there.

But Wal-Mart has outgrown Bentonville. Not physically, but psychologically, politically, sociologically. Just as Wal-Mart has outgrown the rules that have governed business for the last fifty years, so has it outgrown the values that governed its own incredible growth in the last forty years, the values that powered that growth. And just as we have not been able to take a step back and understand that Wal-Mart is fundamentally different from any corporation that has come before, so Wal-Mart itself does not see itself clearly.

The source of almost all of Wal-Mart's troubles can be traced not to some evil conspiracy spun out of the home office, but to the slogan printed right on every Wal-Mart bag: "Always low prices. _Always_." The second _always_ is in italics and underlined, just so there's no confusion about the mission.

Does Wal-Mart pay modestly? Absolutely. They do so on behalf of us—their customers—to enable Wal-Mart to deliver always low prices. Remember that all of Wal-Mart's profit wouldn't get its workers to $12 an hour—still less than $500 a week. So Wal-Mart could pay better—it could offer better health insurance—but it would have to raise prices. And that violates the fundamental mission of the company.

Does Wal-Mart squeeze its suppliers to deliver merchandise at the lowest possible price? Does Wal-Mart hold the trump card of substituting lower-cost imported goods if a supplier is too finicky to do what's necessary to get the costs down? Absolutely. That's the very reason for Wal-Mart's existence—and it's hardly a secret. If a supplier can't cope, sell elsewhere. Not a problem.

Does Wal-Mart extract concessions from local governments for roads and property taxes and zoning as it builds stores? Absolutely. Anything less would be a waste of money—a waste of customers' money.

Does Wal-Mart come into a town and compete hard for business against the local hardware store, and the local clothing shop, and also against the big chain grocery stores and other national discounters? Absolutely. It is common for local merchants to complain that they can literally buy their own stock more cheaply at Wal-Mart—at retail—than their wholesale suppliers sell it to them. But here's the thing: No matter how the competitive landscape evolves, Wal-Mart never looks around and decides to raise prices. Whether the local merchants, or Wal-Mart's big-box colleagues, find a way to compete in a particular town, or go out of business, Wal-Mart does not exploit its customers in victory. Wal-Mart is brutally competitive, but it is not technically predatory. It's not "low prices until the competitors are strangled"—it's "*always* low prices." It is that very Olympian, almost austere, relentlessness that comes directly from Sam Walton that makes Wal-Mart so difficult to compete against. Wal-Mart never takes a breath. If you take a breath, you might have to raise prices.

The mission is so imperative that it now sometimes comes unmoored from ordinary restraints and causes people at Wal-Mart to do things that are appalling, unethical, even illegal. The motivation—always low prices—doesn't begin to excuse the behavior, or justify it. But it does explain it.

Did Wal-Mart lock its employees inside some stores overnight? Absolutely. Lightly supervised employees have a tendency to steal stuff, and theft ultimately costs customers money. Employees who are locked inside stores can't walk off with the merchandise.

Did some managers force store employees to punch out, and keep working? Absolutely. Store-level managers have a certain amount of autonomy, and a lot of responsibility. One of the most urgent responsibilities is to control their labor budget. Bonuses are tied to store performance, and store performance is really built on two big items: sales and staff costs. What better way to keep personnel costs under control than to insist that hourly associates haven't gotten their assigned jobs done in the allotted time, and then force them to finish that work off the clock.

Did Wal-Mart end up using hundreds of illegal immigrants to clean its stores overnight? Absolutely. Wal-Mart hired the least expensive cleaning contractors it could find—it turned out they were cheap for an unpleasant reason.

Even Wal-Mart's long-standing inability to have a calm, rational, constructive relationship with the press is directly related to "every day low prices." Wal-Mart's job is to build stores, find merchandise people need and want, and deliver it to shelves so they can buy it. Everything else is peripheral, irrelevant, perhaps even harmful. Talking to reporters is a waste of time—and anything that wastes staff time wastes money. The view inside Wal-Mart for most of the last forty-four years has been that the kinds of questions reporters ask, and the kinds of stories they write, do nothing to help Wal-Mart sell merchandise—and often sound as if they are going to do just the opposite: Make customers nervous, unhappy, "conflicted." If you have a PR staff of twenty, that's not just twenty wasted salaries; it's twenty people servicing an outside pressure group, the media, which does not in any way help Wal-Mart deliver always low prices.

And there has always been a suspicion inside Wal-Mart that even "nice" stories could be hurtful, even dangerous to Wal-Mart. Even the most apparently innocuous, rosy story—for instance, about how Wal-Mart masterminds the logistics of opening five supercenters a week—could teach competitors Wal-Mart's hard-won secrets. At its worst, the press is hostile to Wal-Mart's mission, vision, and values. At its best, the press is simply a spy system for people who want to best Wal-Mart.

It is remarkable that almost all of Wal-Mart's behavior—even the bad behavior or the seemingly diabolical behavior—can be explained by taking Wal-Mart at its word. It really is all about "always low prices." That's a testament to the shaping power of that one idea, which Wal-Mart has turned into an obsession, almost a corporate fetish. And it's testament to the consistency and discipline of Wal-Mart's culture.

Wal-Mart literally behaves in almost every way as if it were still Sam Walton's curious experiment to see what happens if you cut costs, and cut prices, to the bare margins of survival. Wal-Mart acts as if it is still a company with thirty stores, or three hundred, instead of three thousand.

Wal-Mart is not greedy, Wal-Mart is not spendthrift, Wal-Mart is not complicated, Wal-Mart is not disingenuous. Walk into the stores—walk into headquarters—what you see is what you get. That is what is so frustrating for Wal-Mart's "conflicted" customers, for Wal-Mart's opponents, even for Wal-Mart's leaders. How could a company so modest, so unpretentious, so frugal, a company so driven, so tireless, so determined to drive a hard bargain be bad?

Because as odd as it may at first seem, Wal-Mart has literally outgrown those values. Scale matters—we know that intuitively—but it can sometimes be hard to remember that when size changes gradually.

The behavior of a boy that is charming, or at least harmless, when he is four years old is inappropriate when the boy is fourteen. When the boy grows to the size and power of a twenty-four-year-old NFL linebacker, the four-year-old behavior would be worse than inappropriate, it would be dangerous, perhaps even hostile.

It is one thing to have a few hundred stores clustered in the middle of the country, for which you furiously buy stuff as cheaply as possible, always on watch for someone willing to make you a deal. It is quite another to have so much buying power that instead of simply scrounging for good deals, or for willing suppliers, you can literally reach into the factories of your suppliers and determine how they operate—or even where they operate. The reason the evolution is so confusing is that the fundamental operating principle—the determination to deliver stuff cheap—doesn't change. It's even possible to grant that the motivation of Wal-Mart's buyers doesn't change. And the results on the shelf don't appear to change.

What changes is the scale. What changes is the intangible—the power, the impact that comes with scale.

When the four-year-old boy somewhat unexpectedly jumps on your back for a piggyback ride, well, after the momentary surprise, that's kind of charming. When the twenty-four-year-old NFL linebacker jumps somewhat unexpectedly on your back, that's crushing.

TERRY ENGLISH, the district manager for Wal-Mart who worked for the company for thirty-two of his forty-nine years before retiring in 2004, offers a perfect example of how scale changes everything, from right inside the everyday experience of Wal-Mart's associates and managers.

In the late 1970s and early 1980s, when there were still just a few hundred stores, a typical Wal-Mart might have been open from 9:00 A.M. to 6:00 P.M., six days a week, and had fifty or seventy-five employees. If you caught the shift right, on a typical Thursday in early afternoon, almost everyone who worked for the store would be at work. "When Mr. Walton was around," says English, "he could come to the store and have a meeting with literally all the associates at that store." And a store manager would certainly know not just the faces and names of all the associates—the manager worked with those employees every day, the manager would know them personally.

Today, English points out, many of Wal-Mart's stores are open twenty-four hours a day, seven days a week. A supercenter might have eight hundred employees; it will have staff working literally dozens of different shifts during the week. "You might have two or three or four meetings with associates over the course of the day," says English, "but it's a difficult thing to connect with all the associates. You've got freight hitting the floor, you've got people working overnight." Even a diligent manager would be unlikely to recognize all eight hundred associates—let alone know their names and their personalities.

"When you run a fifty-thousand-square-foot store, you are a working manager out on the floor all the time," says English. "When you run a two-hundred-thousand-square-foot supercenter, you manage managers."

As there was in 1966, so in 2006 there is one person who is the manager of Wal-Mart #2 in Harrison. The job is the same, and completely different. It's all a matter of scale.

There has been a dramatic increase in public criticism, and public wariness, of Wal-Mart in the last five years. Local fights over specific Wal-Mart locations—the sites of stores, their size, the zoning—often have Wal-Mart opponents who are as well prepared as Wal-Mart's local attorneys, opponents who have tapped into years of experience from activists in other communities. Nationally, a coalition of fifty groups, backed with millions of dollars in funding from labor unions and environmental groups, has created a Washington-based group called Wal-Mart Watch, whose purpose is to call Wal-Mart's business practices into question, and to try to hold the company accountable for the impact it has on the global economy—an impact Wal-Mart often insists it does not have, or has no control over. Wal-Mart Watch's seriousness, as well as its pedigree, is clear from the people on the board of directors of its parent organization, who include the executive director of the Sierra Club, the president of Common Cause, and the president of the Service Employees International Union. Wal-Mart's Watch's executive director is the former head of the Democratic Senatorial Campaign Committee.

Wal-Mart has acknowledged the rising level of criticism by launching a public relations campaign of its own. Critical stories in even small newspapers are often answered by letters to the editor from Wal-Mart officials; the company has an aggressive image advertising campaign featuring employees talking about how good a place Wal-Mart has been to build a career, and support a family; Wal-Mart CEO Lee Scott does many more media interviews than any previous Wal-Mart chief—he has probably done more than all previous Wal-Mart CEOs combined. When Wal-Mart proved far more effective at delivering supplies to victims of Hurricane Katrina than the federal government—Wal-Mart's business, of course, is delivering supplies better than anyone in the world—the company went out of its way to accommodate reporters trying to tell that story. Wal-Mart launched a Web site called walmartfacts.com, which is rich in a cascade of numbers, if not context.

Scott himself insistently touts two "facts" that give a sense of the degree to which the company is either being deliberately misleading, or is utterly out of touch with everyday life in America. Scott routinely points out in speeches, in TV interviews, even in the wave of one hundred full-page newspaper ads the company took out on a single day in January 2005, that 74 percent of Wal-Mart associates are full-time employees, in contrast to so much of the rest of the retail industry. He links this with positive pride to the insistence that Wal-Mart's wages for its hourly employees are anything but low, that they are "around $10 an hour, nearly double the federal minimum wage."

Wal-Mart, however, defines "full-time" as any employee who works at least thirty-four hours a week. And even with an hourly wage of $10, someone stocking shelves forty hours a week at the supercenter across Sam Walton Boulevard from headquarters in Bentonville is, after taxes, taking home $1,280 a month. That's without having any money deducted for health insurance. Even in Bentonville, $1,280 a month is austere living. (And, of course, if Wal-Mart's "average" hourly wage is "around" $10 an hour, that means that hundreds of thousands of Wal-Mart workers don't even take home $1,280 a month.)

Lee Scott is right about one point he makes again and again, however: Wal-Mart's opponents give the company no credit for the good it does for America, and the rest of the world.

The vigorous debate between Wal-Mart's critics and its defenders is significant but not because of the deeper understanding it leads to of Wal-Mart's impact, beneficial or bad. Indeed, if you listen closely to the debate, you end up thoroughly confused, or infuriated. You could easily write a book about the ways in which Wal-Mart is good, and a book about the ways in which Wal-Mart is bad. It's the wrong question. It's like asking if the car is good for America.

We love Wal-Mart, as surely as we love the car. During the last two years, as the debate about Wal-Mart has become louder and more urgent, the company's business has grown by the size of Target, including all of Target's own growth during that time. The question of whether Wal-Mart is good or bad for America is the wrong question because, like the car, Wal-Mart isn't going anywhere.

We need to change how we think about Wal-Mart—and not just Wal-Mart but, by extension, a whole class of megacorporations of which Wal-Mart is just the most extreme, vivid example. The easiest response to the Wal-Mart critics comes from people who shrug and say that the United States economy is capitalistic and market based. Wal-Mart is large and ubiquitous—and powerful—because it does what it does so well. Wal-Mart is winning for no other reason than personal choice: Customers vote for Wal-Mart with their wallets; suppliers vote for Wal-Mart with their products. Any consumer, any businessperson who doesn't care for the way Wal-Mart does business is free to buy and sell products somewhere else.

The problem is, that's not true anymore. The CEO of an instantly recognizable consumer products company whose products are sold at Wal-Mart, in the course of a forty-five-minute conversation in which he explained why there was no possible way he could talk about his relationship with Wal-Mart, said, "They have killed free-market capitalism in America."

In many categories of products it sells, Wal-Mart is now the number-one seller of those products in the nation, including some surprising categories like pet food and supplies, home furnishings, and routine apparel. In many categories, Wal-Mart alone is now 20 percent or more of an entire market. Wal-Mart sells 21 percent of the toys

bought in the United States, 23 percent of the health and beauty products, and 27 percent of the housewares. In Texas, Wal-Mart's share of
the grocery market is 14 percent in Austin, 25 percent in Dallas, and
30 percent in Fort Worth.

That kind of dominance at both ends of the spectrum—
dominance across a huge range of merchandise and dominance of ge-
ographic consumer markets—means that market capitalism is being
strangled with the kind of slow inexorability of a boa constrictor. It's
not free-market capitalism—Wal-Mart is running the market. Choice
is an illusion. Wal-Mart's suppliers can't consider themselves serious
players—in dog food or deodorant, in turkeys or toothpaste—unless
they are doing business with Wal-Mart. Once they are doing business
with Wal-Mart, though, they are doing business on Wal-Mart's terms
because Wal-Mart already dominates whatever business they're in.

This is true even among Wal-Mart's megacorporation partners.
The newly merged Procter & Gamble and Gillette has sales in excess
of $68 billion a year—not only bigger by far than any other consumer
products company, but bigger than all but sixteen public companies of
any kind in the United States. The new P&G will be number seventeen, or thereabouts, on the Fortune 500 list in 2006. But remember:
Wal-Mart isn't just P&G's number-one customer; Wal-Mart is as big
as P&G's next nine customers *combined*. Cheerful discussions of partnerships notwithstanding, Wal-Mart owns P&G's business. P&G and
Wal-Mart may in fact have a constructive partnership—but it's a partnership built out of a healthy respect for the fact that P&G needs to
keep Wal-Mart happy. If the relationship should go sour, it would be
too bad for Wal-Mart. It would be devastating for P&G.

That's why businesspeople are scared of Wal-Mart. They should
be. And if a corporation with the scale, vigor, and independence of
P&G must bend to Wal-Mart's will, it's easy to imagine the kind of influence Wal-Mart wields over the operators of small factories in de-

veloping nations, factories that just want work and have no leverage with Wal-Mart or Wal-Mart's vendors.

It can be hard to absorb exactly what kind of advantage scale now gives Wal-Mart, and what kind of reach and speed and opportunity for dominance. Wal-Mart didn't have a single store outside the United States before November 1991. It had only two—in Mexico—when Sam Walton died in April 1992.

Wal-Mart is now the largest corporate employer in Mexico. From doing no business at all in Mexico fifteen years ago, Wal-Mart is now the nation's largest retailer and the largest grocer in the country— bigger than its next three competitors combined. Wal-Mart is the largest retailer in Canada. Wal-Mart is the second largest grocer in England.

The fear of Wal-Mart among businesspeople, and the deference to Wal-Mart, is dramatically magnified by Wal-Mart's way of doing business. Wal-Mart isn't greedy for profit; Wal-Mart isn't, strictly speaking, greedy for power. Wal-Mart is greedy for control. Wal-Mart has created the most elaborate, sophisticated ecosystem in the history of business. The ecosystem isn't a metaphor; it is a real place in the global economy where the very metabolism of business is set by Wal-Mart. The fear of Wal-Mart isn't just the fear of losing a big account. It's the fear that the more business you do with Wal-Mart, the deeper you end up inside the Wal-Mart ecosystem, and the less you are actually running your own business.

Wal-Mart's leadership virtually never acknowledges this control, but the company clearly understands it, and even takes a sly pride in it. Wal-Mart has mastered market capitalism brilliantly. Its obsessive focus on price, its unrelenting discipline of itself and its suppliers, has powered its growth. Now Wal-Mart's scale allows it to constantly and quickly extend the area it controls deeper into the factories and offices and decisions of the chain of companies that feed it, across new lines of business, and across wider and wider geographies. That is the Wal-Mart effect writ large: The expansion of the terrain in which business must follow Wal-Mart's rules allows Wal-Mart to continue to grow. The growth feeds the ecosystem, and the ecosystem powers the growth.

And that is the sense in which Wal-Mart is out of control. It is actually in complete control—of itself, its surroundings, its suppliers, the very business climate in which it operates every day. As a new kind of megacorporation of a scale of economic power we haven't encountered before, Wal-Mart is out of the control of something much more important than wage-and-hour or child-labor laws. Wal-Mart is increasingly beyond the control of the market forces that capitalism relies on to enforce fair play. Wal-Mart isn't subject to the market forces because it is creating them.

I N APRIL 2005, the *Philadelphia Inquirer* wrote a profile of a beloved local company, Tasty Baking, whose signature Tastykake products are a regional delicacy, dating from 1914. The story was about Tasty Baking's turnaround effort. The company has had flat revenue for five years, $159 million in each of the last two. The story included this sentence about the overall snack-cake business in the U.S.: "U.S. consumers spent $850 million on snack cakes during the 52 weeks ended March 20 [2005], the same as the previous year, according to Information Resources Inc., a Chicago company that collects check-out scanner data."

For those unfamiliar with the many nooks of the U.S. economy, it's a remarkable little snack cake of a data: Who knew that someone actually separated and collated all that grocery-store checkout data, right down to the individual snack-cake category? Who knew we were eating $2.3 million worth of snack cakes a day? And could it be a good thing—for our waistlines, if not for Tasty Baking—that our consumption of snack cakes isn't increasing?

The sentence also suggests that Tasty Baking has an interesting challenge because according to the figures, it's already almost 20 percent of the stagnant U.S. snack-cake market.

But here's the problem: The sentence is completely wrong. In the fifty-two weeks from March 20, 2004, to March 20, 2005, U.S. consumers spent $850 million on snack cakes—except for snack cakes Americans bought at Wal-Mart. The $850 million number doesn't include a dollar of snack-cake sales at Wal-Mart. Because Wal-Mart doesn't contribute its sales data to the big pools of information collected by the national consumer sales data clearinghouses anymore. It stopped in July 2001; now it keeps all its category sales data to itself, secret.

Even in this quirky corner of the U.S. economy, the world of snack cakes, Wal-Mart's secrecy is hardly trivial. Wal-Mart is roughly 15 percent of total U.S. grocery spending. If Wal-Mart also sells 15 percent of the nation's snack cakes, then U.S. consumers bought $1 billion in snack cakes that year, and Wal-Mart sold $150 million worth.

Market research firms, including IRI, use labor-intensive techniques involving analyzing the actual purchases of a sample of Wal-Mart shoppers to try to fill the data gap. Another firm, ACNielsen, concluded that in roughly the same time period, Wal-Mart alone sold $2.4 billion worth of something called simply snacks. Wal-Mart also sold $2.5 billion worth of bread and baked goods.

Whichever category snack cakes fall into, it's quite possible Wal-Mart is selling a whole lot of them. Wal-Mart could easily be selling $200 million, or $300 million, or $400 million worth of snack cakes a year. And snack-cake sales are quite likely rising at Wal-Mart—Nielsen says sales of snacks at Wal-Mart grew 12 percent, and sales of bread and baked goods grew 23 percent over the previous year.

So it's not just that the number itself—$850 million in sales of snack cakes to U.S. consumers—is wrong, the interpretation of the number is wrong. Wal-Mart is so big in snacks that snack-cake sales could actually be rising nationwide, even rising dramatically, with all of the increase coming from Wal-Mart. Indeed, with Wal-Mart's grocery business growing, it's quite likely that the $850 million number is stagnant, not because we're slowing our snack-cake consumption but for a completely different, equally important reason: Wal-Mart is taking business away from traditional grocery and convenience stores where we used to buy our snack cakes.

Since Wal-Mart's withdrawal from the data-pooling arrangements, trade publications for industries from candy making to beauty care routinely produce lists of products and product categories, with annual sales, and the change in sales, along with an asterisk or a parenthetical "excluding Wal-Mart." It's like constantly and authoritatively reporting about the state of the global economy, with an asterisk that says "excluding the U.S."

It's a small example of a much bigger problem: Wal-Mart doesn't just change the way business gets done, Wal-Mart doesn't just change the way the economy behaves, and the way we behave, Wal-Mart changes the way we understand the world. And unlike many areas in which Wal-Mart has an impact—factory operations, just-in-time delivery—where it is easy to see how the Wal-Mart effect is beneficial, Wal-Mart's passionate secrecy distorts reality. A university professor trying to answer the most basic questions about Wal-Mart's impact couldn't even get something as innocuous as a list of stores and store-opening dates from Wal-Mart. Indeed, it's almost impossible to understand the U.S. economy and the U.S. workplace with precision because of Wal-Mart's lack of transparency.

Of course, in the arena of information, as in so many other arenas, Wal-Mart does nothing technically wrong. It is a publicly traded corporation, and it complies with the routine rules from the federal government for reporting its basic financial performance. Wal-Mart has made a ritual of announcing its gross monthly sales data, and financial news channels like CNBC often pore through the data trying to discern the mood of American consumers and the future of the economy. And Wal-Mart isn't under any obligation to participate in academic studies, or in consumer sales data-pooling arrangements (the company withdrew, it said at the time, to protect information it considered a competitive advantage).

What Wal-Mart's size, power, and secrecy make clear is how antiquated, and how trivial, is the quantity of information we require from public companies. The problem has crept up on us as the size and dominance of corporations has crept up.

Wal-Mart is now so big that it's possible to ask a whole set of questions that would have been irrelevant, if not downright silly, twenty years ago.

What is the impact of Wal-Mart's wages not on its own workers, but on the wages in an entire town, or in an entire industry?

What is Wal-Mart's impact on the variety and availability of consumer goods?

What is Wal-Mart's direct impact on sending U.S. manufacturing jobs overseas?

What is the impact on local economies of Wal-Mart's abandoning old stores, and even as Wal-Mart freely announces precise numbers for stores it opens, how many stores does it close but leave empty?

What is Wal-Mart's impact on the environment?

What is the impact of Wal-Mart's suppliers on the environment?

These are important questions—they are important precisely because of Wal-Mart's scale—and the answers would be complicated and hugely revealing. The answers would also be contentious and controversial. But as a country, we have the right to ask the questions;

we have the power to ask the questions; indeed, we have the responsibility to ask the questions.

But we aren't even close to answers to even these most basic questions about Wal-Mart because Wal-Mart's secrecy snuffs out most serious academic and economic inquiry, and because the rules about what information should be public have so seriously lagged the sophistication of the corporations themselves.

Consider the example of Wal-Mart and health insurance. Even meaningful information is difficult to get. Wal-Mart, for instance, touts that it makes health insurance available to both full-time and part-time employees, and insists that premiums are affordable. But Wal-Mart does not say that part-time employees—those working fewer than thirty-four hours a week—must work for two years before becoming eligible to buy insurance, or that even after two years, part-time employees cannot buy insurance for their families, only for themselves. Wal-Mart's insurance may or may not be "affordable," but until 2005 it did not even cover some basic things, like the cost of vaccinations for routine childhood diseases.

Even as Wal-Mart had begun using its health insurance benefits as a public image tool, highlighted in the company's newspaper ads, its TV spots, and Lee Scott's speeches, a series of embarrassing stories showed that tens of thousands of Wal-Mart employees, or their family members, actually get their health insurance from Medicaid, or from state government insurance programs for the poor.

Perhaps the most dramatic was the revelation that in Georgia, 10,261 children enrolled in the state's insurance program for poor children had a parent who worked at Wal-Mart. The employer with the next highest number of children was also a retailer, Publix Super Markets—734 children in the Georgia program had a parent who worked at Publix. Even accounting for Wal-Mart's scale, the figure was stunning. Wal-Mart had one child in Georgia's kids' insurance program for every four Wal-Mart employees in Georgia. Publix had one child in the program for every twenty-two employees in the state. In Tennessee, 9,617 Wal-Mart employees were on the state's health insurance program for low-income people.

Wal-Mart has seemed at a particular loss on how to handle the health insurance question. In a presentation to reporters in Bentonville in April 2005, CEO Lee Scott, in answer to a question, said, "There are government assistance programs out there that are so lucrative, it's hard to be competitive, and it's expensive to be competitive." That would be the CEO of the most powerful company in history arguing that his company's insurance program can't compete with the insurance offered poor people by the state of Tennessee.

OUR ABILITY TO see a problem, to understand it, then to figure out how to manage it and how to live with it necessarily lags behind the problem itself. When factories proved to be infernal, dangerous places to work, we put in place rules about hours and safety. When the developers of cities proved unable to organize their efforts reasonably, we put in place rules about zoning. When it turned out that the airline business—precisely because of competition—couldn't be trusted to create safer flying all the time, we imposed an actual technocracy that regulates everything about the safety of civilian jetliners, from minimum maintenance schedules, to onboard staffing, to the materials used in seat upholstery. When the carmakers proved unwilling to make cars more efficient, we imposed fuel efficiency standards.

Initial protests notwithstanding, most efforts like this end up being beneficial not just for the people with immediate problems, but for the people on whom the rules are imposed. Safer factories are hugely more efficient and less costly. Zoning quickly made property of all kinds more valuable. The airline business today suffers from all kinds of problems, but it rightly brags about its safety, which has been critical to enabling the industry to continue to flourish. The most dangerous part of the plane trip, as we all hear routinely, is the ride to the airport in the car. In a world with $60 a barrel oil, we all benefit from even the modest fuel economy standards imposed by Congress—the car manufacturers most of all.

In that sense, Wal-Mart is a problem, but it's also an opportunity.

The five biggest public companies in the United States—with sales of $1.1 trillion—account for 9 percent of the economy. The top twenty companies account for 20 percent of the economy. Those numbers are arresting, and they are moving in the direction of increased concentration. Ten years ago, in 1994, and twenty years ago, you had to add up the sales of the top thirty Fortune 500 companies before they accounted for 20 percent of the economy. Over a longer horizon, the trend is toward dramatically more power in fewer hands. Fifty years ago, the top five public companies in the United States accounted for 6 percent of the economy—today it is 50 percent higher. Fifty years ago, in 1954, not even the total sales of the top sixty companies in the country equaled 20 percent of the economy. We don't often talk about the concentration of corporate power, but it is almost unfathomable that the men and women who run just twenty companies make decisions every day that steer one fifth of the U.S. economy. (The United States has seventy-five hundred publicly traded companies and more than five million companies of all kinds.)

Wal-Mart makes the lack of accountability, of control, even of information, vivid. But Wal-Mart is just a symbol of the era of the modern megacorporation, and we have been living in that era for perhaps fifty years. We don't properly understand the impact of a whole tier of companies—ExxonMobil, GM, GE, Verizon, IBM, P&G, Southwest Airlines—whose operations are so large, and so dominant in certain industries or certain geographies, that like Wal-Mart they stand astride the market forces we rely on to harness them.

The information gap about megacorporations is often stunning, and we've become oddly acclimated to it. Wal-Mart is the largest corporate employer in the United States, with 1.2 million U.S. employees. Wal-Mart, as it happens, is also the largest corporate employer in two dozen of the fifty states. That doesn't necessarily follow: There could be a variety of number-one and number-two employers across the country, different from state to state, and Wal-Mart, coming in, say, as number three in almost every state, could still be the largest in the nation. But as it happens, in at least sixteen states, and likely twenty-four, Wal-Mart is the number-one employer. How many states Wal-Mart is number one in is all but impossible to determine.

In literally weeks of research, it has been impossible to figure out because states, at the behest of corporations, won't tell you. Wal-Mart, to its credit (and as a way of showing how much it gives back to communities through jobs), posts figures on its walmartfacts.com Web site showing the total number of employees in every state, updated every three months. In a few states, government officials happily supply a list of the largest employers, public and private. In at least another fifteen, government officials say that the list of the largest employers cannot be released because it is not public information. In what sense, exactly, are the names of the largest companies in a state, and the number of people they employ, not "public"? What could possibly be a more fundamental place to start understanding impact than a simple measure of size?

It's time to do two things: To acknowledge in public policy terms that there is a difference between a $10 million corporation, a $100 million corporation, and a $100 billion corporation. We need to acknowledge that scale matters. And we need to start a fresh process of understanding by insisting on a level of information from megacorporations that they will vigorously resist providing. As with other shifts in corporate accountability, we can be absolutely confident that as soon as the new era of megacorporation transparency is in place, not only will we benefit, but the companies themselves will benefit. Indeed, in an era when companies relentlessly gather and analyze data about us—all for our own benefit, of course, and Wal-Mart no less than others—it is far past time for those companies to provide far more data to us about themselves.

From what kinds of companies would we demand more information, and what level of information? That's a public policy question, an urgent one that is not even on anyone's agenda. The simple, perhaps simplistic, answer is that a megacorporation is one that is so large—either in terms of sales, or dominance of a certain market, or a certain market within a defined geography, or in terms of employment—that it has the power to reshape that market. The full answer to which companies should provide more information, and what they should provide, requires careful study, analysis, and public debate. What is clear is that companies should not be allowed to decide what information they should release—any more than they should be allowed to determine the safety regulations of their factories, or the pollution rules under which their cars operate. To see that, one need look no further than the stunning collapse and fraud around Enron and WorldCom—publicly traded companies whose public release of information wasn't quite detailed enough to show that they were essentially criminal enterprises.

Resistance from companies will be fierce, not simply because the corporate reflex has always been for a protective secrecy. Companies will fear, rightly, that once fresh cascades of information come out about their impact, there will be a movement to hold them accountable for those impacts—either from public pressure, or from regulation.

Minnesota legislators in 2005, curious about whether the employees and family members of Wal-Mart and other large employers use the state's public assistance programs, discovered that Minnesota state agencies don't gather that data. A bill introduced that would create such a list was vigorously, even angrily, opposed by Wal-Mart, which sent two officials to St. Paul to lobby against it, and sent each legislator a two-page letter outlining its opposition to the law. The letter said the new Minnesota law—similar to laws being drafted now in dozens of states—wouldn't "provide health insurance to anyone," and was simply "a misguided, destructive assault on a business trying to create 100,000 new jobs this year."

A Minnesota state representative supporting the law, Sheldon Johnson, said, "If it's true what people say, that big multinational companies are outsourcing health care to taxpayers, then it would be good to have a handle on which ones. It's just information."

It's just information. The scale of the resistance from companies to revealing more about the size and impact of their operations can be gauged from this one example: The Minnesota law Wal-Mart has worked hard against wouldn't create the slightest burden of any kind on Wal-Mart, or on any Wal-Mart staff in Bentonville. It would only create work for Minnesota's state government workers and, perhaps ultimately, for Wal-Mart's public relations staff.

In his letter to Americans, printed in one hundred newspapers in January 2005, Wal-Mart CEO Lee Scott wrote, "Everyone is entitled to their own opinions about our company, but they are not entitled to make up their own facts." Of course, it is the ultimate irony to be scolded for "making up facts" by a company that has made secrecy an integral part of its corporate culture. At a speech to a Los Angeles business group a month after the open letter, Scott said, "The question of how to assure that American capitalism creates a decent society is one that will engage all of us in the era ahead. To argue, as our critics do, that this quest is somehow served by denying Americans the higher living standards that Wal-Mart's business efficiencies can bring is to make a mockery of American ideals under the guise of pursuing them."

Of course, by extension, to argue that the question of how to assure that American capitalism creates a decent society can be debated and answered in the absence of information and understanding of Wal-Mart's impact is also to make a mockery of American ideals, and of the very principles on which both a market economy, and a democracy, are built.

Wal-Mart is a creation of us and our money. The Wal-Mart effect derives all its vast power from us and our spending. At one level, Wal-Mart is the ultimate form of democracy—we vote yes each time we buy something, and the vote is recorded in the vast database that Wal-Mart is constantly poring over to better understand what will make us buy more. But we vote yes with imperfect information—without the ability to understand what we are voting for when we vote for low prices.

Earlier in the same speech in Los Angeles, Scott said, "Our critics seem to have a broader and, I believe, more troubling aim: to warp the vital debate the country needs in the years ahead about the proper role of business and government in assuring that capitalism creates a decent society."

The most certain way to avoid a warped debate, of course, is to have at hand for everyone a wealth of data, of information, of analysis. Markets, market economies, democracies, even individual industries like the world of snack cakes all require information to work, and they work better and better—for everyone—the more information they have.

Wal-Mart is not just a store, or a company, or a powerful institution. It is also a mirror. Wal-Mart is quintessentially American. It mirrors our own energy, our sense of destiny, our appetite for bigness and variety and innovation. And Wal-Mart is not just a reflection of American society and values. It is a mirror of us as individuals. In a democracy, our individual ambivalence about such a concentration of economic power, even when that power is ostensibly on our side, is a signal. Both as individuals and as a society we have an obligation to answer the unanswered questions about Wal-Mart. Otherwise we have surrendered control—of our communities, of our economy, of some measure of our destiny—to decisions made in Bentonville.

EPILOGUE
PEORIA, SEPTEMBER 2005

The Wal-Mart effect is like the wake of a huge ship passing along the horizon—by the time the waves rock you, the vessel that made them has almost steamed out of sight. It is rare indeed to catch the Wal-Mart effect as it is happening, to be able to see it play out in real time.

In the summer of 2005, the L. R. Nelson sprinkler company, which had made lawn sprinklers based in Peoria since 1911, laid off almost all its remaining factory workers, bringing its U.S. hourly employment down to about 120, from 450 in 1998, with seasonal spikes that went as high as 1,000 to get sprinklers made in busy times.

Whether the name Nelson is familiar or not, the sprinklers themselves are iconic. They are typically the same bright yellow as Caterpillar bulldozers, and they have a heritage of quality, often made of metal, so they could be revived spring after spring.

In announcing what amounted to the end of U.S. manufacturing operations, Nelson president Dave Eglinton spoke with almost unheard-of candor, blaming the layoffs and the relocation of jobs to China squarely on Wal-Mart. "Wal-Mart has said that they would love to buy from us because some of the production is done in the United States, but the cost differential is so great that they told us that unless we supply them out of China, we couldn't do business."

Wal-Mart effectively ordered Nelson to fire its American factory workers; to keep Wal-Mart's business, to survive, Nelson did.

The women who worked at Nelson—and it was mostly women—know exactly how the Wal-Mart effect happens, and exactly what the Wal-Mart effect feels like. They were close enough to the great ship that its wake swamped their lives.

Sally Stone, *now fifty-one, worked at Nelson for twenty years.*

Mary Fail, *while just thirty-seven years old when she was laid off, had worked at Nelson for nineteen years, more than half her life.*

Rose Dunbar, *sixty, worked at Nelson fifteen years.*

Terri Graham, *thirty-two, started at Nelson in 1997.*

Vickie Black, *at forty-one, also worked at Nelson for more than half her life—twenty-one years—and met her husband in the factory.*

The voices of these women offer a vivid firsthand account of the Wal-Mart effect.

MAKING SPRINKLERS

Sally Stone: They always acted like Wal-Mart was our hero. They would say, we love Wal-Mart. We do so much business with them.

Terri Graham: When I first started in 1997, we actually had three different start times—there were so many people working in the factory, parking was a mess, so they staggered start times, 6:00 A.M., 6:30, and 7:00. Then we had staggered quitting times too.

The area I was in was called Turbo, making the Turboheart oscillating sprinkler. The one piece on there, called a cam, is the shape of a heart. That's where that name came from. Turbo was my home.

We would make as many as five thousand sprinklers in an eight-hour shift on one side of the line. Running both sides of the line, we could produce ten thousand in a shift.

Wal-Mart was the biggest customer for those.

That first and second year, it was so busy they had orders for one hundred thousand or more a week for places like Wal-Mart. You had to get it done. It was a constant go go go. Sometimes working six and seven days a week.

Sally Stone: Back then, we made a lot better quality sprinkler, if I may say so myself. The oscillating sprinkler, for instance. We made it all out of metal. It had screws, you could take them out, and fix it. Or you could send it back to the factory and have them fix it. It wasn't plastic. They were like a $40 sprinkler.

I've still got one out in my shed. If something's wrong, I know how to take it apart and put it back together.

Terri Graham: One of the big things the company used to tell us was we are the last company in the United States making these sprinklers in the United States. That gave me a sense of pride.

I was raised on good old American values. You work hard, you're proud of the work you do, you make good quality stuff that lasts a long time.

Rose Dunbar: Eventually, I ended up on the Poppy line, that's the area I stayed with for many years. The Poppy line is the little lawn sprinklers, with three spikes that twirl, the little oscillators.

I loved the work. This was the best job I ever had. It was what I was meant to do. That's how I felt. I couldn't wait to get to work.

I consider myself a 100 percent worker—I work whether I'm happy, or mad, or sad—I worked 100 percent.

I had a ton of friends, I just loved to go there and get the work done.

GETTING WORRIED

Sally Stone: Eventually you could see where they were going to cheaper material. One sprinkler—the Poppy, it's called, like the flower. It has a base, it has three little spouts where water comes out. It spins and sprays at the same time. Originally, it had rubber wheels on it; you could hook it to a hose, and run it around from one spot to another. Then they went to plastic wheels. The plastic wheels were much cheaper than the rubber ones. They would change the screws, the end caps—it would all be cheaper.

Usually it just happened. If you would say something to your team leader—Hey, this is some cheap crap—they'd say, well, they've got to save money.

Terri Graham: The oscillators have a tube that sprays the water. Originally, we would get the tubes, we would work with them. The length was already cut—just a plain straight tube, like a pipe from a wind chime. We would have a couple different machines they would run on. One would punch the holes in a line the water sprays out of. One would bend that tube to the correct shape. One machine would put the jets into the spray tube.

A couple years ago, we quit bending them ourselves. They were bent over in China; they would come in already bent. Then the tubes started to come with the nozzles, the jets already in them. And the end plugs. They came from China.

They were so bad. They leaked terribly. The jets would fly out when you put water in them. I remember telling people, if we were making tubes like that, we'd be fired.

They did get better over time. The last couple years, they got a lot better. But this whole time our name was being damaged by this crap they are bringing in. It was sad to see. We used to make good quality stuff.

Rose Dunbar: Over the years the quality did change. A lot of metal went to plastic. The quality of plastic went down, the quality of the workers went down.

I was head of my line, I could control my workers to a point. It got so frustrating—if they weren't working, if they weren't doing quality work, no one would listen. No one would do anything about it.

In the last couple years, I couldn't focus on doing my quality work because no one cared. That is how I felt. I was butting my head against the wall.

I hated getting up and going to work.

I had more pride in their work than they did.

Sally Stone: They had a big layoff in 2002. We didn't know about the jobs going to China then. They just said they needed to cut the workforce, they were going to have to let some people go.

On a Friday, they gave you a piece of paper—either you were to go to the lunchroom or to the training room. The training room meant you were getting fired.

Those of us who were in the lunchroom, this guy, a sales manager or something, he got up and spoke. He said, We're sorry we have to let some people go. Business isn't that good this year. Because of the weather. They blamed it on the weather. They didn't blame it on China, or Wal-Mart.

Being we are a seasonal business, they always blame it on the weather. They kept us in the dark about this China thing.

And as the guy is talking, we see these people filing out of the other room, the people who had been let go. You would see someone walk by, you'd think, Oh, my God, I can't believe they fired so and so. As the people were walking out, some of them were giving this guy talking to us the finger.

Vickie Black: I thought those layoffs were a red flag. I thought, People, we need to start preparing. I thought, We're not going to be here in ten years, working in the factory.

I started taking classes then—I took biology, psychology, English, and speech. Whatever that would apply to an associate's degree.

Terri Graham: They had told us they had to go to China to compete, to get our costs down because of Wal-Mart. They said, All these other sprinklers are made in China.

They told us they only have to pay the Chinese workers $100 a month. That's less than half what one of us is earning in a week. They can hire ten of them for every one of us.

Sally Stone: One line where almost everybody got fired from—it was the Traveler line. The Traveler is a sprinkler that looks like a little tractor. It's great if you have a hilly backyard. It drives along, like a choo-choo train. That went to China. They were already making the parts for it in China and sending them here. They decided—I guess the parts were made by Chinese—they could just assemble it there.

We knew, at that point, a lot of stuff started going to China. The pistol nozzles—they would come in, we would spray paint 'em, then we would put together the trigger. Then they would come in already finished from China, all we did was throw it in a package—a blister package—or put it on the card.

We knew we used to make that.

Rose Dunbar: Until it started affecting my area, and my work, I kind of took it with a grain of salt. I didn't worry about China. There was kind of joking all over, everything's going to end up going to China. I didn't believe it.

How did we know things were going to China?

When the lines weren't there anymore. The Turboheart, the best seller that we sold to Wal-Mart all these years—those lines left. The machines are literally gone, the tables are gone, they moved the whole thing out. Four Turboheart lines, three are gone. One is still there; the reason they said they keep it, in case Wal-Mart needs it for immediate supply.

Terri Graham: At a meeting this year they said to us, The average person doesn't know what a Wal-Mart "Price Rollback" means. That doesn't mean Wal-Mart is lowering the price, that means Wal-Mart is coming to us and saying *you* will lower *your* price on this product.

The Wal-Mart price rollback—yes, we all knew just what that was from the Wal-Mart TV ads, with the smiley face bouncing around the store.

Mary Fail: I knew it was inevitable, sooner or later we were bound to lose our jobs. It's going to take the consumers to put their foot down, and say, we aren't going to buy any more of this garbage.

"This garbage"—I mean, there is no quality. I've seen parts from China come in that were broken already, that didn't work. Right out of the box. It didn't work when we took it out of the box to package it.

I personally will not buy anything that's made in China.

I even look at food, to see where it's from, see where it's made. The mandarin oranges—the little cans of mandarin oranges? Made in China.

Terri Graham: Earlier this year, they had a few Chinese people walking around the plant and videotaping us working.

That was horrible, horrendous. Right in our faces. They are taking our jobs. Not that we hate the Chinese. But a lot of people are upset with our government, and with their government.

Sally Stone: Nelson is sending some of the people over to China, like the team leaders, the maintenance men, they are going to China to train the people there and set up the machinery for them.

GETTING FIRED

Terri Graham: We found out June 3 that we were being laid off—
Friday, June 3. I worked on until July 22.

The week before my last week, they had taken some of the machines out of our area. It was like having a knife twisted in your
gut. You are watching your job leave.

Sally Stone: The day I lost my job, well, I was working 6:30 A.M. to 3:00
P.M. It was June 3, a Friday.

This time they didn't do it as a group layoff. They thought it
would be more kind to tell you individually. I talked to a supervisor. She said, Unfortunately, you are one of those let go—you can
work till the end of the season.

I said, No, I'm leaving today, I'm leaving now.

I said, I would not want to stick around and do anything for you.

I got five weeks' severance. I was making $11.15 an hour when
I got fired. I knew I could get on unemployment right away. They
were keeping people with less seniority than me. I was there a total of twenty years—they kept people with five years' experience.

Terri Graham: At the end, if I was working regular production, I was
making $10.55 an hour. If I was doing the testing, I was making
$12.05 an hour.

My husband is now working on the edge of town at a sawmill.
He started there in August. He's making less than what I was making at Nelson.

Rose Dunbar: I was not fired. I was lucky—I was there long enough to
get the $5,000 incentive bonus to quit.

I told the human relations person, I don't want to have a meeting, I don't want to know if I'm fired. I'll work until the end, then
I'll go. That's what I told her.

My last day was August 18. I went home and cried for a week. I was overwhelmed. I didn't know what to do.

I started at Nelson at $4.50 an hour. I left at $10.85 an hour fifteen years later—I accepted it, and I lived on it, and I made it do. It was more money than I ever made. I'm not going to see it again.

I'm sixty years old. I'm too young to retire. But I'm not desirable. I'm divorced, my daughter lives with me—she doesn't make much—and my two granddaughters.

But that next week, I got off my butt, and I applied to a couple jobs.

I got a job at a nursing home. I work in dietary, in the kitchen area. I do dishes and some food prep, working forty hours a week. I'm making $8.50 an hour.

I'm going to be okay.

Mary Fail: I've applied for everything from retail to manufacturing. I went in for interviews, I even had an interview with Wal-Mart.

They said no.

I put my application in to work there part time, and they said they want people who are available when they need them, more than part time. They said no.

Why did I apply to Wal-Mart?

Even if you get on part time, you still get discounts on groceries. That is one way I could help support my husband.

I wasn't uncomfortable applying there. It's just a job. I would have worked there if I could have got on.

Sally Stone: They said they would give us help to go back to school— if it's something they approve. I was kind of interested in horticulture and stuff like that. There are jobs around here, there are a lot of nurseries, places that sell flowers to nurseries, but they don't pay.

I would say I'm bitter to L. R. Nelson.

As for Wal-Mart, well, you feel like you are living in communist society. Pretty soon there will be nowhere to shop but Wal-Mart.

I don't shop there unless out of necessity. I feel like I'm a traitor if I shop there.

Rose Dunbar: Do I shop at Wal-Mart now? Not like I used to. Food-wise, I go to Aldi's. I try to go to Big Lots, I go to the Dollar Store. They've grown; they have milk in the dairy case now.

Wal-Mart made me angry. The main thing is, I don't really want to support them. They didn't support us. I don't want to support them anymore.

I don't really think Nelson's and Wal-Mart did everything they could to keep some of us working. That makes me mad.

Terri Graham: Do I shop at Wal-Mart? Unfortunately, sometimes I have to. They have things cheaper than other people. I can't afford to pay $2 more for something.

Until this year, I hadn't had cable in ten years. We hardly ever eat at McDonald's or anything like that. My biggest thing I spent on was movies, I'd usually buy 'em at Wal-Mart because they are cheaper there than anywhere else.

The average person doesn't understand the consequences of these low prices. I went to get a spatula at Wal-Mart. They had six or eight different spatulas. I looked at every one of them; there was only one made in the United States. It was $1 more. I bought it. I do what I can.

I have to go there. I hate it. I'm pinned in there.

Sally Stone: My husband is a farmer. He raises corn, soybeans, Black Angus cows. With his brother. That's not a get-rich-quick scheme, that's for sure.

When I was at Nelson, we had health insurance. I was paying $50 a week for my husband and me. It was an 80/20 deal.

We've got no health insurance right now.

Vickie Black: I worked for L. R. Nelson for twenty-one years. I was nineteen when I started there in 1984. My husband is still a manufacturing engineer at Nelson—we met at the factory. We're a Nelson marriage, we have Nelson children, we're Nelson everything. I don't have many bad memories of L. R. Nelson.

I don't think they could say no to Wal-Mart. If they had, Wal-Mart would have taken their business elsewhere, and that would have been it.

We could lose 110 people now. Or 250 in a year and a half. Maybe by losing 110 now—maybe those other people will still be there in ten years. That was a good chance to take.

This is the way the world works. That's exactly what I think. It is one huge vicious circle. Somebody else has to help do something about it. I don't think just the shoppers can change what's going on.

Terri Graham: I know I'm only a tiny part of the puzzle.

Rose Dunbar: I don't know where this cycle will end.

ACKNOWLEDGMENTS

Many people helped make this book possible.

Tim Calkins, not himself a journalist, had a wonderful and original idea for how to reach people who had worked with Wal-Mart, and he helped me execute it.

Robert O'Harrow, an old colleague from the *Washington Post,* called one day out of the blue in January 2004 and by the end of that thirty-minute phone call had set me on the path to writing this book.

Raphael Sagalyn got me the contract that allowed me to write the book. He has been more than one could hope for in an agent—a source of encouragement and of impeccable judgment about both words and people.

Emily Loose, my editor at The Penguin Press, has quite simply gotten from me a book that I never imagined I could have written. Contrary to the widespread rumor that books no longer get edited, she really did edit the book, before it was written and after, and I'm glad she did.

People in Bentonville and around the country—many quoted in the book—have been hugely generous in sharing their experiences in working with Wal-Mart, working for Wal-Mart, and in providing ways of thinking about Wal-Mart.

My siblings, Andrew, Betsy, and Matthew, provide a built-in cheering section whose enthusiasm never dims.

Bill Taylor and Alan Webber gave me a professional home when they founded *Fast Company* magazine, professional guidance, and incredible latitude during their years editing *Fast Company,* and their friendship since. John Byrne and Mark Vamos gave me the support and time to do the book. I wrote the magazine story "The Wal-Mart You Don't Know" that ultimately led to the book under their editing.

Others have provided indispensable support, which I appreciate and they understand: John Dornan, Myrtle Kearse, Julie Perkins, Keith Hammonds, Anndee Hochman, Zack McMillin, Ruth Sheehan.

G. D. Gearino proved that he still has a great editor within him, hiding behind the great writer, and the great friend.

Helen Sinnott spent six months working as my research assistant, tracking down information I asked for with energy, perseverence, and nary a raised eyebrow.

Lucas Conley fact-checked every sentence of every paragraph, and so provided the kind of security and dependability without which a book like this cannot succeed. The errors that remain are mine, but there are many fewer than there would have been without him.

Nicolas Jonathan and Maya Mercedes were never too busy to stop and provide a bit of comic relief or a freshly inspirational LEGO creation.

Two people, in particular, deserve special mention.

Geoff Calkins has been that rarest of people, a best friend for twenty-five years. He not only read and edited the book, he has patiently heard all of it read aloud, many parts more than once. Another high point, to be sure.

And finally, my wife Trish has never flagged in the months that this book dominated our lives. Her support, her enthusiasm, her love seem to be replenished afresh every morning. I was smart enough to marry the best editor I've ever had. She asked the first question, two years ago, that sparked all my subsequent questions about Wal-Mart. She adds music to both my work and to my life.

SOURCE NOTES

A Note on Sources

Most of the material in *The Wal-Mart Effect* comes from primary sources—from the people quoted or cited in the text. Unless otherwise noted, anyone quoted directly is someone I interviewed. The notes that follow are intended to provide further guidance and to credit the work of others that I have relied on.

The two best existing accounts of the creation, growth, and impact of Wal-Mart are Sam Walton's autobiography, *Sam Walton: Made in America,* written with the business journalist and now editor in chief of Time Inc., John Huey, and *In Sam We Trust,* Bob Ortega's compelling narrative of Wal-Mart's rise, and its consequences, first published in 1998.

I asked Wal-Mart several times to participate in the reporting of the book, at any level that the company was willing, from confirming details to providing the opportunity to interview current managers and executives and tour facilities. The company consistently declined.

Wal-Mart provides information about its financial performance, its store openings, and its employment and purchasing, state by state, at two Web sites: www.walmartstores.com and www.walmartfacts.com.

I have visited dozens of Wal-Mart stores in twenty-three states, sometimes as a shopper, sometimes as a reporter, always as an observer.

Chapter 1: *Who Knew Shopping Was So Important?*

The basic outlines of the story of the "unboxing" of antiperspirants comes from Michael Roth, who helped service Wal-Mart for fifteen years at Playtex, Revlon, and Warner Lambert. Roth was director of marketing for Revlon's antiperspirant business, starting in 1994, when the Revlon brands Mitchum and Almay were still sold with boxes; Wal-Mart made it clear it wanted the Revlon brands out of the box, although Roth was careful to say that "unboxing" wasn't an issue that dominated Revlon's relationship with Wal-Mart. Roth's experience was fleshed out by accounts from two people in the paperboard-packaging industry and two people in the antiperspirant business, all of whom still work either directly with Wal-Mart or with companies that supply Wal-Mart, and asked not to be identified, even though the unboxing started fifteen years ago. Wal-Mart was not the only retailer interested in getting rid of the box, and some antiperspirant makers were more eager to unbox their products—for their own cost savings and for environmental reasons—than others.

Supermarket News (www.supermarketnews.com) publishes an annual list of the seventy-five largest food retailers in the United States, and of the twenty-five largest grocery companies in the world. The figures for the number of bankruptcies in the U.S. grocery business are cited in a *Wall Street Journal* story, "Wal-Mart Tops Grocery List with Its Supercenter Format," May 27, 2003, by Patricia Callahan and Ann Zimmerman. Their story cites an analysis of U.S. grocery store bankruptcies by Burt Flickinger III, of Strategic Resource Group, a New York consulting firm. Flickinger updated the figures to reflect the Chapter 11 filings of Penn Traffic, operator of the Big Bear grocery stores, in 2003, and of Winn-Dixie Stores in 2005. Flickinger, who specializes in retail strategy, pointed out that years before Wal-Mart went into the grocery business, the Davis brothers, who ran Winn-Dixie, invited Sam Walton onto Winn-Dixie's board of directors. "He just went to school on Winn-Dixie," said Flickinger. "Winn-Dixie was a major motivation for Sam Walton to get into the grocery business." Walton was on the board from 1981 to 1986.

A major U.S. market research firm graciously did the analysis of the proximity of U.S. homes, and U.S. residents, to Wal-Mart stores. The firm specifically requested that it not be credited by name, out of fear of upsetting Wal-Mart. The raw numbers themselves are striking:

- Within five miles of a Wal-Mart: 155 million U.S. residents, 59 million households.
- Within fifteen miles of a Wal-Mart: 265 million U.S. residents, 99 million households.
- Within twenty-five miles of a Wal-Mart: 285 million U.S. residents, 107 million households.

The analysis was done when the total U.S. population was 293 million, with 110 million households.

Wal-Mart says that 100 million Americans shop at its stores each week, and 138 million people shop at its stores worldwide each week. John Fleming, Wal-Mart's chief marketing officer, told the *Wall Street Journal* that each year, in 93 percent of U.S. households, at least 1 person shops at Wal-Mart at least once, cited in "Wal-Mart Sets Out to Prove It's in Vogue," August 25, 2005, by Ann Zimmerman.

On its Web site walmartfacts.com, Wal-Mart reports not only the number of employees it has state by state in the United States, updated every three months, but it also reports the number of "supplier jobs" its purchasing of merchandise and services supports in that state for the previous year. The figure of 3 million supplier jobs is the total of each of the state figures that Wal-Mart reports.

The one hundred daily media mentions figure is based on Nexis search results for news stories that cite Wal-Mart (or Walmart) at least twice, in 2005.

Music Trades magazine ("published continuously since 1890") is at www.musictrades.com. The longer story on Wal-Mart and other mass merchants selling musical instruments appeared in the October 2004 issue, headlined "Are Mass Merchants Cause for Concern?"

Robert Spector's 2005 book, *Category Killers* (Harvard Business School Press), includes an account of the birth of Toys "R" Us. The bankruptcy of Winn-Dixie and the merger of P&G and Gillette received widespread coverage in the media. The P&G and Gillette merger was completed on October 1, 2005.

The fact that Wal-Mart keeps track of the number of scans each checkout clerk does comes from Terry English, a thirty-two-year-veteran of Wal-Mart, who spent more than half his career based in McAlester, Oklahoma, as a regional manager of ten stores.

Details of the potentially historic sex discrimination class-action lawsuit against Wal-Mart are available at www.walmartclass.com.

Wal-Mart's www.walmartfacts.com Web site reports the number of items stocked in a typical store.

Chapter 2: *Sam Walton's Ten-Pound Bass*

The easiest way to compare the costs among retailers is the line in their financial statements identified as "selling, general and administrative" costs, known as SG&A. Those are the costs for running the company, not including the wholesale cost of the actual merchandise sold. The revealing figure is not the SG&A costs, but the ratio of SG&A costs to total sales. In the last three years, Wal-Mart's SG&A expenses as a percent of sales have averaged 17.5. Target's

SG&A expenses in the last three years have averaged 20.6 percent. It costs Target $20.60 to sell $100.00 worth of merchandise. It costs Wal-Mart $17.50 to sell the same merchandise. That allows Wal-Mart to charge $3.10 less for exactly the same $100.00 worth of merchandise.

Wal-Mart's www.walmartfacts.com Web site says that in the fall of 2005 there were "more than 40" lawsuits against the company alleging wage and hour violations around the country.

The *New York Times* story "Workers Assail Night Lock-ins by Wal-Mart," by Steven Greenhouse, was published January 18, 2004. In the story, Wal-Mart spokeswoman Mona Williams acknowledged the lock-ins and said they were for employee safety: "Doors are locked to protect associates and the store from intruders." Wal-Mart apparently changed its policy as the story was being reported by Greenhouse to guarantee that in every store where employees were locked in, a manager with a key was always present to let them out, if necessary. The story quoted former store managers saying the main purpose of the lock-ins was to reduce employee theft from the stores, not to ensure their security.

The *New York Times* story "Kmart Closing the Sears Gap" was published February 4, 1986.

Larry English says that all eight children in his family, and his mother, have worked for Wal-Mart at some point. Here is his accounting: His sister Carol worked at the Harrison, Arkansas, Wal-Mart (#2) in high school, and as an invoice clerk as an adult; his sister Reba worked for Wal-Mart in high school; his sister Connie worked for Wal-Mart in high school; his brother Terry worked for Wal-Mart for thirty-two years, retiring as a district manager based in McAlester, Oklahoma; his brother Marty worked for Wal-Mart for ten years, finishing up as an assistant manager of the Bentonville store (#100); his sister Robbin, a contestant at one time in the Miss USA pageant, to which Sam Walton flew the English family on a Wal-Mart plane, worked for Wal-Mart in high school; his sister Traci worked for Wal-Mart in high school; their mother Marcia English worked as manager of the toy department at #2 in Harrison. Larry himself started at Wal-Mart #2 in Harrison, Arkansas, in 1963 and ended his career running the store in Kissimmee, Florida, near DisneyWorld (#817), retiring in 1989. He was never that interested in climbing the management ranks. "I was never what you'd call an 'office' manager, sitting on my butt, looking at the wall," says English. "I'd take a shopping cart, put a shelf across it for a desk, and work off the top of it at the front of the store."

Sam Walton died April 5, 1992, of bone cancer, at seventy-four. In a postscript to his father's autobiography Walton's oldest child, Rob, now chairman of the board of Wal-Mart, writes: "Even in the final weeks of his life, he took great pleasure in doing what he had always done. One of the last people he spoke with outside the family was a local Wal-Mart manager who, at our request, dropped by to chat with Dad about his store's sales figures for the week." Sam Walton is buried in Bentonville Cemetery, with a relatively simple rose-colored granite headstone. The Bentonville Cemetery is adjacent to the parking lot of Wal-Mart's headquarters; Sam Walton's grave is a brief walk from the home office.

The federal investigation into the use of illegal immigrants to clean Wal-Mart stores got wide coverage in the media, as does the slowly advancing class-action sex discrimination lawsuit in federal court in San Francisco. The unionization effort at the Wal-Mart in Jonquière, Québec, has gotten wide attention in the Canadian press. The fact that Wal-Mart said the union's contract demands would require the store to add thirty employees was reported in two accounts in the U.S. media: "For Labor, a Wal-Mart Closing in Canada Is a Call to Arms," The *New York Times,* by Clifford Krauss, March 10, 2005; and "Wal-Mart Shutters Unionized Canada Unit," *Women's Wear Daily,* by Brian Dunn, May 3, 2005.

Chapter 3: Makin Bacon, a Wal-Mart Fairy Tale

Cheryl Knight, still a buyer for Wal-Mart, confirmed in a brief e-mail Jon Fleck's recollection of their early business dealings, writing, "It sounds like you pretty much have the history down." At Knight's request, Wal-Mart's media relations department sent a single-page internal case study of Wal-Mart's business relationship with Makin Bacon. The case study is headlined, "Minnesota Company Founded Upon an Eight-Year-Old's Idea is a Kitchen Partner in Homes Across America Thanks in Large Part to Nationwide Distribution at Wal-Mart Stores."

The man at Armour Bacon who put Jon and Abbey Fleck's bacon dish on fifteen million packages of bacon is Mugsy Holmes, who at seventy-two years old in 2005, is still in the bacon business. Holmes, who was with Swift (which included Armour) for fifty years as it changed corporate ownership several times, was then running Armour's bacon business, from the Chicago suburb of Downer's Grove. He remembers Jon Fleck well. "This guy came to the Armour Swift Eckridge headquarters in Downers Grove Illinois. He had called me and told me he had a wonderful product that would sell a lot of bacon. I told him I didn't have time. He came to the office. I said all right, come on in. He came in, and he wouldn't stop. You couldn't throw him out. He had a good story about

inventing the dish with his daughter. And he'd do anything to get it marketed."
Holmes agreed to put a promotion offering the dish on the back of Armour bacon packages, and told Fleck, "I'm not going to do anything else. They send the
coupon in to you, you do the processing, you redeem it, I don't want one thing
to do with that. I couldn't help but give him the business. He was so intense, he
believed in that thing so much, he was so excited about it, I said I gotta give that
guy a break." Holmes retired from Armour in 1999, and now has a consulting
business to bacon companies called Bacon by Mugsy.

The text of Rob Walton's speech to the American Antitrust Institute annual
conference on June 22, 2004, is available at the organization's Web site, http://
www.antitrustinstitute.org.

The Bentonville/Bella Vista Chamber of Commerce reports that the number
of Wal-Mart suppliers with offices in the Bentonville area is seven hundred.

Details of the settlement of the federal patent-infringement lawsuit by the
Flecks against Tristar Products were reported in the St. Paul Pioneer Press: "Teen
Inventor Gets $150,000 Settlement," by Scott Carlson, April 8, 1997. Although
Tristar paid the Flecks $150,000 and sent them the molds for Tristar's compet-
ing product, in the story Tristar's then president Keith Mirchandani is quoted as
saying, "We decided to settle because it was cheaper than litigating."

Chapter 4: The Squeeze

John Mariotti, the former president of Huffy Bicycles, was with the company
from 1979 to 1992 and tells a story that illustrates the difference between Sears
and Wal-Mart in the velocity in which they distribute and sell merchandise.
"How fast does Wal-Mart work? When I was at Huffy Bicycles, we got a bad
batch of steel one time. We had to recall the bicycles. We called Sears and Wal-
Mart thirty-six hours after the bicycles had been shipped. The Sears bikes were
still waiting to be unloaded. The Wal-Mart bikes had been sold."

The figure for the percent of bicycles imported into the United States comes
from Marc Sani, publisher of Bicycle Retailer magazine.

Welch's director of corporate communications, Jim Callahan, said that the
Welch's juice processing and bottling factory in Lawton, Michigan, "has had its
ups and downs over the years," and said that since Sherrie Ford consulted at the
plant, almost the entire management of the facility has changed. "We have had
some issues at all of our plants," said Callahan, "and I don't think that would be
news to anybody. That's true for any company running a factory. That was true

of our Lawton plant as well as some of our other manufacturing facilities. Right now, Lawton is one of our top plants." Callahan said he had no knowledge of the specifics of Ford's experience, and he said he couldn't comment specifically on Welch's relationship with Wal-Mart. "I have heard people in our sales force say, in answer to the question How difficult is it to do business with Wal-Mart?, they say, 'They force us to do things we should be doing anyway.'" Welch's maintains an office of about six people in Rogers, Arkansas, right outside of Bentonville. Welch's has twice been named a Wal-Mart "vendor of the year," in 1996 and in 2003. Welch's is itself a fascinating corporate entity. It is a wholly owned division of the National Grape Cooperative Association, an agricultural cooperative of 1,350 grape growers. The National Grape Cooperative is owned by its grape growers and buys grapes from those growers to make juice; Welch's, the processing and marketing subsidiary of the National Grape Cooperative, makes the juices, bottles, and sells them.

The material about Levi Strauss launching a new product line called Signature for Wal-Mart, and later for other discount merchants, comes mostly from interviews I conducted with two Levi's executives in July 2003, Mary Kwan and David Love. Kwan, who has since left Levi's, was then vice president of merchandising and marketing for the value channel and had been hired at Levi's specifically to supervise the design and manufacturing of the Signature line of clothing that was launched in Wal-Mart. She had worked at The Limited. Levi's was "going to this channel to reach the hundreds of millions of people who previously had not had access to Levi's products," Kwan said then. David Love is the senior vice president of global sourcing for Levi's; he was in charge of the logistics of getting Levi's product successfully into every Wal-Mart store in the summer of 2003. Although Levi's is not publicly traded, some of its bonds are, and the company issues quarterly and annual financial information much like a publicly traded company. Through the first eight months of 2005, Levi's sales were up 1.8 percent over 2004. Sales in 2004 had continued the company's long decline—although 2004 sales were down less than 1 percent from 2003, at $4.1 billion. The information about Levi's plant closings in the 1980s comes from a story in the *San Antonio Light,* "What Price Layoffs?," by Jeannie Kever, published November 13, 1990. The *San Antonio Light* stopped publishing in January 1993, although the *San Antonio Express-News* maintains an electronic archive of the *Light.* The size of Wal-Mart's Faded Glory brand of blue jeans comes from *Women's Wear Daily,* "Bracing for a Slowdown in Denim," by Scott Malone, December 5, 2002.

Figures for Wal-Mart's historic imports from China are difficult to get. A Wal-Mart executive involved in imports, Tim Yatsko, told the Asia Pulse news service in May 2000 that Wal-Mart imported $3 billion in Chinese goods to the United States in 1999 and $3.7 billion to the United States from China in 2000. Since 2001, Wal-Mart has provided the data. The company imported $10 billion worth of merchandise from China in 2001 and $18 billion in merchandise from China in 2004.

The story reporting L. R. Nelson moving production of its sprinklers almost completely to China, as a result of pressure from Wal-Mart, appeared in the *Peoria Journal Star*, "L. R. Nelson Cuts 80 Jobs: Company Shifts Production of Sprinklers to China," by Steve Tarter, May 24, 2005. Dave Eglinton, president of L. R. Nelson, said in a brief interview with me that Nelson is the "category captain" for sprinklers at Wal-Mart, meaning Nelson staff analyzes sprinkler sales across all brands at Wal-Mart and suggests a total sprinkler category array to the company. He also said that Nelson has twenty-six different product mixes that it provides to Wal-Mart stores, depending on the store's location and what kinds of sprinklers its customers tend to buy. R. E. Keup, Eglinton's predecessor as president of Nelson and now president of Simonton Windows, says that it's not just manufacturing that is cheaper offshore. "Innovation costs money. It's less expensive in the Orient. An engineer in the United States may cost you $75,000 a year, whereas you can get three engineers for that price in China."

Wal-Mart says at its walmartfacts.com Web site that it intends to create 100,000 new jobs in the United States in 2005, on top of the 83,000 new U.S. jobs it created in the United States in 2004. Wal-Mart's full-page newspaper ads that ran nationwide on January 13, 2005, in the form of an open letter signed by Lee Scott, made the same claim. And at a speech to Town Hall Los Angeles on February 23, 2005, Scott also used the 100,000 new jobs figure.

Figures for the growth of the U.S. population come from the U.S. Census Bureau. Figures for the growth of U.S. retail jobs come from the U.S. Bureau of Labor Statistics. The figures for Wal-Mart's employment in the United States come from Wal-Mart's financial statements and information available on its main Web site, www.walmartstores.com. Figures for total U.S. manufacturing jobs come from the U.S. Bureau of Labor Statistics. Historical data on manufacturing employment in the United States comes from the Statistical Abstract of the United States. All of this statistical information is available online.

Chapter 5: The Man Who Said No to Wal-Mart

Jim Wier left his job as CEO of Snapper and Simplicity in the summer of 2005, months after all the reporting on his withdrawal of Snapper products from Wal-Mart had been done. Wier is now a principal at Kohlberg & Co., a private equity firm that owns a portfolio of operating companies, including Singer sewing machines. Kohlberg & Co. was familiar with Wier: For ten years, until June 2004, Kohlberg & Co. owned the majority interest in Simplicity. It sold the company to Briggs & Stratton, a publicly traded NYSE company that makes engines for many of Snapper and Simplicity outdoor products. It's actually a very small world: Before Wier went to work for Simplicity (and its owner Kohlberg) as CEO in 1999, he had spent twenty-five years at Briggs & Stratton.

W. Gene Smiley, an economic historian and professor at Marquette University, has a history of the U.S. economy in the 1920s posted on the Internet, which includes an excellent account of the development of the U.S. retail market. The history is available at the economic history Web site www.eh.net. William Leach's *Land of Desire* (Pantheon Books, 1993) is a remarkable scholarly account of the creation of the mass-market consumer market in the United States.

The Piggly Wiggly story is widely documented, including at the company's own Web site, www.pigglywiggly.com. *Forbes* magazine published a story about this bemusing dawn of retail self-service in Memphis in its issue dated October 1, 1921. *Forbes* reprinted that account in a "Sixty Years Ago in Forbes" feature, on September 28, 1981. The original 1921 *Forbes* story made Piggly Wiggly founder Clarence Saunders sound like an authentic ancestor of Sam Walton: "When Piggly Wiggly opened, everybody laughed at the self-service idea. . . . [T]he scheme came about because, in his plan of rearranging the store and saving as much help as possible, he found that he might as well cut out the idea of waiting on people and let them wait on themselves. And people began to stop laughing when they found themselves buying all their groceries at Piggly Wiggly. . . . With the saving on clerk hire, delivery, and losses on credit sales, Saunders found that he could sell goods quite a bit cheaper than the old-line groceries."

The Outdoor Power Equipment Institute provided data on current sales of lawn mowers. Dan Shell, managing editor of *Power Equipment Trade* magazine, provided the historical perspective on the shift in lawn-mower purchases from independent dealers to big-box stores.

How does Wal-Mart make a lawn mower disposable? Here's another way of doing the math. Depending on where you live, you may need to mow your lawn for five months; a minimum of two cuts a month on average, for a total of ten cuts. Most people, especially in the south where spring and fall are longer, need perhaps twice that number of cuts. Even if you find a teenager willing to mow your lawn for $10 a cut, that's a minimum of $100. If a cut costs $20, and you need fifteen cuts a year, you're spending $300 to have your lawn cut. So for some people, buying a $150 lawn mower and throwing it away every year is cheaper, at least in terms of the checking account, than hiring someone to cut the grass. Of course, throwing away something like a lawn mower always seems unsettlingly wasteful; throwing away a lawn mower every year or two is profligate.

Jim Wier's comment comparing the sales volume Wal-Mart provides a supplier to a cocaine addiction appeared in a story in the weekly *Business Journal* of Milwaukee, "Simplicity Revs Up Snapper," by Rich Rovito, on December 13, 2002.

Chapter 6: What Do We Actually Know About Wal-Mart?

The full texts of all of the papers discussed in this chapter are available online, except for one.

Emek Basker's research can be accessed through her Web site at the University of Missouri: http://www.missouri.edu/~baskere/.

The paper "CPI Bias from Supercenters: Does the BLS Know That Wal-Mart Exists?," by Jerry Hausman and Ephraim Leibtag, can be downloaded from Hausman's Web site at MIT: http://econ-www.mit.edu/faculty/index.htm?prof_id=hausman.

Ken Stone's papers can be accessed through his Web site at Iowa State University: http://www.econ.iastate.edu/faculty/stone/.

The paper "Impact of Wal-Mart Supercenter on a Traditional Supermarket: An Empirical Investigation," by Vishal Singh, Karsten Hansen, and Robert Blattberg, is available through Singh's Web site at Carnegie Mellon University: http://business.tepper.cmu.edu/display_faculty.aspx?id=118.

The paper "Retailer Power and Supplier Welfare: The Case of Wal-Mart," by Paul Bloom and Vanessa Perry, was published in the *Journal of Retailing*, vol. 77, issue 3, September 2001. It is not available online.

The paper "Wal-Mart and County-Wide Poverty," by Stephan Goetz and Hema Swaminathan, is available at the Web site of the Penn State Center for

Community and Economic Development: http://cecd.aers.psu.edu/policy_research.htm.

Inflation figures related to Hausman's paper come from the Bureau of Labor Statistics and the Statistical Abstract of the United States, both available online.

The account of how the CPI gathers pricing data is based on interviews conducted in November 2002 with three officials of the Consumer Price Index, John S. Greenlees, then assistant commissioner for consumer prices and price indexes at the Bureau of Labor Statistics; Dan Ginsburg, then a supervising economist on the CPI; and Pat Jackman, spokesman and economist for the CPI; and also from following an actual CPI "pricer," Cindy Whittington, as she gathered price information. That research was for a story I did on the evolving importance of software to help retailers price merchandise for optimal sales and profit, in *Fast Company* magazine, "Which Price Is Right?," #68, March 2003.

The *New York Times* profile of Iowa State University professor Ken Stone, "His Message for Mom & Pop: There's Life After Wal-Mart," by Barnaby J. Feder, was published October 24, 1993.

The *Des Moines Register* profile of Ken Stone, on the occasion of his retirement, "Stone Leaves Legacy of Taking on the Big Guys," by Hawthorne Vance, was published February 1, 2004. It is the source for the story about the phone calls Stone received from Wal-Mart officials in the early years of his research.

The *Advocate* of Baton Rouge published an account of Kenneth Stone's visit to advise local retailers in advance of the arrival of a new Wal-Mart Supercenter, "Plaquemine Businesses Ready to Meet Wal-Mart," by Timothy Boone, on July 5, 2005.

The reaction from Wal-Mart spokeswoman Mia Masten to Stephan Goetz's poverty study is from "Big Hopes, Big Fears: Wal-Mart's Expansion Inspires Both in the Region," the *Philadelphia Inquirer,* by Mitch Lipka, February 1, 2005.

Chapter 7: Salmon, Shirts, and the Meaning of Low Prices

The National Fisheries Institute, a U.S. trade association for the seafood industry, provides a list of the top ten most popular seafoods each year, with per capita consumption. The list can be found at www.nfi.org, under "media."

The volume of U.S. imports of salmon from Chile and Canada comes from Alex Trent, executive director of Salmon of the Americas, a trade association of salmon producers that promotes eating salmon. Chile passed Norway in 2004 to become number one in the world in the volume of farmed salmon harvested.

Whether Costco or Wal-Mart is the number-one seller of salmon in the United States is unclear. The companies themselves do not provide that kind of product-specific data. Alex Trent of Salmon of the Americas says Costco is number one and Wal-Mart is number two. A representative for Sysco, the large nationwide food distributor, agreed. Gerry Leape, the vice president for marine conservation at the National Environmental Trust, says salmon sales at the two retailers are quite close, and Wal-Mart might now be number one. Leape's staff traveled to Chile in the summer of 2005 in a group that toured salmon farming and processing facilities, and that group included Wal-Mart representatives. Leape is the source for the figure that Wal-Mart buys 30 percent of the Chilean salmon exports to the United States. Rodrigo Pizarro, of the Terram Foundation in Chile, says Wal-Mart buys roughly 25 percent of Chilean exports to the United States.

One question is whether Wal-Mart could, conceivably, buy one third of Chilean imports. Some basic calculations show it is quite possible. Pizarro says that in 2005, Chile will export 340,000 tons of salmon, 40 percent, or 136,000 tons, of which will come to the United States. If Wal-Mart purchases 30 percent of that, Wal-Mart is buying 40,800 tons of Chilean salmon to sell to its customers—which means Wal-Mart would sell 81.6 million pounds of salmon at its U.S. stores in 2005. As enormous (and unappetizing) as that number seems, it gets manageable quickly compared to the scale of Wal-Mart. That volume of salmon comes to sales of 1.6 million pounds per week for Wal-Mart. Whether that number is precisely correct or not—that is, whether Gerry Leape is correct that Wal-Mart buys 30 percent of Chilean imports—1.6 million pounds a week is well within the bounds of reasonability. Americans buy 12.67 million pounds of salmon a week—which would mean Wal-Mart's salmon sales would be 13 percent of the national total, very close to Wal-Mart's overall share of the grocery market. Wal-Mart has one hundred million American customers a week. If just 1.6 percent of those customers go home with a pound of salmon for dinner, that accounts for 1.6 million pounds of salmon sales a week.

The controversy involving Kathie Lee Gifford's line of clothing at Wal-Mart started with the testimony of Charles Kernaghan, executive director of the National Labor Committee, before a congressional committee on April 29, 1996. There are dozens of accounts of what happened in the days and weeks that followed. Several useful ones include: "Wal-Mart, Gifford Deny Sweatshop Allegations," the *Arkansas Democrat-Gazette*, by D. R. Stewart, May 3, 1996;

"Kernaghan Cheers Gifford Move to Monitor Makers of Her Line," *Women's Wear Daily,* by Joanna Ramey, May 23, 1996; "Dirty Little Secrets: Half of Clothes Sold in U.S. Made for Substandard Pay," *Newsday,* by William B. Falk, June 16, 1996.

Figures for the farmed salmon harvest in 1985, and for Chile's exports of salmon to the United States in January 2005, come from James Anderson of the University of Rhode Island.

S. Prakash Sethi, of Baruch College's Zicklin business school, is the author of a book on how multinational corporations can set and enforce standards of conduct for their own employees and for suppliers, *Setting Global Standards: Guidelines for Creating Codes of Conduct in Multinational Corporations* (Wiley, 2003).

Robina Akther, the Bangladeshi factory worker, and her colleague Maksuda have accounts of their experiences working in factories making clothes for U.S. consumers posted on the Web site of the National Labor Committee, www .nlcnet.org. Akther's account is at this site: http://www.nlcnet.org/ campaigns/bangtour/robina.shtml. Reports of their visits to college campuses are also available on the Internet, from, among other sources, the *Yale Daily News,* the *Daily Iowan,* the *Harvard Crimson,* and the *Madison Times.*

Although the fifteen plaintiffs in the lawsuit against Wal-Mart, brought with the help of the International Labor Rights Fund, are anonymous, two people familiar with the lawsuit and with Robina Akther and Maksuda confirm that the women are in fact the plaintiffs Jane Doe III and Jane Doe IV in the lawsuit. The details of the experiences of Jane Doe III and Jane Doe IV working in separate factories in Dhaka, Bangladesh, match the posted accounts of Akther and Maksuda. A simple Google search on the name of the factory where Jane Doe III worked, "Western Dresses," along with the words "Dhaka" and "factory" produces as the first results Robina Akther's accounts of her life in the garment factories. The full text of the lawsuit is available at the ILRF Web site, www .laborrights.org.

Wal-Mart's specific initial response to the ILRF lawsuit, on September 15, 2005, is archived in the "press releases" section of: http://www.walmartfacts.com/ newsdesk/. Wal-Mart's complete "2004 Report on Standards for Suppliers" is available for downloading through the "suppliers" section of another Wal-Mart Web site, www.walmartstores.com. The then current supplier standards for Wal-Mart suppliers are Appendix B of the 2004 report.

The Gap's factory inspection efforts are detailed in the "social responsibility" section of www.gapinc.com.

The group formed in 2005 to challenge Wal-Mart is called Wal-Mart Watch. Its Web site is www.walmartwatch.org. The group is backed by the Service Employees International Union (SEIU), the United Food and Commercial Workers Union (UFCW), and the Sierra Club, among others.

Chapter 8: The Power of Pennies

"The customer is not a moron. She's your wife." Kevin Roberts, worldwide CEO of Saatchi & Saatchi, did say this at the retailing conference in Fayetteville, Arkansas, in October 2004. But he was apparently channeling the advertising pioneer David Ogilvy, to whom the remark is widely attributed. The remark appears in at least one of Ogilvy's books, *Ogilvy on Advertising* (Crown, 1983). The exact quote from *Ogilvy on Advertising* is: "The consumer is not a moron, she's your wife."

The opening of Wal-Mart #5229 in an old Kmart was reported in "Business News in Brief," the *Philadelphia Inquirer,* January 30, 2004. Wal-Mart #5229 is now the Wal-Mart my family and I shop in most frequently. In September 2005, just before this book was going to press, a new manager took over the ever-rumpled store. The name and phone number of the manager of every Wal-Mart store are printed on the receipt for your purchases. When I noticed a new name—Rafael Sanders—I said brightly to the checkout clerk, "Hey, you've got a new boss, a new store manager." Without hesitation, the clerk called out loud enough to be heard across the front of the store, "Rafael! A customer wants to meet you!" She pointed me, with my full shopping cart, at a podium near the front door, where Sanders was working. I wheeled over, and Rafael stuck out his hand in greeting. He didn't even say hello. As we shook hands, he said simply, "We're going to try to do better."

ACNielsen uses its "Homescan" panel of tens of thousands of shoppers—whose purchases it tracks item by item, store by store, much the way it tracks TV viewing habits of another group of Americans—to develop data on sales at Wal-Mart for its client companies. Nielsen's forty-six-page "2004 Wal-Mart Year End Review" includes charts listing the top fifteen selling items at Wal-Mart, both overall and limited to branded items, based on "number of purchase occasions." The items listed come from the half of Wal-Mart's sales where Wal-Mart competes head-to-head with other food and drug retailers—categories that encompass consumables and general merchandise, including groceries, health and beauty products, perishables, and general merchandise. Nielsen's charts do not include merchandise categories of appliances, hardware, toys, pharmacy, or apparel. The most expensive item on Nielsen's overall top-selling list of consumables is the gallon size of private-label whole milk, for $2.93; nine of the fifteen top-selling items cost less than $1.50; six of the fifteen top-selling items at Wal-Mart cost less than $1.00. On the branded list of top sellers, the two most expensive items are Angel toilet paper, twenty-four rolls for $4.84, and Duracell AA batteries, eight for $4.75. Eight of the top fifteen items cost less than $1.50, thirteen of the items cost $3.00 or less.

The three items detailed—Alpha Keri bath oil, no-salt-added canned green beans, and minced clams—are not random. They are all staples of our household. In particular, the canned green beans are an oddity. Our vet prescribed them for our black Lab—one 14.5-ounce can at each meal, morning and night—as an effort at weight control. They work beautifully, and our dog loves them. It also means she eats 730 cans of green beans a year. She may be the single largest individual consumer of green beans in the country. The beans are so inexpensive at Wal-Mart that buying them there saves at least $75 a year, and probably much more.

Supermarket News (www.supermarketnews.com) compiles the annual list of the largest U.S. food retailers and their annual sales. As shown in the study by Hausman and Leibtag, detailed in Chapter 6, a 15 percent savings for buying groceries at Wal-Mart is at the low end of the estimates of the savings of a typical household.

The ratios of sales per employee for Wal-Mart, Target, and Whole Foods are simply total sales for each company divided by total number of employees. Those figures are available from the financial filings of each company.

The texts of Benjamin Franklin's *Poor Richard's Almanack* for many years are available at the University of Kansas's online "Documents for the Study of American History" Web site: http://www.ku.edu/carrie/docs/amdocs_index .html. The closest version of the Franklin adage is from the 1737 *Poor Richard's:* "a penny sav'd is twopence clear."

The information about Americans' credit card balances and bill-paying habits comes from www.cardweb.com, a company that gathers and analyzes data about consumers' use of all kinds of payment cards. The Bureau of Economic Analysis of the U.S. Department of Commerce calculates the average American's rate of saving each month.

The financial performance of Southwest Airlines is detailed in the company's financial statements, available at www.southwest.com. Southwest's launch of service in Pittsburgh in May 2005 is described in "Arrival of the Fittest," *Pittsburgh Post-Gazette*, by Dan Fitzpatrick, May 5, 2005. The bankruptcies of United Airlines, US Airways, Delta, and Northwest have been widely reported and analyzed in the media. The total losses for the airline industry in 2004—$9 billion, or $173 million per week—were reported in an Associated Press dispatch, dated August 7, 2005, attributed to the Air Transport Association. The *Wall Street Journal* reported total layoffs in the airline industry of 135,000 between 2000 and 2005, in "For U.S. Airlines, a Shakeout Runs into Heavy Turbulence," by David Wessel and Susan Carey, September 19, 2005. The *New York Times* reported that Southwest operates with seventy-five employees per airplane, compared to an industry average of one hundred employees per airplane, in "Survival of the Fittest and the Leanest Becomes Strategy for the Airlines," by Micheline Maynard, October 30, 2004. The U.S. Department of Transportation compiles and publishes statistics that show Southwest carries more passengers than any other airline.

Wal-Mart's advertisements in the September 2005 issue of *Vogue* begin on page 383 (the issue has 802 pages). The *Wall Street Journal* detailed the *Vogue* strategy in "Wal-Mart Sets Out to Prove It's in Vogue," by Ann Zimmerman, August 25, 2005. Target's ads in the same issue begin on page 135.

Wal-Mart and Target, along with all retailers, report same-store sales changes as part of their routine public financial reporting.

Wal-Mart's effort at a Target-like makeover is detailed in "Looking Upscale, Wal-Mart Begins a Big Makeover," the *Wall Street Journal*, by Ann Zimmerman and Kris Hudson, September 17, 2005.

The number of Americans for every Wal-Mart store is simply the U.S. population—297 million in 2005—divided by the number of Wal-Mart stores. The number of Americans represented by every congressional representative is the U.S. population divided by the number of representatives, which is fixed at 435.

Wal-Mart's international operations are detailed on the "our company" section of www.walmartstores.com. As of November 2005, the company had stores in nine countries outside the United States, plus Puerto Rico: Argentina (11 stores), Brazil (151), Canada (261), China (49), Germany (88), Japan (405), South Korea (16), Mexico (730), Puerto Rico (52), and the United Kingdom (295). Wal-Mart had 102 stores in Alabama as of November 2005.

The *Business Journal* of Milwaukee reported that 40 percent of Master Lock's locks now come from China in "Opportunity, but No Panacea," April 16, 2004.

Chapter 9: Wal-Mart and the Decent Society

Lee Scott's quote about American capitalism's creating a decent society was part of a speech he gave in Los Angeles on February 23, 2005, to an organization of civic and business leaders called Town Hall Los Angeles. The full text of the speech is available at Wal-Mart's www.walmartfacts.com/newsdesk/ Web site, under the "news center" section, which has a collection of speeches by Wal-Mart executives. It is also available at the Web site of Town Hall Los Angeles, www.townhall-la.org.

The Foote Cone & Belding study of Oklahoma City and Wal-Mart was reported in the business and legal daily in Oklahoma City, the *Journal Record,* in "National Researchers Study Wal-Mart's Impact on OKC Consumers," by Heidi R. Centrella, on March 10, 2004. Leo J. Shapiro & Associates, a market research firm based in Chicago, did much of the research for Foote Cone, and Owen Shapiro was kind enough to provide the company's original reports of their research.

The Statistical Abstract of the United States, available online, provides data about the number of motor vehicles in the United States, going back to 1900, when there were eight thousand. The Statistical Abstract also reports annual fatalities from motor vehicle accidents.

The provisions of the Clean Air Act first required emissions controls on cars in the United States in 1975. The history of the Clean Air Act is available at the Web site of the Federal Environmental Protection Agency, www.epa.gov.

Larry English, who started his Wal-Mart career in Wal-Mart #2 in Harrison, Arkansas, remembers the store being set up to shrink if necessary.

Wal-Mart locking its employees in stores overnight was reported in the *New York Times,* "Workers Assail Night Lock-ins by Wal-Mart," by Steven Greenhouse, January 18, 2004. In another *New York Times* story, "Suits Say Wal-Mart Forces Workers to Toil Off the Clock," June 25, 2002, Greenhouse recounts the lawsuits alleging that Wal-Mart managers forced employees to work off the clock. The story reports Wal-Mart's settlement, for $50 million, of the Colorado class-action lawsuit in 2000. It reports the settlement of a similar lawsuit, involving just a single store, in Gallup, New Mexico. Wal-Mart lost a lawsuit in federal court in Oregon in 2002 over off-the-clock work allegations and was ordered to pay back wages to 83 employees, as reported by the *Oregonian*, "Jury Finds Wal-Mart Broke Laws on Overtime," by Jeff Manning, December 20, 2002. A similar case, filed in Alameda County (California) Superior Court on behalf of 116,000 current and former Wal-Mart workers in California, started a jury trial in September 2005. The *New York Times* reported the resolution of the investigation of illegal immigrants cleaning Wal-Mart stores on its front page, March 19, 2005, "Wal-Mart to Pay U.S. $11 Million in Lawsuit on Immigrant Workers," by Steven Greenhouse.

How deeply ingrained is the suspicion and dislike of the press in Wal-Mart's culture? The first sentence of Chapter 1 of Sam Walton's autobiography, *Made in America*, is about his aggravation with the media. "Success has always had its price, I guess," Walton writes, "and I learned that lesson the hard way in October of 1985 when *Forbes* magazine named me the so-called 'richest man in America.' Well, it wasn't too hard to imagine all those newspaper and TV folks up in New York saying 'Who?' and 'He lives where?' The next thing we knew, reporters and photographers started flocking down here to Bentonville, I guess to take pictures of me diving into some swimming pool full of money they imagined I had. . . . I really don't know what they thought, but I wasn't about to cooperate with them." The man who surely ranks as one of the most important businesspeople of all time begins the story of his life and his achievements with several pages of denunciation of the press.

An online Web site, www.paycheckcity.com, allows you to quickly calculate take-home pay for any pay rate and any state in the nation.

Wal-Mart's annual revenue reported in January 2003 was $233 billion, and in January 2005, it was $288 billion, an increase of $55 billion in two years. Target's annual revenue, reported in January 2005, was $46.8 billion.

Wal-Mart's market share in product categories comes from the research firm Retail Forward and its December 2004 report, "Wal-Mart 2010." Grocery share in Texas was reported in the *Dallas Morning News*, "Grocery Game Plans," February 3, 2005.

That Wal-Mart is the largest retailer and largest private employer in Mexico, and largest retailer in Canada, has been widely reported. See the CNBC documentary *The Age of Wal-Mart*, hosted by David Faber, November 10, 2004. The *New York Times* reported Wal-Mart's scale in Mexico, "Mexico: More Sales Than Its 3 Top Competitors Combined," by Elisabeth Malkin, December 6, 2004. Wal-Mart's UK chain Asda is second in grocery share to Tesco, as widely reported in the UK media, including in London's *Sunday Times,* "Wal-Mart Calls for Probe into Dominant Tesco," by Richard Fletcher, August 28, 2005.

The *Philadelphia Inquirer* article about Tasty Baking Co. appeared April 22, 2005, "Tasty Baking Looks for Winning Recipe," by Harold Brubaker. Joe Dudeck, of IRI, confirmed that the figures for snack-cake consumption released to the media do not include sales at Wal-Mart. Like Nielsen, IRI interviews consumers and tries to estimate sales in product categories for Wal-Mart, but only provides that data to IRI clients. Wal-Mart's withdrawal from sales data-sharing arrangements was widely reported, including "Wal-Mart Cuts Data Supply: Researchers Say Scanner Numbers Hard to Replace," by Ameet Sachdev, *Chicago Tribune,* May 15, 2001.

The basics of Wal-Mart's health insurance are outlined in "States Are Battling Against Wal-Mart over Health Care," by Reed Abelson, the *New York Times,* November 1, 2004. The *Atlanta Journal-Constitution* did the story that revealed that 10,261 children of Wal-Mart employees were getting their health insurance from the State of Georgia, "Wal-Mart Stands Out on Rolls of PeachCare," by Andy Miller, February 27, 2004. Miller's story also reported that Wal-Mart's insurance did not cover things like routine childhood immunizations; a spokeswoman for Wal-Mart told the *Capital Times* of Madison, Wisconsin, that in 2005 Wal-Mart expected to add childhood immunization coverage, "Wal-Mart Workers Need State Health Aid," by Anita Weier, November 4, 2004. The number of Wal-Mart employees on Tennessee's state health-insurance program, TennCare, was reported by the *Knoxville News-Sentinel,* "Big Companies Have a Large Number of Workers in Program," by Rebecca Ferrar, January 30, 2005.

Lee Scott's comment that Wal-Mart cannot compete with state health-insurance programs for the poor was made at Wal-Mart's invitation-only media day in Rogers, Arkansas, in April 2005, and was reported in "Wal-Mart Lashes Out at Competitors and Unions in Conference," by Mary Jo Feldstein, *St. Louis Post-Dispatch,* April 6, 2005.

The figures for concentration of sales of the top U.S. companies, as a percentage of U.S. GDP, come from the Fortune 500 lists. The lists are organized in such a way that the sales reported in a particular year's list are from the previous calendar year—the Fortune 500 list for 2005 reflects sales for 2004. United States GDP figures come from the Statistical Abstract of the United States. The total number of publicly traded companies comes from adding up the companies listed on each of the major exchanges in the United States; the Census Bureau reports the total number of "firms" in the United States.

Helen Sinnott, my research assistant for this book, spent weeks talking to officials, journalists, companies, and chambers of commerce in every state, trying to figure out in which states Wal-Mart was the largest private employer. Wal-Mart provides detailed state-by-state employment data, updated every three months, on www.walmartfacts.com. In the end, Sinnott is able to say, definitively, that Wal-Mart is the number-one employer in sixteen states, and almost certainly the number-one employer in eight more. Together, those twenty-four states account for 198 million Americans—67 percent of the country lives in a state where Wal-Mart is definitely or likely the number-one employer. In eleven states, there is simply no publicly available data that would make it clear where Wal-Mart's employment stands.

Here's the full breakdown:

Wal-Mart is the largest private employer in: Arizona, Arkansas, Colorado, Florida, Illinois, Indiana, New Hampshire, North Carolina, Oklahoma, Pennsylvania, South Carolina, Tennessee, Texas, Virginia, West Virginia, and Wisconsin.

Wal-Mart seems likely to the the largest private employer in: California, Georgia, Kentucky, Louisiana, Mississippi, Missouri, New Mexico, and Ohio.

Wal-Mart is the second largest private employer in: Iowa, Maine, and Nebraska.

Wal-Mart is the third largest private employer in: Alaska and Utah.

Wal-Mart ranks somewhere below third largest in these states: Delaware (#4), Hawaii (#5), Idaho (#7), Oregon (#7), New Jersey (#10), and Rhode Island (#14).

It is unclear where Wal-Mart's employment ranks in the following states, although in most it is probably not the largest: Alabama, Connecticut, Kansas, Maryland, Massachusetts, Michigan, Minnesota, Montana, Nevada, New York, North Dakota, South Dakota, Vermont, Washington, and Wyoming.

Wal-Mart's efforts in lobbying against the public disclosure of which employers in Minnesota have the most employees on public assistance is detailed in "Wal-Mart Fights Benefits Disclosure," by Chris Serres, *Star Tribune* (Minneapolis), June 2, 2005.

Epilogue: Peoria, September 2005

After an initial, brief conversation in the summer of 2005, L. R. Nelson president Dave Eglinton declined to provide any further information about Nelson's operations either in the United States or in China.

I did travel to Peoria to meet and interview the women who tell their stories of working for, and being laid off by, L. R. Nelson in the epilogue.

In Peoria, the staff of the Workforce Network was enormously helpful to me. Workforce Network is the agency, supported in part by the city of Peoria, that helps newly unemployed residents understand their unemployment and educational benefits and look for work. In particular, Beth Fulcher and Jennifer Brackney went out of their way to connect me with laid-off Nelson workers who were willing to tell their stories. Their assistance was indispensable.

Steve Tarter, of the *Peoria Journal Star,* and Debbie Adlof, of the *Community Word* newspaper, provided guidance and background about Peoria.

INDEX